The Walls Have Ears

THE GREATEST INTELLIGENCE OPERATION OF WORLD WAR II

HELEN FRY

YALE UNIVERSITY PRESS
NEW HAVEN AND LONDON

For information about this and other Yale University Press publications, please contact:
U.S. Office: sales.press@yale.edu   yalebooks.com
Europe Office: sales@yaleup.co.uk   yalebooks.co.uk

Set in Adobe Garamond Pro Regular by IDSUK (DataConnection) Ltd
Printed in Great Britain by Hobbs the Printers, Totton, Hampshire

Library of Congress Control Number: 2019941059

ISBN 978-0-300-23860-0 (hbk)
ISBN 978-0-300-25485-3 (pbk)

A catalogue record for this book is available from the British Library.

10 9 8 7 6 5 4 3 2 1

Dedicated to

the Secret Listeners
who fled Hitler and worked for British intelligence

and

to the memory of
Thomas Joseph Kendrick
MI6 spymaster

'In wartime, truth is so precious that she should always be protected by a bodyguard of lies.'

Sir Winston Churchill

Contents

Illustrations

Plates

In the text

Acknowledgements

Huge thanks to Heather McCallum, the Managing Director at Yale and commissioning editor, for publishing this book and for her enthusiasm and support. My sincere thanks to Marika Lysandrou and Rachael Lonsdale at Yale for their meticulous edits, patience and work on the manuscript that has enhanced the story, along with my copy editor Eve Leckey. I am equally grateful to my agent Andrew Lownie for his immense support throughout.

My profound thanks to two very special veteran secret listeners, Eric Mark and the late Fritz Lustig (1919–2018), without whom this book could not have been written. We embarked on a journey that led to the three of us appearing live on the BBC's *The One Show* in January 2013. I was able to interview Fritz's wife, Susan, many times before she passed away in 2013. I also interviewed secret listeners Peter Hart and Paul Douglas. My thanks to veteran former intelligence officer, Cynthia Turner (née Crew), now residing in Australia, for her memories.

This book could not have been written without the help over several years of the grandchildren of Colonel Thomas Joseph Kendrick (Secret Intelligence Service spymaster and commanding officer): my sincere thanks to his granddaughter Barbara Lloyd and her brother, the late Ken Walsh. Much appreciation, too, to Kendrick's great-granddaughters Anne Marie Thorpe and Christina Sutch. Huge thanks to Derek Nudd (grandson of Commander Burton Cope) for providing information from his own naval intelligence research and sharing his transcripts of the diary of naval interrogator Bernard Trench. Also to Anne Walton (daughter of Samuel Denys Felkin).

My gratitude to the following people for providing information and photographs: Lesley Allocca and son Michael Allocca, Dudley Lambert Bennett and son Otto Bennett, Andrew Benson, Richard Benson, David Birnbaum, Professor Hugo de Burgh, Robert Chester, Richard Deveson, Tom Deveson, Liz Driscoll, Andrea Evers, Arthur Fleiss, Dr John Francken, Adam Ganz, Barbara Horwitz, Caroline Jestin, Jennifer Jestin and Loftus Jestin, Andrew Leach, Helen Lederer, Peter Leslie, Robin Lustig, the late Roger Lloyd-Pack, Stephen Lustig, Melanie McFadyean, Stella MacKinnon, Alasdair Macleod, Anne Mark, Miriam Mark, Roger Marshall, Nigel Morgan, Ernest Newhouse, Peter Oppenheimer, Veronica Pettifer, Jessica Pulay, John Ross, Trixy Tilsiter, Sir Michael Tugendhat, Tom Tugendhat, Mimia Umney-Gray, David Wilson. My thanks to Alexia Dobinson who has typed up original reports and interviews.

A huge amount of support has been given by Mark Birdsall and Deborah McDonald of Eye Spy Intelligence Magazine – my thanks to them, and also to Iain Standen (CEO of Bletchley Park), Sarah Paterson and Kay Heather at the Imperial War Museum, Mark Scoble, Nigel Parker, Dick Smith, Neil Fearn, Mark Lubienski, David King, Steve Mallinson, Peter Quinn; Phil Tomaselli for his expertise from MI5, Secret Intelligence Services and Foreign Office sources; Fred Judge, Bill Steadman and Joyce Hutton at the Military Intelligence Museum (Chicksands); Tom Drysdale, archivist at HM Tower of London; and Colonel John Starling and Norman Brown of the Royal Pioneer Corps Association.

My thanks to the Trustees of the Museum of Military Intelligence for the honour of being able to serve as one of their ambassadors. I am grateful, too, to fellow trustees of the Friends of the Intelligence Corps Museum for their support as part of saving the heritage.

The fifteen years of research for this book have led to a special friendship with producer Rebecca Hayman, whom Fritz Lustig and I first met during the filming for the documentary, *Spying on Hitler's Army* (Channel 4 and PBS). Most poignantly, it was Rebecca who recorded Fritz Lustig's last public interview, with Sir David Jason in the grounds of Trent Park (North London) in 2017, for the TV series *David Jason's Secret Service*. A special relationship has also developed with veteran secret listener Eric Mark, with whom Helen Lederer and I filmed for BBC1's series *Home Front Heroes*.

Having written the wartime history of MI9/MI19's bugging operation and as the official biographer of Thomas Joseph Kendrick (*Spymaster*), I became very active and took a leading role in the campaign to save Trent Park in 2015, and served as deputy chair of the Trent Park Museum Trust. Special thanks to the late Tony Pidgeley CBE, founder and chairman of the Berkeley Group, without whose generosity there would not be a national museum on site to honour Trent Park's wartime intelligence role. Trent Park has now been recognised by Historic England as being on a par with Bletchley Park for shortening the war.

Thanks to my dedicated family for their loyal and practical support over the years. A special commendation goes to my eldest son who accompanied me on several trips to the National Archives in 2010. He worked methodically and carefully through the transcripts of conversations from Trent Park, Latimer House and Wilton Park.

I have been incredibly privileged and honoured to have worked on this story for two documentaries with Sir David Jason OBE, for ITV's *Britain's Secret Homes* (filmed at Latimer House in Buckinghamshire), and Channel 4's *David Jason's Secret Service* (October Films, 2017). Sir David is inspirational, enjoys a good discussion on spies, and has huge respect for the men and women who worked at the M Room sites. His particular hero is the wartime spymaster himself: Thomas Joseph Kendrick. The favourite drink of Kendrick's colleagues – especially the Naval Intelligence team – was the exotic cocktail 'pink gin'. So, may we raise a glass of pink gin to the nation's hitherto unsung hero, Thomas Kendrick, as we picture him on the terrace of one of his secret sites with Ian Fleming's own spies of the Naval Intelligence . . .

Abbreviations

ADI(K)	Air Intelligence (internal section)
ATS	Auxiliary Territorial Service
CIA	Central Intelligence Agency
CSDIC	Combined Services Detailed Interrogation Centre
DDMI	Deputy Director of Military Intelligence
DMI	Director of Military Intelligence
ETOUSA	European Theater of Operations, United States Army
FANY	First Aid Nursing Yeomanry
FBI	Federal Bureau of Investigation
FIU	Forward Interrogation Unit
GR	General Report
GRGG	General Report, German Generals
GRX	General Report, POWs of different services
HUMINT	Human Intelligence
JIC	Joint Intelligence Committee
NCO	Non-Commissioned Officer
NID	Naval Intelligence Division
OKW	Oberkommando der Wehrmacht
OSS	Office of Strategic Services
PID	Political Intelligence Department
POW	prisoner of war
PWE	Political Warfare Executive
PWIS	Prisoner of War Interrogation Section

ABBREVIATIONS

RASC	Royal Army Service Corps
RCA	Radio Corporation of America
RMLI	Royal Marine Light Infantry
RNVR	Royal Naval Volunteer Reserve
SD	Sicherheitsdienst
SHAEF	Supreme Headquarters Allied Expeditionary Force
SIR	Special Interrogation Report
SIS	Secret Intelligence Service
SOE	Special Operations Executive
SR	Special Report
SRA	Special Report, Air Force POWs
SRGG	Special Report, German Generals and senior officers
SRM	Special Report, Army POWs
SRN	Special Report, Naval POWs
SRX	Special Report, POWs of different services
SS	Schutzstaffel
USAAF	United States Army Air Force
WAAF	Women's Auxiliary Air Force
W/T	wireless transmissions

Decades of Silence

Paratrooper: I was very amused yesterday when they [interrogation officers] showed me a drawing of the sloping ramp rocket projector.

Infantry soldier: That doesn't convey anything at all. I've no idea how big it really is.

Paratrooper: The track along which the projectile travels was tiny, just as the projectile was. You know these heavy trench mortars, these grenades with a long wing (??) . . . a projectile just like that! How I laughed . . . I was quite helpless with laughter. The sloping ramp looks similar but . . . quite different . . . They know nothing about it, which is a relief to me.

11 March 1943. In a cell at Latimer House in Buckinghamshire, two German soldiers, a lower-rank infantry officer captured in Tunisia the previous year, and a paratrooper captured in Algeria a few months before, are discussing the interrogations they have undergone. The previous day, British agents had hauled the paratrooper into an interrogation room and shown him a sketch of some rocket launch ramps.[1] He had given nothing away and was now boasting about it. As he told his cellmate, the British had got the dimensions of the projectile and its track entirely wrong, and, thankfully, knew absolutely nothing of Germany's launch ramp designs. What's more, the interrogating officers had tried in vain to soften him up to make him talk. They were unbelievably stupid.

What the prisoners did not suspect was that behind the walls of their cell a team of secret listeners were recording, transcribing and interpreting every word. That these two prisoners had been brought together in the one room was no accident, and the interrogations which had been so inadequate were not what they seemed. Above all, their boastful conversations were not private. The captured soldiers had unwittingly handed over another piece of vital information to MI6, playing their part in an elaborate hoax, a brilliantly conceived and spectacularly successful strategy to extract information from German prisoners of war.

The recording of prisoners' private conversations following an interrogation was one part of an enormous clandestine operation run by one man: Thomas Joseph Kendrick. When war was declared on 3 September 1939, Kendrick already had three decades of experience in espionage and running spy networks across Europe for Britain's Secret Intelligence Service (SIS/MI6).[2] His eventful career was veiled in total secrecy and would not have appeared out of place in the gritty world of a John Le Carré novel.

Kendrick was both soldier and spy, having served Britain in intelligence since the age of twenty-one at the end of the Boer War, into the 1910s in South Africa, and again during the First World War in France. He had been formally on the payroll of SIS since 1923.[3] In 1925, he was posted to Vienna as the British Passport Officer – a cover for his SIS intelligence work.[4] He oversaw spy networks across Germany, Czechoslovakia, Hungary and Italy and handled a number of double agents.[5] Kendrick was the ideal spymaster – quick-witted, gregarious, cultured and a gifted pianist who charmed his way through Austrian high society and gathered useful contacts for his spy network.[6] Like a spider, he spun his fine web in every discreet corner of Europe and stole secrets for his country. With an old-fashioned sense of humour, he could amuse a room full of guests and regularly entertained in his Viennese apartment. Gregarious, yes – but he was also discreet, trained in the art of human espionage and able to think on his feet.

Within hours of Hitler's annexation of Austria on 12 March 1938, termed 'the Anschluss', the British Passport Office was inundated with hundreds of Jews seeking exit from Austria. Kendrick struggled to run his spy networks and send intelligence back to MI6 chief Hugh 'Quex' Sinclair in London because he and his staff were working up to twelve hours a day to save the country's Jews and political opponents of the Nazi regime. Foreign Office reports credit them with saving between 175 and 200 Jews a day, something for which they have yet to be fully recognised.[7] Kendrick forged documents to enable the country's Jews to emigrate, even if they did not qualify, and stamped and approved their papers, including applications that were not complete.[8]

Adolf Eichmann, who later masterminded the Final Solution, had been dispatched to Vienna with orders from the Führer to rid Austria of its Jews by actively assisting their emigration. Eichmann turned to Kendrick as the British Passport Officer who could aid his plan. He struck a deal with Kendrick in which a thousand Jews were given illegal visas to enter Palestine without the knowledge of the British authorities.[9] Palestine was a thorny issue for the British, with strict quotas at the time. Kendrick was acting on humanitarian grounds but was reprimanded when the Foreign Office discovered his actions over Palestine.[10]

Kendrick became the 'Oskar Schindler' of Vienna. As he struggled amidst the catastrophe facing the Jewish population, the Gestapo (Secret Police under Himmler) were looking for the 'elusive Englishman' whom they knew was SIS's man in Vienna.[11] In August 1938, Kendrick's luck ran out. He was betrayed by one of his own agents, Tucek, who was acting as a double agent.[12]

On 17 August 1938, the Gestapo arrested Kendrick as he and his wife tried to cross the border at the town of Freilassing in the Alps.[13] He was taken back to Vienna and interrogated at Gestapo headquarters in the Hotel Metropole. Over four days, he was forced to undergo eight-hour interrogations with no break.[14]

Kendrick survived, but he was expelled from the country for spying – an allegation which he and the British government always denied.[15] After his release on Saturday 20 August, Kendrick was immediately smuggled out of Austria in the consulate general's car and taken to Budapest before the German authorities changed their mind. From Budapest, he took a flight to Prague, then Rotterdam and on to Croydon airport. Back on

British soil, he was promptly whisked off to the Foreign Office for a debriefing and disappeared from the public eye.

In September 1938, Prime Minister Neville Chamberlain signed the Munich Agreement with Adolf Hitler, in an attempt to avoid war. Sinclair knew that war was inevitable – all intelligence pointed to it.[16] It was not a matter of *if*, but *when*. With pragmatic foresight, he purchased Bletchley Park in Buckinghamshire from his own private funds. Here, a dedicated team of mathematicians and cryptologists would break the seemingly unbreakable German Enigma codes, enabling the encrypted messages between Hitler and his commanders to be read.[17] This provided vital intelligence that impacted on the war and shortened it by at least two years.[18]

Kendrick arrived at MI6 headquarters at 54 Broadway to a flurry of activity and entered the nondescript grey building, a dingy warren of corridors with several floors of offices. Sinclair had an important task for him. Kendrick was an old master at running a complex bureaucratic system; he could draw on his experience in dealing with German prisoners in the First World War and on his knowledge of Nazi Germany during the 1930s. His brief would not change – he was still to spy on Nazi Germany, but this time from within Britain's borders.

The M Room operation (M stood for miked) was an early and ingenious brainwave by British intelligence. In January 1939, with war looming and the invasion of Czechoslovakia on the horizon, the intelligence branches of the War Office, Admiralty and Air Ministry agreed to open a unit to record the unguarded conversations of unsuspecting prisoners in their cells.[19] This unit would fall under the remit of human intelligence (HUMINT) and initially came under the auspices of MI1, the forerunner of MI6.[20] Sinclair recognised enemy prisoners of war as one of the most valuable sources of intelligence, but the challenge was how to obtain information from them when they would be reluctant to give anything away during interrogation, especially in the early part of the war when victory could go either way.[21] The British needed information on a vast range of subjects, such as enemy operations and battle plans, Axis military capability and rearmament programmes, new weapon capability and technological developments in relation to aircraft and U-boats, details of encrypted codes and communications between Hitler's armed forces and the Abwehr (Secret Service), and crucially any plans in the pipeline to invade Britain. If early intelligence could be gained, it would feed into warfare planning and strategy on air, land and sea, enabling the Allies to stay one step ahead. It would also allow British scientists to develop counter-measures to new German technology, and corroborate the intelligence coming out of other top secret sites, like Bletchley Park.

To succeed, the new unit needed a skilled commander-in-chief who was fluent in German, had an intimate knowledge of the German Wehrmacht, was acquainted with Germany's rearmament programme in the 1930s, and understood human beings in all their complexity. Kendrick was the perfect candidate. He knew how to court high society – diplomatic, social, intellectual and cultural – but was not a diplomat. Sinclair had also seen in Kendrick a man who could steer British intelligence through the minefield of human egos and the eccentric, stuffy demands of heads of departments with an efficiency and subtle skill that would produce results.

Kendrick had already been through one world war with Germany. Yet, in spite of that, and his experiences at the hands of the Gestapo in 1938, he bore no hatred for Germany or the German people.[22] His wife Norah was the daughter of a prominent German businessman and some of her family were still living in Germany during the Second World War.[23] Kendrick was not willing to sanction unorthodox methods or torture at his secret sites. He was a pragmatist whose sole aim was to find clever ways of getting his prisoners to spill the beans.

In January 1939, Kendrick began the arrangements for a bugging operation located in a special compound within the Tower of London[24] – designed to spring into action within twenty-four hours of the outbreak of war.

CHAPTER I

The Tower of London

The upholding of the Munich Agreement did not last. The invasion of Czechoslovakia on 15 March 1939 brought Britain closer to conflict. Chamberlain issued an ultimatum that if Germany invaded Poland, Britain would declare war.

In May of that year, just a few months before the outbreak of war, MI1(a) and MI5 had liaised over accommodating prisoners of war in the Tower of London.[1] Guidelines for their interrogation by Naval Intelligence had already been prepared,[2] and Kendrick had liaised closely with Ian Fleming of the Naval Intelligence Division at the Admiralty. Fleming had selected the Naval Intelligence team that would work at Kendrick's secret wartime site.[3] Kendrick had also authorised a team of specialist engineers to enter the Tower of London and 'wire it for sound'[4] and liaised with the Post Office to supply listening apparatus. To maintain absolute secrecy, the engineers who installed it were required to sign the Official Secrets Act, as did all personnel who worked in the M Room. Anyone who broke the silence could face up to 14 years' imprisonment.

The day that German forces invaded Poland, on 1 September 1939, Kendrick (then in the rank of major) opened his clandestine unit at the Tower of London. Within the historic walls of this iconic fortress that had seen the deaths of royals, traitors and spies, Kendrick launched a bugging operation against the enemy on British soil that combined all three services of army, air force and navy. Their joint cooperation would be carefully masterminded and choreographed by Kendrick

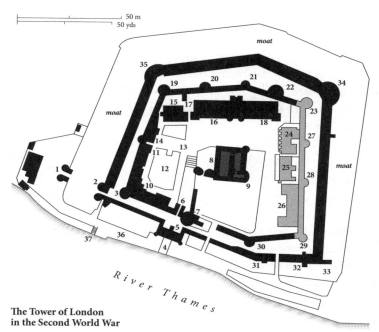

50 m
50 yds

moat

moat

moat

moat

River Thames

The Tower of London in the Second World War

1 Middle Tower
2 Byward Tower
3 Bell Tower
4 Traitor's Gate
5 St Thomas's Tower
6 Bloody Tower
7 Wakefield Tower
8 White Tower
9 Chapel of St John the Evangelist
10 Queen's House
11 Gaoler's House
12 Tower Green
13 Block (site)
14 Beauchamp Tower
15 Royal Chapel
16 Waterloo Barracks
17 Jewel House
18 Oriental Gallery
19 Devereux Tower
20 Flint Tower
21 Bowyer Tower
22 Brick Tower
23 Martin Tower – *Commandant Anthony de Salis's office was in here*

24 Officers' Quarters – *believed to be 'F. Block'. The ground and first floors were used for British staff (other ranks). The second floor was reserved for thirty German officers and forty-five other rank prisoners, and a barrack room for the prisoners' Mess Room. Today, it is the Fusilier Museum*
25 Old Hospital Block – *used for prisoners who needed to be segregated*
26 New Royal Armouries – *more prisoners' accommodation, to enable the special centre to hold a total of 120 German prisoners*
27 Constable Tower – *its use in the Second World War is not known, possibly as overflow for No.28 and No.29*
28 Broad Arrow Tower – *three rooms used and 'wired for sound' back to an M Room*
29 Salt Tower – *four rooms used which were wired to an M Room on the top floor*
30 Lanthorn Tower
31 Cradle Tower
32 Well Tower
33 Develin Tower
34 Brass Mount
35 Legge's Mount
36 Tower Wharf
37 Queen's Stair

himself, in a delicate balancing act that made each service feel it was in control.

Joining Kendrick in the Tower were Flight Lieutenant (later Group Captain) Samuel Denys Felkin, Squadron Leader Edmund Pollock and three captains of the Intelligence Corps: William Rose, G. Buxton and J.B. Carson.[5] Arriving within a fortnight were Major Arthur Richard (Dick) Rawlinson, in charge of interrogation of enemy prisoners,[6] Lieutenant Colonel Bernard Frederic Trench (RMLI), Lieutenant Commander Edward Croghan (RNVR), and army Captains Charles Corner and Leslie Parkin.[7] Trench already had a pre-war history in intelligence as a naval spy, recruited by Mansfield Smith-Cumming, the first head of SIS.[8]

Edmund Pollock had been a British businessman and hotelier in Vienna before his arrest by the Gestapo on 13 March 1938. His hotel confiscated and business assets frozen by the Nazis, Kendrick, who was a personal friend, managed to secure his release and escape out of the country through diplomatic channels.[9] Pollock, an ex-officer of the Royal Air Force, had been decorated with a First World War Military Cross. At the Tower of London, Pollock was initially placed in charge of the Air Intelligence section AI1(K), to be succeeded within weeks by Denys Felkin who would serve in that role until the end of the war.[10]

Denys Felkin (b.1894) had also lived in Vienna, was a close friend of Kendrick and had worked for him as an agent during the 1930s.[11] From 1914–15, Felkin had served in the Artists' Rifles and at the end of the First World War he had become a pilot in the Royal Flying Corps. Once the hostilities were over, he was posted to the Reparations Committee in Berlin where he acquired fluency in German and worked alongside the British diplomat and economist Sir Andrew McFadyean. In 1931 while in Paris, Felkin met American socialite Charlotte Warner Burchard, the cousin of Princess Henry XXXIII of Reuss.[12] They married in Paris in December that year. In 1934, the Felkins moved to Vienna where Denys became manager of the Ideale Radiator Gesellschaft. His posting was believed to be a guise for intelligence work because he had no technological training relevant to the company.[13] He used the work to travel and monitor the rise of the Nazi regime in neighbouring Germany. Then, still pre-war, he was transferred to Paris as manager of the Paris Radiator Company – again believed to be a cover for (unknown) intelligence work.

Charles Corner and Arthur Rawlinson had served in the First World War – Corner with the King's Royal Rifle Corps and Rawlinson with the West Surrey Regiment. The latter had transferred to intelligence duties in France from 1917 to 1918 with MI1(a), the section of military intelligence that dealt with prisoners of war.[14] In the inter-war period, Rawlinson had had a career as a screenwriter and worked on the script for the British film, *The Man Who Knew Too Much* (1934). At the outbreak of the Second World War, Corner and Rawlinson were both called up to an emergency commission and posted to MI1(H). Soon after his time at the Tower of London, Rawlinson became deputy director of Military Intelligence (Prisoners of War) and later head of MI19.[15]

Leslie Parkin was a charismatic character who fitted well into the world of espionage, especially the wartime bugging operation. Born in 1893, he was a fine pianist who had taken lessons with Russian-born concert pianist, Benno Moiseiwitsch. Liz Driscoll has vivid memories of her uncle:

He spoke several languages (German, French and Persian) with an intimate knowledge of Persia, Poland, Russia, Belgium, Holland and Germany from the 1920s and 30s. I remember him as a kind, entertaining, generous and talented uncle who loved animals and children, drank south-African sherry and who was a wonderful pianist.[16]

Parkin had served on special duties in the First World War, and worked in Germany as general manager for the Eastern Telegraph Company in Hamburg in the 1930s. He and two other businessmen were expelled from Germany in April 1939 in reprisal for the British expulsion of secret Nazi police agents. It is probable that the Nazis had also suspected him of spying. Parkin was an expert in telegraphy and technology, proving indispensable for the technological side of the M Room. His knowledge of Nazi Germany meant that he could interrogate or befriend the prisoners.[17]

Lieutenant Richard Pennell (RNVR) conducted interrogations at the Tower from late October 1939. He had originally joined the Royal Naval Reserve as a Midshipman in January 1931 and attained promotion to Lieutenant in 1935. At the Tower, he aided Trench in carrying out interrogations for the Naval Intelligence section, designated as NID 11 by the Admiralty, and later NID 1 (P/W).[18] Pennell eventually moved to other naval intelligence operations; in July 1942 he saw action in the Channel and in October of that year took part in Operation Jubilee (the Dieppe Raid).[19] Promoted to Lieutenant Commander in 1943, he went on to command HMS *Tartar* and the escort destroyer HMS *Quantock*.[20]

Although initially small, the unit was a highly sophisticated and exceptionally well organised operation. It would soon be expanded by Kendrick and continued to run for the duration of the war. Around him was a dedicated team of men and women, some of whom he had known from his pre-war days in Vienna, whilst others had served with him in intelligence in the First World War. Between 1939 and 1942, Kendrick's team of secret listeners were British-born men who were fluent in German. At their work stations, they recorded the prisoners' conversations but by 1943, the information coming out of the M Rooms across Kendrick's three bugging sites (Trent Park, Latimer House and Wilton Park) was highly technical and the German dialects so hard to understand that British secret listeners struggled to decipher and transcribe the recordings properly. Kendrick needed native German speakers to monitor the thirty bugged rooms at each of the sites.[21] He turned to the companies of the British army's Pioneer Corps where several thousand German-speaking émigrés, mostly Jewish refugees, were serving and 'digging for victory'.[22] They had fled Nazi Germany and Austria prior to the outbreak of war and wanted to fight Hitler but, instead of being stationed on the front line, had been placed in a labour corps of the British army. Their chance to play a more direct role came in 1943 as Kendrick sought to recruit 101 of them for 'special duties'. They became an extraordinary team who were deeply loyal to him. Secret listener George Pulay and his family already owed their lives to Kendrick for getting them out of Vienna.[23]

Having signed the Official Secrets Act, ex-refugee secret listeners, like Fritz Lustig, remained silent for over sixty years and never talked about their work in the M Room. During their time as secret listeners, they did not set eyes on a single German prisoner of war, yet they came as close as possible to them behind the walls of the M Room.[24] They eavesdropped on over 10,000 German POWs, from U-boat crew, to Luftwaffe pilots and army officers to high-ranking generals and Field Marshals. The prisoners were captured in many theatres of war, from North Africa, Italy, Greece and France to Belgium and Holland. They included German pilots shot down over the English skies and U-boat crews pulled from the freezing waters around Britain.[25]

THE WALLS HAVE EARS

A special section of the guards was responsible for bringing prisoners in and out of the Tower. They had no idea of the clandestine side of the operation and asked no questions. The daily administration of the special compound, initially known as the *Prisoners of War Collecting Centre in London*, came under the jurisdiction of commandant Captain Count Anthony Denis Rodolph Fane de Salis, an officer of the Guards who was based in Martin Tower on the north side of the complex.[26] De Salis (b.1897) was from an old aristocratic family, the son of British diplomat and landowner the 7th Count de Salis; he was a regular in the army during the First World War, commissioned Lieutenant on 1 March 1918, and given a special appointment from 1 June 1920 to 8 January 1921.[27]

Security at the Tower was increased and no civilian was permitted in the compound unless in possession of a special pass signed by de Salis or the adjutant.[28] An extensive part of the Tower was given over for the prisoners' special interrogation and holding quarters: the Old Hospital Block (for prisoners who had to be segregated), four rooms in the Salt Tower, three rooms in Broad Arrow Tower, the small Warden's room at the middle Drawbridge, store rooms in the Moat near Wharf Guard (Nos.1–11), the first floor of F. Block's No.3 barrack room (for other ranks of staff), and the ground floor company store as their Mess Room.[29] The second floor of F. Block was reserved for prisoners as follows: No.4 barrack room to house 30 German officers, No.5 barrack room for 45 prisoners of other ranks, and No.6 barrack room as the prisoners' Mess Room, No.3 Sergeants' room was used for stores and No.4 Sergeants' room for Quartermaster Sergeant officer John D. Hodges, and the Wharf Guardroom and Detention Room for use by the guards only. A shelter was constructed outside the entrance to the barrack rooms for use as a kitchen until the construction of a cookhouse had been completed. Cooking was undertaken by two Auxiliary Territorial Service (ATS) women. The special compound could hold up to 120 prisoners at any one time.

Prisoners were exercised in the dry moat between St Thomas's Tower and the Well Tower. In wet weather when the moat was too damp, they were taken to the wharf front near the Byward Tower and to a point opposite the Cradle Tower.[30] Procedures were in place to deal with any prisoners who escaped, including the immediate ringing of the bell to the Warders' Hall in Byward Tower. In the event of a fire in the prisoners' quarters, the detainees were to be assembled under strong guard in the Salt Tower. In the event of an air raid warning, 'prisoners will remain in their quarters. Sentries will be doubled. Every precaution will be taken to ensure that the prisoners do not attempt to expose a light'.[31]

Prisoners brought into the Tower were swiftly interrogated. A number of softening techniques were used to encourage them to give away their intelligence.[32] After interrogation, the prisoner was taken back to his room which he shared with one or two other prisoners. The British interrogators were frequently seen by them as incompetent or stupid for conducting a 'phoney' interrogation,[33] with the result that prisoners went back to their room and talked to their cellmate about what they had not told the interrogator – unaware that the rooms were fitted with bugging devices.[34] The tiny microphones were hidden in the fireplaces and light fittings, and wired back to listening apparatus in another room, the M Room, which housed the listeners who were recording the prisoners' conversations.[35] Information about the number of listeners at the Tower is not given, nor are details about the technical equipment used and who supplied it.

In his wartime diary, Guy Liddell (MI5's director of counter-espionage) wrote on 12 September 1939 that Kendrick was 'kicking his heels at the Tower of London while waiting for the arrival of German prisoners of war. I suggested that we might perhaps pool our resources with SIS in the matter of the interrogation of prisoners, of whom there are over 200'.[36] Kendrick was not kicking his heels for long.

THE FIRST GERMAN PRISONERS

The first prisoners arrived at the Tower on 17 September 1939: forty-three officers and other ranks were brought from U-39 which had been sunk off north-west Ireland on 14 September after an attempt to sink the British aircraft carrier HMS *Ark Royal*.[37] The first enemy U-boat to be sunk in the war,[38] all the crew of U-39 survived, including its captain Lieutenant Commander Gerhard Glattes and Chief Quartermaster Peter Aussen. A nominal register of all the crew was compiled by Captain de Salis.[39] On 20 September, they were interrogated at the Tower by Lieutenant Colonel Bernard Frederic Trench and Lieutenant Commander Edward Croghan.[40] Very little information was achieved from these interrogations because the captain 'had had opportunity to impress upon his crew the importance of reticence'.[41] The interrogations were completed a week later on 27 September.

On the evening of 22 September, thirty-eight German officers and other ranks of U-27 were brought into the compound after it had been sunk.[42] It was the second U-boat to be sunk in the war, with an expectation that the crew would provide early intelligence on Germany's dockyards, ports, technology and new U-boat construction.[43] After being searched to remove items that could be used in an attempted escape, the prisoners were allowed to keep their gas masks, steel helmets, identity discs, badges of rank, decorations and pay books.[44]

The prisoners faced intensive days of interrogation by Trench and Croghan, which ended on 27 September.[45] Amongst them was chief wireless operator, petty officer Werner who was interrogated about his training and duties.[46] He told Trench and Croghan that he had trained for a year at Flensburg and aboard U-27 had worked up to ten hours per shift on irregular watches. He revealed details of German short wave, medium wave and long wave transmissions and reception, including the naval Enigma machine.[47] He explained that messages were coded, coming through in double or triple code. After the first decoding of a message, the version obtained had to be decoded again, and the process repeated even a third time:

> Codes were changed frequently, in cyphered messages no call signs were used, the addresses being mentioned not at all, or at the beginning, in the middle, or at the end of message. Some of the cypher traffic from Kiel and Nauen contained political and war news. Messages in code were handed to the 1st officer or captain, who had the table of settings for the Naval Enigma machine. Messages could only be sent by express order of the captain, and were in 4-letter groups.[48]

Werner explained that on its last mission, U-27 had maintained complete silence to avoid the anti-submarine detection on British destroyers. So exceptionally good was the equipment used that the only possible defence for U-boats was to lie on the sea-bed, but this was seldom possible.[49]

Werner's colleague, First Lieutenant Beckmann, attempted to send a letter back to Germany from the Tower but it was intercepted and translated. In it, he said: 'The treatment here is good, and there is no need to worry. This is in itself an astonishing fact, considering the colossal anti-German agitation of the English people through their newspapers.'[50]

Most of the crew of U-27 were held until 28 September, then transferred to one of Britain's regular prisoner-of-war camps. Over a thousand POW camps were eventually opened across Britain to hold enemy prisoners until their repatriation at the end of the war.[51]

Before their transfer from the Tower, commanding officer Glattes of U-39 and commanding officer Franz of U-27 were taken out for lunch by Statham (?) and Havard (?) of Naval Intelligence and were thoroughly pumped.[52] On 28 September, interrogators at the Tower were joined by Lieutenant Pennell, RN.[53]

Four prisoners arrived on 1 October: General Freiherr von Reitzenstein, Sub-Lieutenant Körner, and Petty Officers Heckt and Schnalfeldt. Von Reitzenstein's Dornier aircraft (a Do.18) had been shot down by a sub-flight of Skuas from HMS *Ark Royal* and he and his crew were then picked up in the North Sea by a naval vessel. On the morning of 3 October, they were interrogated by Naval authorities. That afternoon, Kendrick placed von Reitzenstein and Körner in the same room, hoping that they would talk. If they did, the hidden microphones would pick up everything. They initially exchanged pleasantries, then had a bragging contest. Kendrick noted that von Reitzenstein appeared to win by a small margin and was 'obsessed with the idea that he is a very clever young man, and anxious to impress this fact on everybody'.[54]

Von Reitzenstein had endured a five-hour interrogation earlier that day, during which he had talked fairly consistently, but with a considerable amount of embellishment. With lots of guffawing and chuckling, he and Körner were convinced that they had successfully deceived the interrogators and repeatedly said: 'Herrgott, was haben wir die verkackert' (*My God – what shit we served them up!*).[55]

They had not fooled the interrogators. Kendrick found them 'crude and incapable of deceiving anyone'.[56] Although files are scant between early and late October 1939, some gaps can be filled by the personal diary of interrogator Bernard Trench. He noted that he met with Peter Fleming, elder brother of Ian Fleming (later the inventor of James Bond), at the Admiralty to discuss prisoners of war escaping.[57]

During October, Trench and fellow interrogators questioned surviving crews of U-40, U-42, U-12 and U-14.[58] On 27 October, Squadron Leader Edmund Pollock submitted a report to Fighter Command Intelligence (Air Ministry) about the interrogation of two surviving crews from a British attack on German seaplanes on 21 October. One had been shot down by two Spitfires of No.72 Squadron, the other by a Spitfire from No.46 Squadron. Pollock commented, 'all these prisoners are very reticent, and it is hard to obtain information'.[59]

At this early stage of the war especially, prisoners were not willing to give much away during interrogation. The Geneva Convention (1929) required them to give only their name, rank and number. Throughout the war, no unorthodox methods or torture were to be used by interrogators, as laid down in British military guidelines and in accordance with the Geneva Convention.[60] The guidelines stated that POWs 'shall at all times be humanely treated and protected, particularly against acts of violence, from insults and from public curiosity. Measures of reprisals against them are forbidden.'[61]

On 15 November 1939, Pollock interrogated an unnamed German pilot who was part of a Staffel (squadron) that had attacked a British convoy off Grimsby.[62] The Staffel consisted of nine He.115 aircraft that had set off from List, each carrying two 250-kilo bombs. During interrogation, Pollock gleaned that the He.115 had two BMW radial engines with ordinary ignition systems and carburettors. The prisoner had not been told the object of the raid before leaving and was most surprised when attacked by British fighters. He told Pollock: 'The experience was terrifying. As soon as we were attacked, my one aim was to see how quickly I could get down to sea level and land. I hoped that your fighters would then stop shooting.'[63] He survived with minor injuries.

Until early November 1939, Kendrick and Felkin's reports on interrogations and bugged conversations were written up as general summary reports. From early November, full transcripts of the conversations between prisoners were produced and this became the format for the rest of the war. They were designated as Special Reports (SRs), and have survived in the National Archives, kept separately from prisoners' interrogations. They provide a unique insight into life for German prisoners in the Tower. The earliest surviving copy of a Special Report signed by Kendrick is dated 2 November 1939.[64] It is a verbatim conversation between two unnamed air force officers the previous day, thought to have been Oberleutnant

Awater (observer) and Lieutenant Fischer (pilot). The following patchy remarks were overheard:

First Voice: Ja also mit dem Funkgeraet . . . (*Well, about the radio apparatus . . .*)

Second Voice: Ja wissen Sie, damals in Paris, da hatten die innerhalb einer halben Stunde genauen Bericht ueber den Einschlag. (*You know, in Paris at the time, they got an exact report about the hit within half-an-hour.*)

First Voice: Ob der Deutsche Funk hier arbeitet? (*I wonder whether the German radio works here.*)

Second Voice: Mit gedaempften Schwingungen? (in querying tone) (*With subdued(?)/muffled(?) oscillations(?)/waves(?) . . .?*)

First Voice: Ja mit ungedaempften Schwingungen bringen die es nicht fertig. (*Yes, with oscillations(?)/waves(?) which are not subdued(?)/muffled(?) they wouldn't manage it.*)

Kendrick noted that there was a pause whilst the prisoners arranged their beds for the night. After some small talk, the conversation continued:

First Voice: Ich glaube, man kann England von Deutschland aus beschiessen. Sagen Sie mal, wieviel schafft denn die 8.8? (*I think one can shoot at England from Germany. Tell me, how far can the 8.8 reach?*)

Second Voice: Ja, so 14 kilometer (*Well, about 14 kilometres.*)

First Voice: Das ist zu klein. (*That's not far enough.*)

Second Voice: Ja, mit der Gleitrakete, dann soll es schon geh?? (*Well, with the gliding rocket [Gleitrakete] it should be possible.*)

A copy of this first Special Report was sent to the War Office, Trench of the Admiralty, and Felkin of Air Intelligence AI1(K).[65] Although the conversations provide only patchy information, any snippets, however insignificant, were necessary to start building an intelligence jigsaw on, for example, Germany's fighting capability, bombing capacity, radio communications, and technological advances in warfare. Unguarded casual conversations between prisoners could yield information that was generally withheld during interrogation.

When Awater was first brought to the Tower, he was interrogated by both Kendrick and Felkin and gave what they considered to be a trustworthy account of the formations of the German air force, synthetic fuel used in German aircraft and a description of one of the first attacks on Hanover: 'The British flew over an aerodrome at Hanover fairly soon after the outbreak of war and machine-gunned a German machine which was practising landings on the aerodrome and then before it could be attacked by fighters disappeared again above the clouds. He states that he actually saw this himself.'[66]

Other remarks heard at the Tower that day include a prisoner commenting: 'We can't make an escape from here. We must try when we are in camp . . . not I, I am married and would not like to be put in a prison. If we make a getaway, we can under certain circumstances be shot. God forbid!'[67]

In another conversation, the prisoner said: 'Keep your chin up, later on I am going to ask for a razor and good cigarettes, newspapers and books. The German government can pay for it afterwards. We've got to live after all.'[68]

Petty Officers Grimm and Unger of the German air force discussed with each other details of their interrogation by Felkin. Unger, who had arrived at the Tower on 7 November, told Grimm: 'We also talked about an exchange (i.e. with English prisoners in Germany). He [Felkin] does not believe that anything like that will be done.'

Unger then asked Grimm, 'Do you still intend to fly if you should have the opportunity of returning to Germany?'

Grimm replied: 'Is there likely to be an opportunity? What do you think?'

Unger added: 'He [Felkin] asked me whether I knew anything about the attack on Kiel and which ship had been hit. I would not tell him even if I knew.'[69]

Later that month, the same prisoners were in conversation with petty officer Hochstuhl who had been in the Tower since 23 October.[70] Hochstuhl commented that Hitler had lost a lot of blood already in Poland.[71]

Unger replied: 'Dear Lord, redeem us from our torment and let there be peace! Either there shall be peace or England shall perish!' Then comments were overheard about British and German losses:

GRIMM: The English newspapers never say how many ships they have lost. I estimate 50,000 tons a month. I estimate that perhaps 4 or 5 U-boats have been lost.
HOCHSTUHL: With crews?
GRIMM: Yes, we had over 90 [U-boats]. Now we have many more.[72]

The comments might seem trivial, but they provided an emerging picture about Nazi Germany. Snippets like these enabled British intelligence to gauge Germany's naval strength and leak it to other prisoners in the hope that those prisoners might provide further information. Germany herself would not readily admit to how many U-boats had been sunk. The Admiralty, for example, found it difficult to obtain independent verification of the number of U-boat losses without mention of them in prisoners' conversations which provided at least a marker for the Admiralty to judge whether the losses which they had collated matched those mentioned by prisoners. British intelligence also used the bugged conversations to build a picture of the enemy threat. During the course of the war, the intelligence-gathering process and reports generated would become more detailed and refined.

SECRET WEAPON

A bugged conversation on 26 October between two unnamed U-boat officers in the Tower produced sketchy results. They discussed how men were being commandeered for submarine service in the German navy, and how Russians and Europeans could never be bed-fellows.[73] They did not believe that England would be bombed and were 'amused at the sight of civilians in Plymouth carrying respirators and wearing steel helmets'. However, that same day, Awater and Fischer of the German air force made the first reference to a 'secret weapon' in a bugged conversation.[74] It was written up by Kendrick as a report on 9 November 1939:

They [the prisoners] apparently do not know whether our fighters mount cannon or only machine guns. They think the war will end when the Führer comes out with his secret weapon.[75]

The prisoners did not appear to know, or chose not reveal, precisely what that weapon was. Three days later, Felkin wrote in an intelligence report: 'Hitler's secret weapon is talked about a lot. They [POWs] believe in it, but say there is no possibility of bacteriological warfare.'[76]

These particular bugged conversations are highly significant because they provide intelligence that predates the Oslo Report which had been written by German physicist Hans Mayer and secretly passed to the British Legation in Oslo on 4 November 1939.[77] Copies of the report were swiftly sent by the British Legation to MI6 and Naval Intelligence.[78] The Oslo Report was believed by historians to be the first crucial evidence confirming development of Germany's secret weapon. The bugged conversations turn this on its head, although the conversations do not mention the Peenemünde Army Research Centre in the Baltic by name (as the Oslo Report does). The conversations from the Tower are believed to be the first wartime reference to Hitler's secret weapon from any known intelligence source.

Several more references to a secret weapon would be made by prisoners held in the Tower before the end of December 1939. Hochstuhl commented to Ambrosius: 'Let us hope that the secret weapon comes through soon.'[79] The following day, Ambrosius, Meyer and May were in a room together, and Ambrosius commented: 'They [the British] have a wholly [sic] fear of the secret weapon. They think it is the mines.'[80]

The references were dismissed because they had come from lower-rank prisoners and it was thought that they were expressing vague fantastical hopes of a super weapon. Even so, a secret weapon was mentioned periodically in 1940 in bugged conversations, copies of which were sent only to MI6.[81]

EXPANDING THE UNIT

On 26 October 1939, the unit was renamed the Combined Services Detailed Interrogation Centre (CSDIC), a rather unglamorous and awkward title that was designed to mask its secret role.[82] Transcripts of conversations continued to be signed off as originating from MI1(H) for several months to come, in spite of the change of name. In December 1939, the unit came within the branch of military intelligence MI9, designated MI9(a), after a meeting between the Director of Military Intelligence, Deputy Director of Military Intelligence, MI5, MI6, Director of Naval Intelligence and Director of Intelligence (Air Ministry).[83] Rawlinson was assigned to all matters regarding prisoners of war from an intelligence aspect.[84]

The Tower of London could never be a valid location for this unit in the long term; it could only hold 120 prisoners at a time in the special area designated to MI1(H). Successful campaigns on enemy-occupied territory would mean that Kendrick and his team would have insufficient staff or quarters to interrogate and process the numbers of prisoners. Kendrick had already been seeking a larger site, amidst concerns of a German invasion and heavy bombing of the capital. To move to a site that was not so prominent would divert attention away from the secret nature of the unit. The new site was Trent Park at Cockfosters in North London, where the War Office requisitioned the mansion house, stable block and part of the parkland for 'special purposes'.[85] Once the property of Sir Philip Sassoon, a wealthy Baghdadi Jew whose family had made a fortune trading in opium, the estate and businesses had been inherited on the death of his father, Edward, in 1912.[86] During the 1930s, Sir Philip had hosted lavish bohemian parties for famous guests of his era, amongst them Charlie Chaplin, Stanley Baldwin and Winston Churchill.

During the war, the Tower continued to receive the occasional German prisoner on behalf of the intelligence services; the most famous of whom was Hitler's deputy, Rudolf Hess, who was held there for four days in May 1941.[87]

In late autumn 1939, work began on the construction of temporary wartime structures next to the main house at Trent Park. These would accommodate the interrogation block, cells and administration offices. Former interrogator, Matthew Sullivan, described the scene:

> The cell block, including high-fenced exercise yards and raised watch towers, was adjacent to the mansion which belonged to Sir Philip Sassoon, connoisseur and man of affairs. The interrogating officers lived here and in the cottages and had use of the large park.[88]

An M Room was initially constructed next to the interrogation block. The house and estate were described later by one of the German generals:

> [There] is a large nursery with a wonderful fruit and vegetable garden and greenhouses under whose wide glass roofs fragile peach tree branches were suspended like thick spiders' webs. The castle court-yard, laid with large paving stones, was bounded on the southern side by a double barbed-wire fence, and shelter-trenches had been dug on the longer side. An additional double and higher barbed wire fence bounded the western and northern sides of a square lawn about 120 x 70 metres in size. In fog and limited visibility, only the smaller courtyard was available for the use of the prisoners while the larger one was available during fine weather. Longer walks through the fields and woods were organised on several days each week in the company of officers, but only after giving one's word of honour not to attempt to escape.[89]

While Trent Park was being fitted out, December saw a busy period at the Tower with the interrogations of thirty-five surviving crew of U-35 which had been scuttled at the end of November 1939.[90] They arrived early in the morning of 3 December with their captain, Werner Lott.[91] The following day, Pennell and Trench interrogated three of the officers who were described as 'very pleasant and communicative'.[92] Their morale was high and they did not expect the war to last long. The interrogations continued over the next five days. On 9 December, fifteen prisoners from U-35 were transferred to unnamed prisoner-of-war camps. The others remained at the Tower for further interrogation.[93]

From its inception, Trent Park was never to be referred to as a prisoner-of-war camp or a prison, but as 'Cockfosters Camp' or 'Camp 11'.[94] Like Bletchley Park, the fact that its existence remained unknown for decades was a testament to its success.

CHAPTER 2

₥ Room Operations

Before Trent Park could function for any intelligence purposes it had to be made ready; the installation of listening equipment was begun in the house and an M Room was prepared. A handwritten report entitled 'Listening and Recording Equipment at Country House' laid out the requirements for the new site.[1] Five interrogation rooms and six bedrooms were to be wired with concealed microphones. An approach was made to the Radio Corporation of America (RCA) to supply the specialist equipment.[2] The American company was based in New Jersey but had offices in the United Kingdom at Electra House on Victoria Embankment in London and had previously carried out work for SIS.

The equipment was transported on the next available transatlantic journey because of the urgency of the operation. A top priority import licence was granted and the equipment, consisting of nineteen cases of wireless apparatus, was shipped in two cabins from New York at the end of 1939.[3] A cypher from the Military Attaché in Washington to the War Office confirmed that it had left New York for MI1.[4]

The work of installation began during the latter part of 1939, and was carried out by Mr Barnes and his team (Ackroyd and Doust) from the General Post Office Research Department at Dollis Hill (London).[5] All installation staff were required to sign the Official Secrets Act.[6] Maintenance of the equipment became the responsibility of the Post Office Research Station to avoid a breach of security. As the first

Christmas of the war approached, Kendrick began the preliminary phase of moving the administration side to Trent Park. A few weeks later, he received a letter from RCA to inform him:

> We have pleasure in handing over to you the complete installation at T.P [Trent Park] in full operating condition including both recording and reproducing or play-back sections . . . The only other copy of this letter and the attached report in existence is one in our own secret files which it is of course necessary for us to keep. We should point out that certain drawings are in the possession of the Post Office and the Office of Works and you will no doubt consider whether you want to collect them and destroy them.[7]

The original drawings have not been declassified and may still survive in archives of the War Office or intelligence services, though perhaps they have been destroyed as directed.

The two long reception rooms of the house, labelled S.1 and S.2, were fitted with false ceilings, in line with the rest of the architecture to avoid arousing suspicion.[8] Further alterations took place in May 1940 when rooms in the mansion were divided up and more soundproofing added. Work included the installation of false panels and ceilings, microphones concealed in the fireplaces, the lamp fittings, even in the plant pots, under the billiards table and in the trees in the grounds.

WITHIN THESE WALLS

On 9 December 1939, Captain de Salis relocated to Trent Park from the Tower of London as its camp commandant until 1943, when he was succeeded by Major Denis Bevan Topham.[9] With a larger site, Kendrick rapidly expanded its intelligence-gathering capability to become a highly efficient and impressive operation for amassing and processing vast quantities of information. He gradually increased the staff to 515 army personnel, including administrative staff, typists, couriers, translators, engineers, cooks, administration staff and guards.[10]

Although he was the overall commander, Kendrick also headed the army intelligence section of the site. Some of the officers under this section were recruited because he had known them in the pre-war period.[11] Amongst them were Charles Juulmann and John Burgoyne, both drafted into the Intelligence Corps in 1940. Their backgrounds provide a snapshot of the kind of profile Kendrick sought for the officers who joined his team. Charles Juulmann, born in Estonia, had served with the Signals Service, Royal Engineers in the First World War.[12] In 1923, he was naturalised as a British citizen and was attached to the Intelligence Department, British Army of the Rhine (Cologne), where his commanding officer was Thomas Kendrick. In the late 1930s, Juulmann was working as an 'examiner' at the British Passport Office in Berne, Switzerland, possibly as cover for SIS work. In 1940, he was commissioned into the Intelligence Corps and attached to Kendrick's unit.

John ('Sandy') Burgoyne joined Kendrick's unit in early 1940. A talented linguist, he had studied French and German at the University of Edinburgh.[13] In May 1939, he enlisted as a private in the Royal Scots (Home Defence), and transferred to the Intelligence Corps on 24 February 1940. On 2 March 1940, he received a letter from the director of Military Intelligence:

You are selected to fill an appointment as Intelligence Officer Lieutenant, M.I.1.H at Cockfosters Camp. You should be at Enfield West tube station (Piccadilly Line) at 10 a.m. on Monday March 4th, where you will be met and given further instruction.[14]

During this period, the secret listeners were drawn from commissioned officers of all three services: Army, Navy and Air Force. They were selected because they had studied languages at either Oxford or Cambridge Universities, or were ex-German refugees who had arrived in Britain from 1933 and already been granted British nationality. That would change later in the war when Kendrick required only native German speakers to cope with the dialects and technical language used by the prisoners.

STOOL PIGEONS

The interrogation of prisoners was only deemed successful when used in conjunction with the M Room operation and the use of stool pigeons.[15] 'Stool pigeon' was the term given to someone who was acting as a fake fellow prisoner. One person believed to have served as a stool pigeon in the Tower of London in 1939 and then at Trent Park, was Brinley (Brin) Newton-John – the father of English-Australian actress Olivia Newton-John – who spoke fluent German.[16] From autumn 1940, he interrogated captured German pilots at Trent Park, using the pseudonym Dike or Dyke, but he also befriended them by using his knowledge of upper-class German society to gain their confidence.

Occasionally, MI9 had to assess whether a stool pigeon was suspected of not being a genuine prisoner, as was the case after one bugged conversation in December 1940. A note, which identified him only as SPF/4, read: '. . . whilst there is no reason to think that A674 [POW] suspects his companion [SPF/4] of not being a genuine POW, it is not of course impossible that the statement may have been made to lay a trap, though we do not feel this is the case.'[17] The note refers to something the prisoner said to the stool pigeon which could have been false information. The stool pigeon in question might have been Brin, who later transferred to Bletchley Park.[18]

In 1940, Kendrick selected four stool pigeons after interviews with ex-refugees who were serving in the British army's Pioneer Corps. They were Stefan Georg Klein, Werner Theodor Barazetti, Josef Lampesberger and Georg Schwarzloh[19] who all transferred to Trent Park where they took on a new identity as German 'prisoners of war'. The value attached to stool-pigeons is highlighted by the case of Georg Schwarzloh, a former German policeman in the Hamburg police and an anti-Nazi who had worked for Czech counter-intelligence before fleeing to Britain. He was brought to MI5's attention by a former employee who commended him for intelligence work. However, by some misunderstanding, Schwarzloh had been arrested by the British authorities and categorised as a Class A internee ('dangerous Nazi'). He was then interned and subsequently transported to an internment camp in Canada. Schwarzloh was considered so important as a potential stool pigeon that MI9 wrote to the Home Office, requesting his urgent return to Britain: 'We are anxious for various reasons that one Georg Schwarzloh, who is at present interned in Canada, should be returned to this country . . . [we] request that this alien might be included in the next batch of internees coming to this country.'[20] He was brought back from Canada and served at CSDIC until the end of the war.

The use of stool pigeons was expanded over the course of the war, such that Kendrick engaged a total of forty-nine Germans for this work from among both prisoners and refugees who had fled Nazi Germany.[21] Records of the names and details of these individuals are extremely rare, but some are known, amongst them Freiherr von Bassus, and two others named only as Reinhardt and Petrie.[22] In return, stool pigeons received preferential treatment and outings as a reward, funded by SIS's Special Fund.

M ROOM APPARATUS

The new intelligence site was kitted out with fifteen type 88A pressure microphones, nine portable disc recorders, five high quality headphones, one amplifier for loudspeaker monitoring, four switchboard assemblies, one mainframe assembly and a transformer.[23] The operators were supplied with 525 12-inch double-sided acetate recording discs for recording conversations, and 58 steel recording styli, 10 sapphire recording styli and spare parts. Very little is known about the microphones that were used, except from a report which stated: 'It was proved in practice, as was anticipated in laboratory work, that the moving coil type of microphone was the only practicable type for concealing purposes. Firstly, its size and shape were suitable, and secondly, it could be fitted and forgotten; only 2 failures were experienced over a period of three years.'[24]

The equipment allowed for complete versatility and flexibility. Any or all operators could listen singly or together into any one of the bugged rooms, including the interrogation rooms. Each of the eight machines could record conversations in any of the wired rooms.

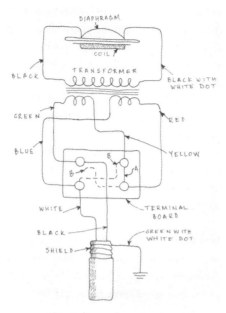

Circuit diagram for a microphone

A separate playback room was equipped with four playback units with turntable and variable speed motor, amplifier, hypersensitive pick-up, power control switch and pilot lamps and twin output jacks.[25] Eight headsets and eighty silent styli were also part of the equipment supplied. This allowed two translators to listen simultaneously to the recordings.

Kendrick's own office in the Blue Room at Trent Park had a playback machine similar to those in the M Room. At any time his office could be connected direct from the M Room to any of the bugged cells and interrogation rooms and listened to using either headphones or loud-speaker. He also controlled the instruments in Interrogation Room 6 via a switch which he held under lock and key; this meant that if any of the machines in the M Room broke down, his machine could be used as a replacement. With the M Room fully kitted out, the RCA wrote to

Kendrick: 'Dust is anathema to disc sound recording and so should be avoided. Thus the M Room should never be swept and that is why we have included a vacuum cleaner in the equipment.'[26]

The M Room consisted of three rooms and six listening stations, with the secret listeners working in twelve-hour shifts.[27] The technical side of recording and listening-in was taken care of by Captain Copping of the Royal Corps of Signals. Psychologist Lieutenant Colonel Henry Dicks advised on interrogation of particular prisoners. In overall charge of the M Room was Major Cassels who had already been called up on Emergency Reserve to Military Intelligence (War Office) in February 1939.[28] He was posted to CSDIC on 26 February 1940. Secret listener Fritz Lustig recalled how they operated:

We sat at tables fitted with record-cutting equipment – this was before electronic tapes were invented. We had a kind of old-fashioned telephone switchboard facing us, where we put plugs into numbered sockets in order to listen to the POWs through our head-phones. Each operator usually had to monitor two or three cells, switching from one to the other to see whether something interesting was being discussed. As soon as we heard something which we thought might be valuable, we pushed a switch to start a turntable revolving, and pulled a small lever to lower the recording-head onto the record. We had to identify which prisoner was which by their voices and accents and keep a log, noting what our 'charges' were doing or talking about. In that log, we noted down the time of day and the subjects that we had recorded, so that the next shift could see at a glance what had been happening. As soon as a record had been cut, somebody else had to take over the monitoring, and the operator went to a different room to transcribe what he had just recorded. At the end of duty, the log-sheet was handed to the next shift so the other listeners could tell what had happened on the previous shift. Whenever a record was 'cut', a note was made in a column on the log sheet. It enabled the day's activities to be seen at a glance for any of the cells.[29]

The secret listeners did not take shorthand notes because British intelligence needed to record every detail, as personal judgements were not permitted. Each acetate record held up to seven minutes of conversation. A carefully transcribed text could take over an hour to complete. If it was not possible to identify certain words, then a line or a series of dots indicated on the transcript the inability to recognise a word or phrase.[30] The secret listeners were not allowed to guess what that word might be. After transcribing the conversation, a senior operator checked the draft for any errors, omissions or superfluous material. It was then passed to the editorial section on site.[31]

The 'cut' record from the M Room was kept for two months before being returned to the Post Office Research Station at Dollis Hill for re-conditioning and re-issue. The records with evidence of wartime atrocities were kept permanently. These included any reference to concentration camps, the killing of Jews, Poles and Russians, the places of mass murder (e.g. towns and villages) and who carried it out (the SS, death squads, or German army).

EDITORIAL SECTION

The editorial section was responsible for handling all Special Reports coming out of the M Room. A register was kept of all draft reports which were then carefully checked to ensure they were all finalised and dealt with.[32] The register showed the date on which a report was received and the date it was finally disposed of by the section. After registering a Special Report, it was passed to the interrogators straightaway so they could check for valuable information that they needed – especially for intelligence that they had not been able to obtain during interrogation. When they had finished their checks, the reports were sent to the draft room for translation and typing by ATS personnel. The ATS officers had to have a good knowledge of current colloquial German. They also compiled extensive glossaries of technical and slang terms that could be consulted by any member of the section. The reports were translated into English, and both the German and English typed up.

Any queries at translation stage were sent back to the M Room to clarify. The verbatim bugged conversations were referenced under SRN (navy), SRM (army), SRA (air force), SRX (different services), and those of senior German officers under SRGG and GRGG. The transcripts of interrogations were called Special Interrogation Reports (SIR), and intelligence summaries were known as General Reports (GR).[33]

A final check was made by a different officer from the one who had originally checked the translation and carbon copies were then made. An average of 80 copies could be made of each report; in the early days these were then dispatched to, for example, Air Intelligence, the War Office and the Admiralty, MI5, MI6, MI8, MI9, MI14 and Bletchley Park.[34] As the war progressed, the number of departments receiving copies dramatically increased, especially after D-Day.[35] A card index was kept of every POW, showing his movement and companions in his cell whilst at a CSDIC site. A subject index was also compiled of all subjects covered by POWs. A copious amount of information was being amassed that would flow into Intelligence for the duration of the war. An entry in the MI9 war diary in 1940 recorded: 'Reports received at Cockfosters are evidence of the increasing value of the work done by the organisation.'[36] The Editorial Section of the M Room was a huge manual intelligence operation – all carried out by personnel and without the aid of any early machines or computers.

Transcripts from bugged conversations were exceptionally productive in providing the first information on new German technology, warfare, operations and military capability that could not at this stage of the war have been ascertained from interrogation alone.[37] Prisoners were usually held for a few days or up to about a week, or sometimes (but rarely) longer, until they had unwittingly given away all they knew. When they talked to their cellmates mainly about their families or private matters, it was a sign that they had no more important material to impart. They were transferred to a regular POW camp elsewhere in Britain where their conversations were not bugged.

Felkin managed the team of RAF interrogators in the Air Intelligence section at Trent Park. He was known to the prisoners by the pseudonym

'Oberst King'.[38] He possessed three qualities which made him an excellent interrogator for Air Intelligence: charm, patience and a sixth sense.[39] The interrogations were sometimes 'phoney', designed to make the prisoner think the British did not know very much or were stupid. An interrogator sometimes revealed only partial information, knowing that it would plant a seed in the prisoner's mind such that he would talk about it in more detail once back with his cellmate. The prisoners were held two to a room, often from different services to encourage the talk. Did the German prisoners ever suspect? They had been warned back in Germany that if ever captured, the British would probably bug their conversations. But the prisoners soon became complacent and let down their guard. In a memorandum, Kendrick reassured intelligence chiefs that security consciousness had been encountered amongst the prisoners, but 'this attitude was frequently broken down by careful grouping of POWs and by devising ways and means of disarming suspicion'.[40]

NAVAL CODES, ENIGMA AND BLETCHLEY PARK

On 12 December 1939, the remaining prisoners of U-35 were moved from the Tower of London to Trent Park.[41] Four days later, Trench and Croghan arrived at Trent Park to see them again. Croghan took Sub-Lieutenant Roters and engineer Stamer out for a walk and chat in the grounds whilst Trench talked to U-35's telegraphist Erich May.[42]

On 28 December 1939, Trench met with Alastair Denniston, the first head of the Government Code and Cypher School (GC&CS) at Bletchley Park. Denniston, who had a background in naval intelligence and codes from the First World War, was concerned about breaking the German naval Enigma code in the new war. Trench noted in his diary: 'Colonel Denniston came in to tell me about his camp.'[43] It is possible to infer from this entry that, prior to this, Trench had no knowledge of Bletchley Park.

Two days later, on Saturday 30 December, naval interrogator Pennell was sent to Bletchley to discuss ways of securing Enigma intelligence from Erich May who was being held at Trent Park.[44] Prisoners had been talking amongst themselves about German codes, decoding methods and cyphers (all picked up by the hidden microphones), but the interrogators at Trent Park needed to understand exactly what intelligence was required by the code-breakers.

The entry in Trench's diary is an indication of the early intelligence cooperation between Trent Park and Bletchley, and of a relationship that would continue throughout the war.[45] Both sites were highly top secret and not all personnel at Kendrick's site were cleared for knowledge of Ultra – the wartime signal intelligence obtained at Bletchley Park from cracking the high-level encrypted messages of the enemy.[46]

On New Year's Day 1940, Pennell went out to Trent Park to see Erich May and tried the softer approach.[47] May had already been taken for trips into central London and had confided to another prisoner:

He [Lt Pennell] invited me alone to his house where he is living for the time-being only with his butler. His wife is on the west coast. He has a number of country estates, one in the West of England, and another in South Africa and his fine house in London. We had a very good meal and drank only champagne and port. He is a fine fellow. I believe him when he says he only has a personal interest in me.[48]

May's preferential treatment was designed to soften him up. During the interrogations, which were more like friendly discussions, Pennell sweet-talked him into giving away more information about the naval Enigma machine.[49] Copies of these conversations were sent direct to Commander Denniston, and cryptographers Dilly Knox, Oliver Strachey and Frank Birch at Bletchley Park.[50] On 8 January, May disclosed to Pennell:[51]

There are spare wheels kept in a box and they are easily inserted. The wheels are numbered and changed roughly every two days. The change takes approximately sixty seconds and the wheels can be put on the shaft in any order . . . The layout of the 'stechus' is given below:

1	2	3	4	5	6	7	8
0	0	0	0	0	0	0	0
0	0	0	0	0	0	0	0
9	10	11	12	13	14	15	16
0	0	0	0	0	0	0	0
0	0	0	0	0	0	0	0
17	18	19	20	21	22	23	24
0	0	0	0	0	0	0	0
0	0	0	0	0	0	0	0

I remarked to May that our Enigma machine functioned very slowly and was unsuitable for urgent operation signals and consequently we used a table. He said that their Enigma was as quick as anything (I must confess it sounded quicker than our GG cypher when it is used by submarine officers).

May took a piece of paper and drew the German method of working with letters for codes. He explained that when a petty officer presses Z on the key and Q lights up, his opposite number writes it down in the corresponding column.

In turn, Pennell gained May's trust by confiding in him about top secret British naval codes.[52] The strategy was not risky because Pennell knew that May would not be going back to Germany until the end of hostilities and could not impart the information to the German navy. Pennell's decision to befriend May proved correct. May would turn out to be one of the most important prisoners with knowledge of German naval Enigma. Pennell worked on the logical assumption that the German navy probably used an Enigma machine similar to that of the Royal Navy. The Naval Intelligence team at Trent Park continued to pump U-boat crews for information on Enigma and codes during 1940.[53]

On one occasion, pilot Wilhelm Meyer and wireless petty officer N125 chatted together about codes used by the German navy. It was N125 who inadvertently told Meyer:

Do you know the special U-boat morse code? This is used for rapping signals, when one is locked up anywhere. If you want to give a dot, you give a dot, and for a dash you give 5 dots. For instance, if you want to give your name, you give 5 dots twice, one dot, 5 dots, one dot, 5 dots, 5 dots, dot, dot, 5 dots, dot.[54]

John Godfrey (head of Naval Intelligence Division) recognised the value of the information being gathered at Trent Park and later wrote: 'I have reviewed the results obtained from naval prisoners of war since the outbreak of war, and can unhesitatingly confirm that they are of such operational importance as to make it vital to develop this source of information to the full.'[55]

Information from the interrogation and secret recordings of U-boat wireless operators continued. This included operators from U-32 and U-31. Copies of their reports were sent to cryptographer Frank Birch at Bletchley.[56] The close working relationship and sharing of intelligence between Kendrick's unit and Bletchley continued for the duration of the war.[57]

PILOT WILHELM MEYER

In December 1939, 31-year-old pilot Lieutenant Wilhelm Meyer was transferred from the Tower of London to Trent Park along with U-boat prisoners. He had been amongst the first captured Luftwaffe pilots to be brought to the Tower, having been shot down over the river Thames on 20 November 1939.[58] Pulled unconscious out of the freezing water, he had been taken first to the Royal Herbert Hospital for medical treatment because of injuries.[59] Whilst at Trent Park, he was interrogated about the crew's call-sign, wavelengths on radio transmissions and communication with ground control. His interrogation by Felkin was written up in a special report and sent to the Air Ministry.[60] It confirmed for the Air Ministry that Meyer's crew had received no navigational aid on their flight to England. They had flown by sight to just north of Borkum and then on a plotted course between Deal and Dover where they crossed the coast of England. Assistance for their return flight (had they made it) would have been given over shortwaves.

By the end of 1939, the unit began to give its prisoners codenames in the transcripts, such that it is often not possible today to identify the original prisoner (there are some exceptions), as in the case of Meyer. There was still much talk amongst the prisoners about U-boat production, torpedoes, minesweepers, U-boat tactics, the manufacture of German aircraft (Heinkels and Junkers) and belief that the war would end soon.[61]

In one conversation, a wireless operator commented to a German pilot: 'What is the X-Gerät?'[62] Pilot (A129) replied: 'It has to do with dropping bombs on unseen target.' This is thought to be the first reference to X-Gerät by any prisoner and its significance is discussed in the next chapter.

Another prisoner had bailed out on the island of Hoy (Scapa) on 30 November 1939 when his plane crashed, killing all other members of the crew. He revealed that he had really been flying in a Ju.88, not the He.111, a machine that was little known in 1939. Felkin wrote: 'The interrogator realised that this man was a born talker and kept him under interrogation – with excellent results – for 103 days.'[63]

On 23 December a conversation was recorded between Meyer, Ambrosius (German air force) and May (U-35) in which Meyer asked a somewhat rhetorical question: 'Do you think listening apparatus are built in here. I don't think so. It is the one thought that is always with me.'[64]

With the exception of Meyer, the other prisoners did not suspect that the place was 'wired'. The conversation turned to their treatment by the British as prisoners of war. Meyer recounted how, when he had gained semi-consciousness after being pulled out of the Thames, he had asked for a cigarette and was given an expensive cigar. He told his mates: 'When we were fished out of the water, we were undressed at once and firmly rubbed down, and everyone gave us a part of his linen, and then we got eggs and bacon. It tasted good. They are kind-hearted people after all.'[65]

May replied: 'Damn this war! We might have been comfortably sitting at home now. But the English won't rest until they have completely crushed us.'[66] At nine o'clock that evening, Meyer was taken out of the room by a guard. Ambrosius was alone with May and piped up: 'He is a very decent fellow.' To which May replied: 'I like him quite well. He is a man at least.'

Hochstuhl was one of the few prisoners who became suspicious of the reason for being held in the Tower. In a conversation recorded on Christmas Eve, he expressed doubts to Meyer about why he had been brought to the Tower, then released to a regular prisoner-of-war camp and brought back again:

> HOCHSTUHL: I have had unpleasant experiences here. Even though the treatment is not too bad, I don't trust these fellows any more. I don't trust the quietness of it here: I have had my experiences in the Tower. They use all sorts of means here to get information out of us. I think it is despicable when they put English officers into German Air Force uniforms.
>
> MEYER: Did they do that?
>
> HOCHSTUHL: Yes, in the Tower . . . I am very sceptical about our being brought together just on Christmas Eve, for we are not generally so well treated. I don't trust these people. They are doing it for some special reason.[67]

The reference to English officers being put into German air force uniform refers to the M Room's use of stool pigeons to provoke specifically oriented conversations for intelligence needs.[68] A report summarised the importance of stool pigeons:

> A good stool pigeon could accomplish a great deal to help an interrogator. He could put the prisoner in the frame of mind best suited to the tactics upon which the interrogator was relying. And even the most difficult prisoners could, with continued briefing, conduct a complete interrogation. Not the least of his

value lay in his ability to flatter a prisoner into giving a full account of a recent interrogation, as a result of which details given at the interrogation could be embellished and assessed for their accuracy.[69]

The use of stool pigeons is discussed in more detail in the next chapter.

On Boxing Day 1939, Meyer, Ambrosius and May passed the time playing cards. Their conversations that day were recorded as Special Reports No.9 and No.10.[70] Talk was of naval and air force matters.

Meyer told May, 'We must rely on the Air Force. When Hermann [Goering] sends all his Squadrons over at the same time, that will give them a surprise. And then perhaps the new Heinkel will be ready, with four engines.'

Meyer replied, 'Our Air Force comrade (Hochstuhl) is a very queer fellow, he is suspicious of everybody, he even looked at me mistrustfully.'

May said, 'All I should like to know is what they want me for. If they want to know anything about U-boats, then I haven't the faintest idea. The officers are probably doing their duty, but we are not going to let ourselves be pumped.'

'They are much too dumb anyway,' Meyer replied.

The comment that their captors were 'dumb' was precisely what British intelligence wanted them to think.[71] In believing that the British were incompetent, stupid or both, it enabled the M Room project to roll out successfully and undetected.

It appears from comments at this time that the prisoners were taken to brothels. May said: 'We are going to that brothel next month.' To which Ambrosius replied: 'We shall probably frequently wish we were back here.'[72]

Ambrosius also commented: 'It is surprising that they have not yet photographed us in case we should escape.'[73] To which Meyer replied: 'I would make for Ireland.'

Relaxed and quite complacent, the prisoners continued to talk about bombs, military strategy, German aircraft and U-boats:

> MAY: We have more now – say, ten shipyards where U-boats are built – then two boats could be launched every week. But they are only just starting to build. There is the *Germania* shipyard in Kiel, the *Deutsche Werke* in Kiel – they have not yet built and should now be starting – then there are two shipyards on the Baltic. In Bremen, U-boats are built by the *Deschimag*, then building is going on in Hamburg by . . .
>
> MEYER: Blohm & Voss.
>
> MAY: Yes, and then they are building in Wilhelmshaven at the *Siegmunds* shipyard. They are also building in Kiel at the *Kieler Kreigsmarinewerft*. That is already six shipyards.[74]

These comments gave British intelligence an important insight into Hitler's rearmament programme and piecemeal information that could be used to corroborate intelligence coming from other sources.

On 12 January 1940, Ambrosius was interrogated by Felkin. Immediately afterwards, he was placed in a room with Erich May. Ambrosius recounted his interrogation and told May that the interrogation officer had shown him poor-quality photographs of military installations and commented: 'They must have poor apparatus. I told them so. They were taken from a height of 7 to 8 thousand metres. Our photos are better: when they are taken from, say, 4,000 metres, you can see every house on them.'[75]

The interrogation officer had then shown Ambrosius a selection of better-quality photographs of Kiel and Wilhelmshaven, taken from 3,000 metres. It led to Ambrosius speculating with May as to whether the British could successfully bomb German runways and installations based on such photographs.[76]

Apart from interrogation, British officers sometimes 'befriended' a prisoner if it was thought the softening-up process would reveal information. The prisoner might be taken for a walk and chat, or for an alcoholic drink alone in relaxed surroundings. The result of these friendly chats often came out in the conversations between fellow prisoners afterwards. The British officer might talk about politics and try to gauge the prisoner's opinion on certain matters which might lead to him inadvertently giving something away. The intelligence officer might tell the prisoner that the Führer had not kept his word about having no design on Czechoslovakia.[77] This was something that could not easily be refuted and such evidence of deceit was intended to plant doubt and criticism in the mind of the prisoner.

Captured German officer Lieutenant Fritz Wenzel found himself in a cell with his old comrade, Hans Engel; as former interrogator Matthew Sullivan recalled:

> They had a great deal to say to each other and naturally took the precaution of talking softly and frequently changing position. They also had a good look around the walls, but despite the most meticulous search, they never succeeded in finding any trace of a microphone; so perhaps they were over-cautious. The brilliant device of incorporating a microphone in the electric light fitting was never detected by any prisoner.[78]

Prisoners were sometimes befriended at Trent Park:

> The game played with him [Fritz Wenzel] was an hour's pleasant walk in the park with a British naval officer . . . Wenzel of course giving nothing away – unless afterwards to the listening socket in the cell. Why otherwise was he at Cockfosters for a month? Not just so that he could catch up on his reading from the excellent library![79]

In another case, a German armaments officer of a coastal unit was held in confinement almost exclusively with his interrogator who took him out,

> for trips to armament establishments near London and for meals in restaurants . . . The report on this prisoner, one of the few who really

did not know he was being interrogated, became for the next six months the book of reference on bombs, fuses and aircraft armament. It was first learned from this officer with surprise that Germany had radar at the beginning of the war.[80]

The subtle demythologising of a prisoner's confidence in Nazi Germany was a common tactic. Sullivan wrote of Felkin:

His favourite time of day was at night. Over a glass of whisky in Room A, which was fitted out like a sitting room, he would slowly convince a POW that Germany had lost the war. This he proved by taking the prisoner for a night out in London to show the German that the city, far from being in ruins, as Goebbels claimed, was bustling with activity and night life.[81]

Such excursions served as a subtle propaganda tool and were important alongside the gathering of intelligence to provoke the prisoner into questioning the Nazi leadership and whether Germans had been brainwashed. A prisoner might even begin to express his concerns about the Nazi leadership to his cellmate. When this happened, it confirmed that the various ruses being used by British intelligence were indeed working.

CHAPTER 3

Trent Park

The first prisoners to arrive at Trent Park comprised mainly U-boat crew and Luftwaffe officers.[1] Relatively few army prisoners were captured during this first phase of the war; their influx did not gather momentum until after the successful British campaigns in North Africa in 1942. By the end of the first year of the war, Kendrick had submitted 1,533 reports, the majority emanating from the Air Intelligence section at Trent Park.[2] The material was classified into categories Top Secret, Most Secret or Secret, determining who had the right to see it. Female staff undertook much of the clerical administration of typing up interrogations, summary reports, and Special Reports from bugged conversations.

Kendrick's first intelligence report showed that the secret listeners had gathered extensive and detailed knowledge about Germany's military capabilities.[3] An appendix to the survey gave a comprehensive list of the main topics emerging from bugged conversations on which reports were available. They included aerial and magnetic torpedoes, aerodromes in German-occupied countries, armour, artillery, Austria, Bulgaria, British POWs, cavalry, conditions in Germany, enemy aircraft equipment, Gestapo, Goebbels, Goering, hand grenades, Himmler, Hitler, Hitler Youth, identification of [German] units, Jews, losses (army, German air force and navy), Mussolini, navigation on aircraft, parachute troops, Poland, production of enemy aircraft, rockets, 'S' boats, small arms, SS, strength of enemy armed forces, tanks, training of enemy forces, U-boats, weapons, Western Front, Zeppelin.[4]

The transcripts occasionally provide details of daily life. Three U-boat prisoners were overheard telling each other not to give anything away to the British in interrogation.[5] One of them, designated N209, was security-conscious and told his mates: 'We have a microphone in our room, built in above the fireplace. I unscrewed the lid. Up to now I've been in room B.1. There is an aviator in the room opposite. He is a W/T [wireless telegraphy] operator called A40. An air force officer keeps visiting him and talks to him by the hour.'[6] N210 signalled his name through to N184 by tapping on the wall. The transcript then notes that N184 said to him: 'N210 come close to the wall and try to talk. Do you hear me? . . . Did you tell anything about our boat? [silence] That's too hot. They have a microphone in here after all.' (Begins to knock on the walls to find the microphone.) Guard enters: 'Did you knock?' N184 replied to the guard: 'Yes, I want to go to the lavatory.' He is taken to the toilet and on his return resumed his conversation through the wall, discussing how there were thirty experienced U-boat officers in the camp.[7]

The discovery of microphones was rare, but if a prisoner was known to have found one or was actively looking for bugging devices, he was swiftly transferred away to another camp.[8]

Up until the end of December 1940, 685 German airmen were brought to Trent Park.[9] What they provided was contained in over a thousand reports and often related to technology aboard their aircraft: 'It can be said without fear of contradiction that there was hardly an aircraft, an aircraft engine, bomb or piece of aircraft armament which was not known by ADI(K) through the interrogation of prisoners, often a considerable time before the emergence of such a weapon in operations.'[10]

Luftwaffe pilots talked about their respect for the British Spitfire which was holding its own in the skies over England. The following extract comes from a recorded conversation between a wireless operator (A26) and a pilot (A29).

A26: The Spitfire overtakes us.
A29: A first class machine! What a pity we haven't one like her.

A26: She has better manoeuvrability and . . .

A29: (interrupting) Goes faster?

A26: Yes . . .

A29: If the Spitfire goes up to 10,000 metres, or even 9,000 metres, the fighters will not catch up so easily; even the 109 will find it difficult enough.[11]

Luftwaffe pilots now pinned their hopes on Germany's new Focke-Wulf fighter which was expected to go into action shortly. In the same conversation, pilot A29 admitted to A26 that he had flown the new Focke-Wulf fighter. A26 then commented that there was another new machine. To which pilot A29 replied: 'The HE177 dive bomber; it is to go to the formation that I was to join. But they [the British] mustn't find out anything about it and we mustn't talk about it in camp. It is still being kept dark, even in Germany.'[12] The following was overheard about the Spitfire and Luftwaffe formations for attack on coastal cities and docks:

A344: The Spitfire is better at banking than the '110'. Our W/T operator only has four weapons in the moveable turret. He can't shoot straight in front. The Air Force has equipped the '109' with bombs. It is a marvellous idea and works quite splendidly. During the attack we flew in *Staffel* formations. One *Staffel* always flies 2,000 metres lower than the other. We set fire to all the oil stores in Portland, Weymouth and Plymouth. They shot down six of us.[13]

A comment made by a Luftwaffe pilot to his cellmate on 28 March 1940 revealed: 'The whole of North Germany is one big aerodrome. The further north one goes, the worse it becomes.'[14]

Major General Francis H. Davidson (the new director of Military Intelligence) commented on Kendrick's first report: 'I have inspected the whole show and thought it very efficiently run: and the general spirit of this Survey (and the weekly reports) shows the true spirit of attacking intelligence.'[15]

BATTLE OF THE BOFFINS

In the spring of 1940, the operations at Trent Park discovered new technology being used by the German air force – Knickebein, X-Gerät and Y-Gerät – which, according to Felkin, had far-reaching consequences.[16] Knickebein made use of a radio navigation system developed for civil aircraft for use in bad visibility, broadcasting two adjoining radio beams in line with a runway.[17] If the plane was to one side of the runway line the pilot would hear 'dot' pips in his headphones, if on the other he would hear 'dashes', and when they merged into a single unbroken tone, he would know that he was approaching along the centre line of the runway. In the bombing aid system, two such guide beams were sent from widely spaced transmitters, aimed to cross over the target. The bomber flew along one guide beam, and when the other beam signal could be heard (on another receiver) the pilot knew he was over the target. The British did everything possible to jam Knickebein and render it ineffective.[18]

X-Gerät, the new Y beam technology fitted to Luftwaffe planes, was developed when the British became too good at interfering with Knickebein. It functioned like an early radar system enabling pilots to conduct more precise bombing raids across England:[19] the bomber flew along a main guide beam, intersected by cross signals set at specific distances from each other and from the target. On getting the signal from the first intersecting beam, a timer was started. On crossing the second, a further impulse would be fed into the timer. As the distance between the intersecting beams was known, this showed the ground speed of the aircraft irrespective of headwind or tailwind, so at the moment the bomber reached the target (again at a known distance from the second intersecting beam) the timer automatically released the bombs.

An early reference to X-Gerät was recorded in February 1940 between a Lance Corporal (A35) and a Wireless Operator (A38). A35 commented to A38:

They [the British] have just shot down a machine in which an X-Gerät is installed and they can try it out as much as they like, for it is so secret that only he knows about it, or the crew knows it and if the crew keeps its mouth shut they'll never find it out. They can try it out and examine it as much as they like. It is a sort of apparatus that they will never find out.[20]

Twenty-eight-year-old scientist, Professor Reginald Victor (R.V.) Jones was engaged as head of the Scientific Section of MI6. Working from his office at MI6 headquarters at 54 Broadway, he was to advise on the technical intelligence being gathered at Trent Park.[21] He also became a key scientific advisor to Churchill and the Cabinet on X-Gerät, Knickebein, and eventually V weapons, after Churchill became Prime Minister in May 1940.[22]

The significance of the discovery of this technology cannot be overstated. It provided British intelligence with knowledge of new technology being used by the Luftwaffe in sufficient time for 'the British authorities to prepare countermeasures against a method of bombing which in the autumn of 1940 constituted a very real threat to British War Industries.'[23]

On 10 April 1940, Kendrick received a glowing letter from Norman Crockatt (head of MI9) about the discovery of X-Gerät, with congratulations to 'those officers under you who contributed so largely to one of the most successful pieces of intelligence investigation I have ever come across.'[24] Crockatt later reported: 'The secret recordings produced some of the earliest information of the German experiments in Air Navigational aids (March 1940), and has played an important part in the successful development of the British counter-measures.'[25]

A German bomber pilot (A807) told another pilot (A777) that the British interrogation officer already knew that two beams were sent out from a base in Cherbourg, but nothing more detailed than that. Pilot A777 replied: 'They know that all the construction work is carried out by the French. He has a rough idea of it, but he doesn't know exactly, especially about the new Y-Gerät.'[26]

The prisoner had just unsuspectingly given away the existence of Y-Gerät which the Germans had devised to overcome English interference in earlier technology. It was harder to jam than a system of cross beams, allowing ground controllers to determine the position of the bomber by measuring time delay of responding (reflecting) signals from the aircraft, giving distance from the ground station and instructing the pilot by radio.[27] For bombing purposes, Y-Gerät was claimed to be accurate to within an area of 200 square yards. The prisoners did not appear to know the precise location of the beam transmitters, but they did know that there were two positions: Zentrale A and Zentrale B. 'A' was west of Cherbourg and 'B' in the neighbourhood of Kassel. Once British intelligence knew the location of these transmitters, the information was passed to the RAF which authorised air sorties to attack the transmitters. Although a map of the system had been captured by the British, it was barely legible. It was only from the bugged conversations that British intelligence was able to reconstruct most of the beam lines of the Y-system.

The Y-system operated from Kassel to Hull, Sheffield, Liverpool, Birmingham and London, and from a point just west of Cherbourg to London and Sheffield. At least four tracks were drawn from Poix and at least seven from Fécamp. This system was effective for the Luftwaffe until the British learned to transmit false 'reflecting' signals from Alexandra Palace in North London. Within a year, all German aircraft had been equipped for the Y-system but prisoners were still talking about Knickebein.[28]

NAVAL INTELLIGENCE SECTION

In 1940, British warships and submarines battled hard for supremacy at sea. Losses from attacks by the German navy and U-boats inflicted serious damage on the Royal Navy, merchant shipping and supply lines into Britain. It was a difficult battle that would last most of the war. During the period of Kendrick's first survey to the end of 1940, 447 German naval officers and 31 Italian naval officers passed through Trent Park. They comprised survivors from thirteen U-boats and one armed German trawler.[29]

Italian naval POWs provided very little by way of information, except to give an indication of low morale amongst their crews. The German

POWs, on the other hand, yielded the most valuable intelligence. From their conversations, British intelligence established details of the strength and movement of German U-boats and their losses during the Norwegian campaign, and monitored the progress of Germany's new battleship construction programme.[30]

On technical matters, the most important naval information for this period was the discovery of the new magnetically-fused torpedo.[31] Some of the prisoners spoke about it in detail. In simple terms, it could be fired from a U-boat and explode underneath a British ship as soon as it detected the magnetic field from that ship. The Admiralty had already added a degaussing coil to its ships to de-magnetise them as protection against German magnetic mines lying on the sea bed. To counter the new threat from magnetically-fused torpedoes, the Admiralty added extra degaussing coils. This was done in sufficient time before the Germans had the chance to use them effectively in action and is one example of how intelligence from the M Room about new technology had a direct impact on the Battle of the Atlantic.

On 12 March 1940, Burton Scott Rivers Cope joined the Naval Intelligence section at Trent Park.[32] His grandson, Derek Nudd comments: 'It was the nature of the job that he left few footprints.'[33] Burton Cope, born to English parents in Munich in 1885, was a fluent German speaker and had served in Naval Intelligence in the First World War. In the inter-war years, he worked abroad for Cunard White Star Lines and was living in Paris with his Swiss wife Marie Louise Girard and young daughter when the Second World War broke out. They returned to London and Cope was sent to Trent Park where the small Naval Intelligence section then comprised the interrogators Lieutenant Colonel Bernard Trench, Lieutenant Commander Edward Croghan, Lieutenants Richard Pennell and Wilfred Samuel, all of whom already had at least two months experience of interrogation at Trent Park before Cope arrived.[34] Lieutenant Commander Philip Wood Rhodes was engaged in liaison between the Director of Naval Intelligence and MI9. By the end of the year, they had been joined by Sub-Lieutenant Dick (Richard) Weatherby and Miss E.R. Heath (civilian assistant).

From April 1940, letters to and from naval POWs went via the Naval Intelligence section at Cockfosters for censorship.[35] The censor discovered that the prisoners were coding their letters to Germany but, as the codes had already been broken by the British, they were allowed to go through as British intelligence wanted to see the coded replies from Germany.[36] The letters revealed precise attempts by Germany to deliberately plant trained POWs amongst the ordinary prisoners to instruct them in methods of cooperation with airborne troops when Germany began the invasion of Britain.[37]

The Naval Intelligence section at Trent Park expanded to include John Weatherby and Ralph Izzard, formerly of the *Daily Mail* newspaper, as interrogators.[38] After D-Day, Izzard served in liberated Europe with Ian Fleming's 30 Assault Unit, a special commando unit that raided Germany and its occupied territories to obtain its new technology, equipment, documentation, scientists and technologists in a race before they fell into Russian hands.[39] Izzard is said to have provided the inspiration for a scene in Fleming's Bond novel, *Casino Royale*.

The female team were Evelyn Barron, Jean Flower, Claudia Furneaux, Esme Mackenzie, Gwen Neal-Wall, Celia Thomas and Petty Officer Ruth Hales.[40] The WRNS spoke fluent German and knew as much about the German navy as the male interrogators.[41] In a rare interview, Evelyn Barron revealed the work of the female team: 'We did not do translation work, we were the interrogators. The German prisoners found it most unnerving to be interrogated by a woman!'[42] Apart from CSDIC Cairo and one female interrogator with MI9 at Wilton Park, the Naval Intelligence section is the only unit known to have used female interrogators in the Second World War. Their insight and analytical skills in processing the intelligence gained from prisoners improved the work of the unit. Furneaux was also known to have accompanied U-boat officers on a pub-crawl in London, as a reward for their cooperative behaviour.[43] The naval section was soon joined by Brian Connell, who was fluent in four languages, Czech refugee Harry Scholar, and Charles Wheeler, a young officer in the Royal Marines.[44] Colin McFadyean, an idealist, fluent in German and French, had been appointed in September

1939 by Ian Fleming to head the German section in Naval Intelligence;[45] he joined the team at Trent Park in March 1942.[46]

Donald Burkewood Welbourn joined the Naval Intelligence team as an interrogator on the personal recommendation of Commander Cyril Francis Tower (the officer in charge of the German section).[47] When a U-boat crew arrived at CSDIC, they were first stripped, searched and given a bath. Welbourn commented:

> They were often in need of clean clothes, since the stench of the typical leather clothing of U-boat crew, compounded of sweat, diesel oil and many other things, has a pungency which does not commend itself. An interrogator would be present, since a lot could be learned at this stage; nothing but German coins in the pockets suggested a boat straight from Germany. Letters from home, condoms, notebooks, all added scraps of information about the man and his boat.[48]

Once the crews had been given clean clothes and civilian rations, they were put in a cell with another mate. A little later, they were interrogated. The time between first arriving in the cell and their interrogation was a crucial period when M Room operators listened into the conversations for idle chatter. This careless talk gave the interrogators a head start. 'If, when a man came in for interrogation,' commented Welbourn, 'we could start by giving him the number, and sometimes the nickname of his boat, with the captain's name, his base and a pretty good description of where she had been before, he might think that we already knew so much that the effort of not talking was not worthwhile.'

THE NORWEGIAN CAMPAIGN

On 9 April 1940, Norway and Denmark were overrun by German forces. Between 9 April and 10 June 1940, in what is known as the Norwegian Campaign, British forces sought to repel German troops with the aid of French and Finnish resistance fighters. Although there was some success at Narvik (northern Norway) with heavy losses inflicted on the U-boats and German destroyers, the campaign ended in military failure for the Allies and marked the beginning of six years of German occupation of Norway.[49] The sinking of the British aircraft carrier HMS *Glorious* off Norway in June 1940, with the loss of over 1,200 men, was one of the biggest naval disasters of the war.

In spite of the overwhelming losses, some enemy POWs were captured during the Norwegian campaign. They were brought back to Trent Park, interrogated by Trench, Croghan, Samuel and Pennell,[50] and their subsequent conversations were bugged.[51] Amongst them were survivors of U-49 which had been sunk near the port of Harstad (Norway) on 15 April 1940. At the end of April, steps were taken to increase the number of interrogators at Trent Park to cope with the work expected following the capture of POWs from the Norwegian campaign.[52] Captain Steege, Lieutenant Hornby, Lieutenant Jeune and Lieutenant Burrows were added to the team of army interrogators.[53] They were trained by Captain Alexander Scotland (Intelligence Corps and MI9), an expert in the interrogation of German POWs during the First World War.[54] In early 1940, he was based at Cockfosters[55] in a small interrogation quarter at Ludgrove Hall – a small country house in Games Road, and once part of the Trent Park estate.[56]

The new interrogators were dispatched to various ports around Britain, attached to the RAF and Royal Navy, to interrogate selected POWs for MI9. The MI9 war diary noted: 'The operations in Norway have resulted in considerable increase in the activities of MI9(a). Much useful information has been received from this source.'[57] There is no elaboration on the kind of information gained.

On 10 May 1940 came the news of the fall of Holland, Belgium and Luxembourg to Nazi forces. This caused 'considerable work for MI9 and arrangements for the reception of numbers of POWs, including parachutists',[58] as fighting in the Low Countries increased the number of enemy prisoners being brought to Trent Park; most were captured in Holland. All Whitsun leave for MI9 staff, including those at Trent Park, was cancelled.[59] By mid-May, it was reported that:

The fighting in the Low Countries in the last week has materially affected the activities of MI9 . . . The advent of a number of enemy POWs captured in Holland has necessitated the rapid organisation of a corps of interrogators who have been dispatched to the various ports of arrival and in conjunction with the RN and RAF have been interrogating selected enemy POWs.[60]

The MI9 war diary noted: 'The agents' house at Cockfosters has also been requisitioned.'[61] Files do not name the house, but it was part of preparations to expand the secret capabilities and facilities of this aspect of MI9's work.

Prisoners from the Norwegian Campaign were still being interrogated in June 1940 and provided detailed information on the U-boat war in the region, related in particular to two battles at Narvik, and revealing what the Germans knew about British submarines operating in the area.[62]

ARMY INTELLIGENCE

With much of Western Europe under Nazi occupation, Britain was next in line for invasion. Kendrick's first survey report for 3 September 1939 to 31 December 1940 draws on information provided from only 113 German officers and other ranks.[63] Prisoners captured in this period described tank battles in France prior to the evacuation of the British Expeditionary Force at Dunkirk from May to June 1940. Other conversations dealt with the type of tanks used, railway guns and the 'liquid air' weapon.[64] Some German army prisoners spoke about the airborne assault by German troops during the invasion of Holland and the heavy losses of men and aircraft. All types and sizes of missile were mentioned, revealing that German bombs were gradually increasing in size to 3,600 kilogrammes each. In addition to high explosive devices, references were made to other special types of weaponry such as liquid air, oxygen, cable and flame bombs.[65] Some prisoners expressed doubts that Germany could win the war by bombing techniques alone, thus providing an insight for British intelligence on the reality of the German military capability.

The most frequent discussions concerned a possible invasion of Britain, morale in the German forces, and the use of gas in warfare.[66] As expectations of an invasion heightened, so talk of the possibility and tactics became more frequent in prisoners' discussions, especially in July and early August, then again from mid-September to November 1940.[67] Prisoners discussed the points at which the invasion would be made, the different communications to be used during it, and methods of invasion: the use of gliders, cement-strengthened barges to carry tanks, and underwater tanks and long-range guns mounted along the French coast.[68] The secret listeners picked up preliminary references to a possible cancellation of Hitler's autumn invasion plans, providing British military command with the first signs that Britain's shores may yet be safe.[69]

In the period up to July 1940, the morale of the German armed forces appears to have been consistently high. Fighting morale was still defined by the belief in an early victory against Britain and that prisoners would be home by Christmas.[70] As this became more unlikely, a mood of pessimism prevailed until renewed hopes of an invasion of Britain's shores surfaced in conversations. Bugged conversations during 1940 monitored the behaviour of German troops in Nazi-occupied countries; in Belgium and Holland, German troops requisitioned whatever they could. In France, the Resistance organised acts of sabotage: captured POWs talked at Trent Park about how aircraft were damaged at night and the German telephone wires were cut; in the neighbourhood of Hitler's headquarters, the lights went down and it was reported that 350 people were shot as a result. British intelligence learnt that French inhabitants were hiding English airmen and, according to one prisoner, '. . . telephone wires tapped and information transmitted to England by an espionage organisation, twenty members of which have been arrested in Brest'.[71]

Thirty-six Italian POWs passed through Trent Park during the period of Kendrick's first survey, and as he himself commented, they yielded virtually no useful intelligence, except comments which revealed that they had a poor opinion of Italy's war capabilities.[72] Italian prisoners and intelligence will not be explored further in this book.

During the Battle of Britain, German prisoners' conversations began to reveal a more general picture of the extent of German losses incurred in the heavy daylight raids and losses on night flights. In one report, a prisoner quoted Kesselring (a Field Marshal) as saying that during 1940 Germany was losing 280 aircraft a month from accidents alone. It was difficult for British military commanders to independently assess German losses from the dog-fights over enemy territory; this would require flying reconnaissance missions over those areas, but British pilots were occupied with combat and defending the country. During an air raid alarm on 2 September 1940, two prisoners at Trent Park discussed a battle overhead. Prisoner B said: 'You can see it from here, a Spitfire up there. Just there – underneath. It has flown in a sort of arc. There it comes again over here.'[73] Prisoner A replied: 'Oh! There is a Zerstörer [More M.G. fire and roaring of engines is heard]. There it is again, the Spitfire, always following up.'

The secret listeners picked up that the Germans had tried out a type of 'nerve gas' with temporary soporific effect at Maastricht during the invasion of Holland in May 1940.[74] Although the majority of references to gas were of a general kind, British intelligence discovered from bugged conversations that Germany would not employ gas in an attack against Britain unless Britain used it first.[75] Other prisoners spoke about the alleged use of an 'anaesthetising gas' in Belgium.[76]

FRANZ VON WERRA

Germany's flying ace Franz von Werra was captured on 5 September 1940 after his plane was shot down over Kent during the Battle of Britain. His daring escapades were later immortalised in 1957 in the British film, *The One That Got Away*. He was held in barracks in Maidstone for a few days, where he attempted his first escape. He was transferred to Trent Park and interrogated by Felkin, but there is no evidence that he tried to escape from there. Von Werra was found to be 'the most optimistic of the believers in Hitler's victory'[77] and was even considered by MI9 to be 'a completely successful product of Nazi education'.[78] It was reported from his bugged conversations between 16 and 19 September 1940 that:

> He approves pogroms and the beating of prisoners in concentration camps … Von Werra's opinions are quoted at length for their psychological interest. His supreme confidence is exceptional.[79]

Von Werra was transferred from Trent Park to Grizedale Hall, a prisoner-of-war camp in Lancashire known as No.1 camp, run by Lieutenant Colonel Morton. On 7 October 1940, von Werra escaped from Grizedale Hall, was recaptured five days later and promptly sentenced to three weeks in solitary confinement at Camp No.13 in Swanwick, Derbyshire. In January 1941, he was transferred with other German prisoners of war to a camp in Canada though he again escaped and eventually made his way back to Germany. Later that year he saw active service on the Eastern Front and continued his dangerous missions. He died on 25 October 1941 after crashing into the sea, north of Vlissingen, off the Netherlands coast.

The intelligence work was demanding. Army intelligence officer Charles Deveson was one of the few to speak about it in general terms during his lifetime. His son, Richard, commented:

> My father always emphasised how taxing the work was – the long hours, the need for intense concentration, the time-pressure, the often harrowing nature of the material and the unpleasantness of some of the prisoners (though others were quite reasonable).[80]

Born in London in 1910, Deveson had studied English at Oxford and taught at an exclusive boys' boarding school in Prussia. He returned to England in 1936. At the outbreak of war, he was enlisted into the Royal Armoured Corps but, by 1941, was transferred to the Intelligence Corps and sent to Trent Park. Kendrick asked him to sign the Official Secrets

Act and then, it is said, Deveson was handed a pistol across the desk and told: 'If you ever betray anything about this work, here is the gun with which I expect you to do the decent thing. If you don't, I will.'[81] The secrecy of Trent Park and its clandestine operation had to be protected at all costs.

Amongst his files, Charles Deveson left brief pencilled notes about his work at Trent Park.[82] Information was gathered by the unit on every conceivable subject, and in many cases the first indication of a new enemy weapon or device was given away in the recorded conversations. On naval matters, he listed U-boat types, tactics, names of commanders, methods of attack, torpedoes, mines (magnetic and acoustic), codes, cyphers, gunnery, human torpedoes and details of the major units of the German navy, which included the sinking of the *Bismarck*, *Scharnhorst* and *Tirpitz*. On military subjects, he mentioned tanks (details of new models and tank production), rockets (location of sites and description of firing ramps), very detailed information on the Gestapo, and character studies of senior officers (including Rommel and Rundstedt) and their relations with Hitler. General material was picked up for use in Black Propaganda: bomb damage, morale, atrocities, Hitler's headquarters, and conditions in occupied countries.[83]

In terms of Air Intelligence, Deveson mentioned the information gathered on the Battle of Britain, air tactics, navigational methods, new kinds of aircraft, advanced information on the bombing of Coventry and Glasgow, bombs and guns, and details about night fighters.

EXPANSION OF THE M ROOM

In late 1940, plans were discussed to expand the M Room operation to two further sites in Britain.[84] It was believed that Trent Park would prove inadequate for the large influx of prisoners captured in the coming campaigns of the war.[85] Two estates in the heart of the Buckinghamshire countryside were considered: Latimer House near Chesham, and Wilton Park at Beaconsfield. The nearest railway station to the former was Chalfont & Latimer on the Metropolitan Line and, to the latter, Seer

Green or Beaconsfield. Both sites were therefore within easy reach of London, discreet and well hidden to preserve the secrecy of the operation. A meeting took place at Latimer House in January 1941 to establish its suitability as a second site for CSDIC.[86]

A month later, construction work was already under way and Latimer became known as Camp 30 or No.1 Distribution Centre (No.1 DC),[87] while Wilton Park became Camp 300 or No.2 Distribution Centre (No.2 DC).[88] A short distance from each of the stately houses temporary prefabricated wartime buildings were constructed for CSDIC: two parallel blocks of cells, interrogation rooms, an administration block, an M Room, a block for Naval Intelligence, a cookhouse, guard block and Nissen huts were distributed within the grounds. As with Trent Park, the sites were secretly 'wired', with the bugging devices hidden in the light fittings of the cells and wired back to the M Room.

Latimer House and estate belonged to John Compton Cavendish, the 4th Lord Chesham. On 12 September 1939, he had entered into negotiations with New Scotland Yard for the red brick mock-Tudor house to be given over as a convalescent home for air raid casualties from the Metropolitan Police. Having been requisitioned, it was soon occupied by a unit of the Northamptonshire Yeomanry and then became the headquarters of IV Corps. Security surrounding IV Corps was paramount and Lord Chesham was required to vacate the estate. He purchased the Old Rectory opposite and moved there, but little could he foresee that he would never live in Latimer House again: at the end of the war, it was subject to a compulsory purchase order by the government for the sum of £30,000, in spite of Lord Chesham contesting the decision for five years. During 1941, the estate was vacated by all army units and construction work began.

Wilton Park in Beaconsfield, some nine miles from Latimer, was a thirteenth-century estate that once belonged to the Whelton family. It was later purchased by the Du Pre family. Josias Du Pre had carried out profitable trading through the East India Company with such success that he was able to commission the building of a large Palladian-style mansion, dubbed the 'White House', at Wilton Park. During the Second

World War, the estate was requisitioned from Colonel William Baring Du Pre. This estate too was subject to a compulsory purchase after the war, as buildings on the site were used in the government's denazification programme for prisoners being repatriated to Germany. The White House fell into disrepair and was demolished in 1967.

The intelligence services and Chiefs of Staff held various meetings during 1941 to discuss the expansion programme. Their conclusions survive in a series of memoranda by the Joint Intelligence Committee in Cabinet Papers.[89] The memoranda were marked 'strictly limited circulation' and to be 'KEPT UNDER LOCK AND KEY' because they were highly classified. The intelligence chiefs concluded that the unit was:

> Of the utmost operational importance, vital to the needs of the three fighting services and should accordingly be given the highest degree of priority in all its requirements, that the normal formalities regarding surveys, plans and tenders should be waived and that any work required should be put in hand at once and completed by the earliest possible date irrespective of cost.[90]

Amongst the signatories of this recommendation to the Joint Intelligence Committee were Stewart Menzies ('C'), John Godfrey (head of NID) and Francis Davidson (DMI). The Joint Intelligence Committee approved the request and Kendrick did not need to go through the usual channels for authorisation.[91] The priority of extending the bugging operation was underlined by John Godfrey when he reported: 'I regard this as of such importance as to override normal considerations of cost and I hope that you will be able to use every endeavour to see that this expansion is given absolute priority.'[92]

Godfrey's counterpart at the Air Ministry, Archibald Boyle, wrote to the Director of Military Intelligence, Major General Francis Davidson, on 19 December 1940:

> The value of the information obtained has been inestimable, and at all costs must continue to be obtained to the fullest possible extent.

I want to emphasise how important it is from the Air point of view, for nothing to stand in the way of the development of this Centre to a maximum output in a minimum space of time.[93]

A memorandum that survives in Cabinet Offices files indicates that unlimited funds had been authorised for this expansion to two new sites.[94] To make the sites operational was estimated at a cost of over £400,000 (equivalent to around £25 million today).[95] Clearly, funding of that level would not be released to a unit that was speculative or might not have produced results. This intelligence unit was considered indispensable for the war and was not therefore to be restricted by a lack of funds.

However, a problem soon arose: two new aerodromes were in the process of being constructed near Wilton Park and at Bovingdon, just three miles from Latimer House. Kendrick wrote to Crockatt (head of MI9) explaining the issues:

If an aeroplane passes in the vicinity of the house, even at an appreciable height, M Room operation is momentarily blacked out. This has occurred in a number of cases when conversations on subjects of primary importance were being recorded. The loss of a phrase or a significant word may render unintelligible some vital source of information.[96]

Kendrick's concern was discussed at a meeting of the Joint Intelligence Committee.[97] Intelligence chiefs agreed that construction of the aerodrome at Wilton Park had to be cancelled. Bovingdon aerodrome was already sixty per cent completed at a cost of £300,000, and so to minimise interference with Latimer, it was downgraded to a ground training station for Bomber Command, with flying restrictions in place.[98]

JUSTIFYING THE M ROOM

Norman Crockatt wrote in his evaluation report: 'The regular and continuous supply of SR and SP reports . . . provides accurate and completely untendentious information on the general topics outlined. Providing a regular supply is maintained, these methods produce better results than would intensive direct interrogation of POWs who have already been subjected to this by Navy and/or Air Force.'[99]

Kendrick circulated a questionnaire to various departments of military intelligence asking whether the information obtained from the bugged conversations was of relevance or important to that department. MI6 stated that the interrogation reports and Special Reports were 'of considerable importance and their method of presentation is excellent'.[100] MI14, which specialised in intelligence about Germany, replied that they were:

> . . . of vital importance in connection with enemy preparations for combined operations. It is of importance in adding to our records of personalities, Field Post Numbers, locations . . . concerning enemy morale, the German scene, relations between party and the army, political opinions, etc. In this connection these reports are frequently of considerable interest in so far as they provide possible material for the broadcasts to the German army.

Moreover, the German text of the conversations was of special value 'in certain cases where the English text unavoidably leaves a doubt in the reader's mind as to the exact shade of meaning'.[101]

The Air Ministry provided guidance on the kind of information it needed from the M Room and what topics the secret listeners should record. The topics of interest to the Air Ministry included knowledge of tactics of German air force bomber and reconnaissance pilots by night and day, heights at which they attacked targets, routes most frequently used and methods of identifying targets, use made of beams, and flak.

A reply from the Political Intelligence Department (Foreign Office) highlighted the importance of M Room intelligence for propaganda purposes, especially for information which they could not obtain any other way: 'These reports are our only first-hand information concerning the state of mind of the clients for our propaganda.' It went on to say that, 'the present dialogue form of SR reports is of greater value, but in order to conceal the method by which these reports are obtained we are glad to have the summarized intelligence reports as it enables us safely to give them a slightly wider, though still restricted circulation.'[102]

Norman Crockatt commented that there was much material which 'had no Service value, but deals with Party scandals, local colour, erotic stories and low-class jokes. Such material, we are assured, is of great propaganda value'.[103]

The MI5 counter-intelligence department, working out of Room 055A at the War Office, confirmed:

> Not only do we obtain technical knowledge from the reports, but we get also a line on the standard technical training given to German air force personnel . . . The German text is of great value, not because there exists grounds for criticism of your translations, but because the text in the original language occasionally conveys something which is lost in translation.[104]

Much of the achievement of this period was due to the interpersonal skills of Kendrick himself. At the sites, he frequently entertained the top brass of British intelligence as well as important personnel from the Admiralty, Anti-aircraft Command, War Office, Foreign Office, Air Force and Army. By hosting lunches, he built up the necessary rapport for total cooperation between himself and other departments. A tour of parts of the site, within certain limits, enabled them to see first-hand the nature of the work and how it had a bearing on intelligence gathering for their departments.

Lieutenant-General Sir Frederick Pile of Anti-aircraft Command headquarters, Stanmore, wrote to Kendrick after one such luncheon: 'In future, when I read the reports I get, their value will be enhanced at least fifty per cent by knowing how these reports are arrived at . . . I get more value out of them than out of any of the intelligence summaries which reach me.'[105]

The M Room operation was running like clockwork.

CHAPTER 4

Prized Prisoners, Idle Chatter

The results of the M Room were to prove crucial during 1941, especially for the Battle of the Atlantic. Prisoners captured during this period still comprised mainly U-boat crews and Luftwaffe personnel.[1] German air force prisoners spoke about specific bombing raids. One prisoner commented: 'When it is full moon, it is better to attack Plymouth and the other seaports, then you can see every street, every lay-out and every building.'[2] Plymouth was one of the cities to receive devastating attacks from the German air force, reducing much of the city centre to rubble.

In the first two months of 1941, the bugged conversations from U-boat personnel gave the first indication that Hitler planned to intensify U-boat attacks from March and carry out a blockade of Britain to starve the country into submission.[3] They also provided advance intelligence that U-boats were about to start attacking shipping escorts as well as the supply convoys.[4] Kendrick's first six-monthly report for 1941 noted that the number of prisoners from the German navy amounted to 288, 5 from the Italian navy, and 238 German air force personnel.[5] Their interrogation and bugged conversations enabled British intelligence to keep abreast of the movements, numbers and losses within the U-boat fleets, as well as U-boat tactics in attacking convoys.[6] Invasion of Britain was no longer a major theme of conversation amongst the prisoners, and if mentioned, doubt was expressed that it would take place at all.[7] Throughout 1941, several copies of the transcripts were sent to each of MI9, the Admiralty and Air Intelligence, and when necessary to MI6.

These organisations sifted the intelligence and sent it to the relevant departments within their organisation.[8]

During May 1941, a very different picture began to emerge. Prisoners spoke about heavy U-boat losses and the increased difficulty of attacking British shipping from the air because of improved defences by the RAF. One prisoner sought to explain the losses in these terms: 'We were great poets and philosophers, we had Schiller and Goethe, but we have never achieved unity in Germany. That brought us to the edge of the precipice.'[9]

Prisoners still believed they had outsmarted their interrogators. A bomber mechanic captured on 21 February 1941 told his cellmate: 'He [the interrogation officer] asked what engine the Do 217 had. I said, I don't know. As a matter of fact, I do know that it has the Bramo double-row radial engine.'[10]

The following month, a Commando raid, codenamed Operation Claymore, was mounted against the Lofoten Islands. The Norwegian islands were under German occupation and important to Germany's war industry because of the production there of fish oil and glycerine. The raid resulted in the capture of 43 German naval, military and air force personnel. In addition, 169 German civilians and 323 Norwegian patrols (including eight women) were brought back to Britain by the raiding force.[11] All were interrogated at either Trent Park, a command cage (under the aegis of Colonel Scotland), or by MI5 at its interrogation sites.[12] The raid resulted in the capture of documents and, by the end of March, a further influx of prisoners from the operation.[13]

This period also saw the arrival at Trent Park of crew from three U-boats, other German naval personnel and a heavy influx of German air force personnel from the night-fighter successes.[14] Air force prisoners spoke, for example, about three big attacks by the RAF on Wilhelmshaven, a key German port and naval base. One told his cellmate: 'A lot of damage was done – a lot of houses were smashed and about 400 killed and injured.'[15]

Construction work continued as a priority at MI9's two new sites. The MI9 war diary noted that work was 'actively continuing to complete the two new sites at Latimer House and Wilton Park, and part of the premises at Latimer was to be available by 19 May 1941'.[16]

GERMAN WARSHIPS AND U-BOATS

Intelligence from naval prisoners was an absolute necessity in fighting the U-boat menace. The intense battle at sea continued: in the first six months of 1941, two former crew members from the *Admiral Graf Spee*, an armoured cruiser, passed through Trent Park.[17] Inevitably the two prisoners discussed the movements, tactics and details of the German battleships, the *Gneisenau*, the *Tirpitz* and *Scharnhorst*.[18] Not only did they discuss how the battleships refuelled at sea, they also helpfully leaked technical details about their armour, armament, construction and engines. Other prisoners provided descriptions of the damage inflicted on German vessels at the port of Brest, and of submarine schools located at Kiel, Neustadt, Pillau and Gotenhafen.[19]

Survivors of the battleship *Bismarck* described her last voyage in considerable detail, including the damage inflicted during her fight with the British warships *Hood* and *Prince of Wales*, and her sinking on 27 May 1941.[20] The *Bismarck* and her sister ship *Tirpitz* were two of the largest battleships ever built by Germany. British commanders had been closely tracking their movements: the *Bismarck* was tasked with raiding British shipping from North America to Britain and became one of the main surface threats in the north Atlantic. She engaged and destroyed the British battlecruiser HMS *Hood* at the Battle of Denmark Strait on 24 May. Two days later, the *Bismarck* was pursued relentlessly by the Royal Navy and attacked by torpedo bombers from HMS *Ark Royal*. The following morning, 27 May, the British cruiser *Dorsetshire* finished off the *Bismarck* which had been reduced to a helpless hulk by fire from the battleships *King George V* and *Rodney*. German accounts provide an alternative explanation and say that she was scuttled.

When survivors were spotted in the waters the British destroyer *Maori* moved in to pick up 110 Germans from an original crew of 2,200.

They were transferred to Trent Park for interrogation and clandestine monitoring by M Room operators.[21]

The significant number of U-boat losses led to a shift in attitude amongst the prisoners. They began to express doubt to each other about the use of U-boats as a decisive weapon in deciding the outcome of the war. They also provided precise details of losses and numbers of U-boats still operational at sea.[22] In May 1941, one prisoner, described by CSDIC as an anti-Nazi, discussed with his cellmate precise numbers of U-boats, saying that its full strength was fifty, of which twenty were at sea, twenty in port and ten in dock.[23] Other prisoners confirmed that more than seventy U-boats had been in operation, but thirty-five had been sunk, and there was a shortage of trained U-boat crews. References to the loss of a specific U-boat often reached British intelligence through the M Room operation weeks before any official announcement had been made in the German press. It enabled British intelligence to keep abreast of the German threat and fighting capability.

From the M Room came information about mines and torpedoes, including Germany's target areas for mine-laying in British waters.[24] It was discovered that the Germans had introduced a new type of mine with delayed action, acoustic and water-pressure, as well as an improved version of the magnetic mine. Accompanying this information was considerable detail about the various heights from which certain German aircraft dropped mines. As a result, it enabled the Director of Torpedoes and Mining to form an accurate picture of the situation and 'recognise the new object directly it arrived and have an officer on spot without any delay and to issue a warning and guidance at home and abroad'.[25] The information gleaned therefore proved to be crucial.

Due to the improvement of British defences, the German air force had largely abandoned dropping mines from a low altitude. To maintain accuracy from a higher altitude, the Germans were developing a mine-bomb, fitted with fins and without a parachute.[26] Information picked up in secret recordings and interrogations revealed that the enemy was about to make alterations in mining attacks. Praise of this work was received from Godfrey (head of Naval Intelligence), who wrote to the Director of Military Intelligence:

> Without them [the Special Reports] it would have been impossible to piece together the histories of [enemy] ships, their activities and the tactics employed by U-boats in attacking convoys. The hardest naval information to obtain with any degree of reliability concerned technical matters … I wish to convey to the staff at the CSDIC my warm appreciation of their work.[27]

Stewart Menzies (head of MI6) wrote to Norman Crockatt to reinforce the importance of the work at Trent Park:

> From my point of view, the reports are of distinct value, and I trust the work will be maintained and every possible assistance given to the Centre [CSDIC]. It is essential that the Service Departments should collaborate closely by providing Kendrick with the latest questionnaires, without which he must be working largely in the dark.[28]

INTELLIGENCE ABOUT THE GERMAN AIR FORCE

Naval prisoners from two Kondor aircraft discussed the new German 109 fighter and the long-distance bomber HE177.[29] Further discussions on navigation and communication on aircraft provided extremely useful information to MI9. Prisoners continued to mention Knickebein, Elecktra and X-Gerät, and Britain's interference with navigational beams.[30] One of the most significant pieces of intelligence in this period related to the new heavy bomb termed 'Max' (2,500kg), mine-laying techniques and 'the introduction of 1lb incendiaries with a small explosive charge'.[31] At the end of April 1941, two bomber pilots were recorded talking about bombs on aircraft. After interrogation, A830 (captured

8 April 1941) told his cellmate A777 (captured 13 March 1941), 'They knew about our new 5,000kg bomb here', prompting A777 to ask: 'Really! What aircraft carries it?'

'It is not carried. It is towed. It has sort of little wings which somehow fall off at the moment the bomb is released ... Here they know that 5,000kg bomb exists, but they maintain that we have no aircraft capable of carrying them. They don't know that it has wings and is towed,' replied A830.[32]

Most of the information coming out of the M Room was of direct relevance to the Air Ministry and 'enabled Air staff to keep abreast of enemy technical developments and in some instances to take effective counter measures.'[33] Gauging the impact and effects of RAF bombing raids on German cities was not easy once a British pilot had completed his sortie and returned to base. It was here that British intelligence relied on the M Room operators to pick up these details from German prisoners who revealed that substantial damage had been inflicted on places such as Kiel, Wilhelmshaven, Hamburg, Mannheim and Berlin.[34] Morale amongst the German air force was already in decline in 1941 due to heavy losses sustained during their attacks on British shipping and in raids over Britain. Prisoners began to criticise Germany's bombing strategy. Kendrick noted, 'Outspoken pessimism about the outcome of the war is rarely met, but occasional discussion of the possibility of losing the war is in strong contrast to the prevailing mood during 1940 when such talk was virtually unheard of.'[35]

Friendly conversations between a British army officer (one of Kendrick's officers) and a U-boat commander were recorded in the grounds of Trent Park. Prisoner N511 (as he was known) had been present at the launching of the battleship *Prinz Eugen*. He revealed an idolisation of Adolf Hitler when the Führer had stepped on board:

I shall never in all my life forget the moment when I saw the Führer. An electric shock went through and through me and it is just the same when he speaks ... As he stood there on the platform and looked around it was really quite unforgettable. The Führer casts a spell over anyone he looks at.[36]

The weakening of belief in an early victory, often promised by Hitler, led some prisoners at Trent Park to express a considerable measure of political criticism.[37] Kendrick noted: 'Hitler remains for the majority of prisoners above controversy, but towards the end of the period under review, there were several unusually irreverent references to Hitler by Naval personnel.'[38]

In terms of German military strategy, naval prisoners spoke freely to each other about the movement of German aircraft to Romania and U-Boat personnel to Bulgaria. Relations between Germany and Russia were said to be strained and heavy fortifications were being constructed on Germany's Eastern Front. There was talk of the deployment of a new long-range bomber, HE177, against cities like Moscow and increased references to the movement of troops to the East. This was accompanied by some withdrawal of aircraft away from the West. From these conversations, British intelligence could monitor Hitler's military build-up for the invasion of Russia, so that British intelligence was already prepared by the time news broke of the German invasion of Russia on Sunday 22 June 1941. By this time, British intelligence had had in its custody for six weeks the highest-ranking German prisoner ever to be captured in the war – Hitler's deputy and designated successor, Rudolf Hess.[39]

RUDOLF HESS

On 10 May 1941, Kendrick received a call from Stewart Menzies (head of MI6) that Rudolf Hess had bailed out of his Messerschmitt over Scotland. It took a few days before Hess's real identity was verified. Kendrick temporarily left Trent Park for four months to become one of Hess's three minders on behalf of the intelligence services, under the codename 'Colonel Wallace', with SIS colleague Frank Foley and 'Captain Barnes' (whose real name remains obscure).[40] Much mystery still surrounds Hess's mission to Britain, widely believed now to have been to negotiate some kind of peace deal through the Duke of

Hamilton, whose estate lay close to where Hess bailed out. What is unknown is whether Hess came with or without the sanction of Hitler. Historian Michael Smith argues that Hess was lured to Britain by MI6.[41] If true, it would mean that Hess's flight on 10 May 1941 was expected.

Hess was transferred by train from Scotland to London and held in the Queen's House at the Tower of London for four days. He was then transferred to Mytchett Place near Aldershot, where bugging devices were installed to monitor him. Although some of the information covering subsequent months in the care of Kendrick, Foley and Barnes at Camp Z, as his holding site was codenamed, is available, much of the Hess material remains classified. However, there is a single brief report in Foreign Office files, dated 23 May 1941, and signed by Denys Felkin of AI1(K) whilst based at Trent Park.[42] The report was destined for the desk of Flight Lieutenant E.H. Baring, Personal Assistant to Air Vice Marshal Charles Medhurst (Assistant Chief of Air Staff Intelligence). It informed Baring that Hess had been declared 'a vulnerable case' and as such over a hundred military guards were guarding him. Felkin then wrote: 'So far nothing can be ascertained about either the second occupant of the aircraft, or regarding the Canadian Bearer Bonds.'[43]

Hess was found to have been carrying the bonds when he was captured, but Felkin's comment about a second man in the plane is odd given that Hess was believed to have flown to Britain alone.

Cynthia Turner (née Crew) worked for Felkin at Latimer House in 1944. She commented: 'It was generally understood that one of our senior RAF officers, Squadron Leader Spenceley, was sent to interview him [Hess].'[44] Whilst this was based on hearsay around the site, Spenceley did work for Felkin in ADI(K) and his interrogation report of Hess has not been released.[45] Theories surrounding Hess will remain as long as the files are withheld from the public domain.

M ROOM INTELLIGENCE: JULY–DECEMBER 1941

In the six months from 1 July 1941 to 31 December 1941, the secret listeners transcribed 1,324 Special Reports.[46] Although no German army prisoners were captured during this period, matters relating to army intelligence were often provided by U-boat crew or Luftwaffe pilots. They gave away evidence of civilian resistance in Holland and Norway (both under German army occupation) and German fears of sabotage, and in north-west France there were suggestions of attacks on U-boats in their pens. Conditions in Germany itself seemed favourable with little evidence of any hardship yet being suffered from the war. In southern Germany and Austria, food conditions were less favourable and there were suggestions that the religious persecution of Jews was unpopular.[47]

Kendrick's six-monthly survey shows that the unit dealt with 341 personnel from the German navy and U-boats. Other ranks amounted to 301 individuals, captured from various German naval vessels: the *Bismarck, Alstertor, Gonzenheim, Egerland, Lothringen* and *Ketty Brövig*, and also prisoners taken from Raider 35 (*Pinguin*) and Raider 16. Special Reports revealed that a new fearsome warship, the *Tirpitz*, had completed her trials and was ready for Atlantic operations. Damage from RAF bombing of the battleships *Gneisenau* and *Scharnhorst* was discussed by prisoners, as well as the refit of the German heavy cruiser *Admiral Hipper*. Criticism was expressed from both U-boat and other naval POWs that the German High Command had shortened the period of training for new recruits and was drawing heavily from the Hitler Youth.

In this period, Trent Park dealt with survivors from nine U-boats:[48] U-651, U-138, U-556, U-570, U-501, U-111, U-95, U-433 and U-574. The volume of intelligence was extensive; it included information on the movements and exploits of the U-boat fleets, with prisoner estimates of U-boats in operation varying from twenty-five to fifty. As the Admiralty tried to gauge an accurate number, references were made to various U-boats that had been sunk by Britain. A former wireless transmissions operator said that sixty U-boats had been lost. MI9 considered his conversations to be reliable because he had been passing messages between Kondors and U-boats and was considered well-informed. Another U-boat prisoner captured on 27 August 1941 revealed that Germany had forty

U-boats in operation with another twenty undergoing repair. He placed the total number of U-boats at 200, with the vast majority being used for training purposes.[49]

The secret operators overheard a new development revealing that Italian submarines, stationed at their base at Bordeaux in the south of France, were to be replaced by German U-boats. This enabled the Admiralty to track the whereabouts and movement of U-boats. It was also said that new U-boat pens were being built at Lorient and St Nazaire.[50] Confirmation of these bases could only come from prisoners' conversations because the bases were so well hidden that they could not be seen from aerial photography by RAF reconnaissance missions. The bugged conversations therefore identified clearly where these sites were so the RAF could bomb them with greater precision. Indiscriminate bombing of such sites was not only a costly waste of resources, but carried the risk of the air crew being shot down in enemy territory or killed.

By the end of 1941, it was known from conversations that Germany had U-boat bases in Italy and a U-boat flotilla in Greece. A construction company in Hamburg was turning out one new U-boat a week, each fitted with new wireless-controlled torpedoes.[51] Large and medium tonnage mine-laying U-boats were in production as well as small U-boats, similar to E-boats. The Admiralty was particularly eager to understand how U-boats were refuelling without returning to their base. Prisoner conversations revealed that German ships were supplying underwater and surface raiders with food, munitions and fuel.

Towards the end of 1941, the prisoners talked about a German merchant ship moored at Vigo on the north-western coast of Spain, to which U-boats could fasten at night and take on fuel and other supplies. This seemingly trivial piece of intelligence was important for the Allies because it provided knowledge of how Germany was refuelling its U-boats when they were on active missions far from their main base.

A prisoner who had once served on Raider 16 provided details of tactics and armament of German raiders which operated from a base on the island of Kerguelen in the Antarctic. A captain of a German supply vessel spoke about raiders located in the vicinity of Panama in the south Atlantic. From this information, the Admiralty was able to focus on areas off the coast of South America. A surviving wireless operator from the *Pinguin*, the most successful German commercial raider of the war, known as Raider F at the Admiralty, talked at great length with his cell-mate about German naval wireless transmissions and codes.

AIR INTELLIGENCE

New information emerged from the crew of a Kondor (naval patrol vessel) about the re-training of Luftwaffe pilots for attacks by aircraft with torpedoes. Other prisoners discussed how Germany was having difficulty attacking Atlantic convoys because of protection by British aircraft, the use of the balloon barrages and improved anti-aircraft barrages. British intelligence learned from their captives that Germany had suffered substantial air force losses on the Eastern Front, usually as a result of low-level flying attacks. By the end of the year, German aircraft losses were so heavy that their planes were withdrawn from action on the Eastern Front. The urgent question now was to establish how and where Germany would redeploy their remaining aircraft – would there be another Battle of Britain in the skies over England?

German air force prisoners at this period, although relatively small in number at a total of ninety-seven, were from specialised units such as the Kondor, night fighter and torpedo and mine-laying units.[52] They gave away details of operational flight areas over Britain, and how the airspace over the country was divided between various German night fighter patrols. This enabled the Air Ministry to understand the Luftwaffe's fighting strategy, find ways to counter it and prepare to defend that area. One prisoner gave away the code used for German W/T communications between the night fighter aircraft and the home station, thus enabling Britain to decode those messages and pre-empt Germany's attacks. He also revealed how British W/T messages had been intercepted[53] thus alerting the Air Ministry to the fact that Germany was able to decode some of its messages and the codes needed to be changed. German pilots who had flown in operations over the Eastern Front spoke about a small anti-personnel bomb used in low-level attacks, and some conversations also described another bomb, fitted with a photo-electric cell to correct deviations from the desired target during its fall.

Bugged conversations showed that losses sustained by the German air force had begun to affect morale amongst pilots. They realised the difficulties in attacking Allied shipping and complained to each other that air attacks on Britain were now 'tantamount to a death sentence'. But the majority of naval prisoners continued to show an absolute loyalty to Hitler. Even the defeat of German troops in Russia did not dampen their spirits, although they now expressed doubt whether Germany could win the war solely by an Atlantic blockade. Such a shift in opinion showed that Germany was probably not yet in a position to gain naval supremacy. Altogether, at this time prisoners' comments gave a significant indication to British intelligence that Germany was losing its grip on any chance of air and naval supremacy.

CONCENTRATION CAMPS

Since its inception, the M Room had picked up periodic references to the Nazi concentration camps and egregious crimes against humanity.[54] One important testimony came in 1941 from a 'turned' prisoner whom MI9 used as a stool-pigeon, soliciting comments from fellow prisoners in the cells. His name has never been disclosed, but he was a survivor of Belsen concentration camp where he had been incarcerated for his political views.[55] It was from him that MI9 got some of its first-hand eye-witness accounts. Germany was experiencing a shortage of good mechanics and so, although an inmate, he had been taken on as a member of staff to carry out repairs to the commandant's house. He was finally released and conscripted into the German forces, then captured by the British.

Naval interrogator Donald Welbourn wrote of this prisoner in his unpublished memoirs:

He was the first person to tell us about the Beast of Belsen, and of the lampshades made from tattooed human skin. The Foreign Office did not want to believe our reports. All this information came out very quickly, together with the fact that this prisoner wanted to do everything in his power to make sure that the Nazis did not win the war.[56]

At the Wannsee Conference the following January, Hitler and leading members of the Third Reich ratified the Final Solution to escalate the programme of annihilating Europe's Jews. In late December 1941, the secret listeners had recorded a conversation between a German infantry soldier and an artillery soldier about Bergen Belsen concentration camp. These prisoners had been captured in Operation Archery, the British Combined Operations raid on the Norwegian island of Vågsøy.

The infantry solider, codenamed MI19, told M130: 'There's a POW camp near Hameln. I should say that, without exaggeration, there were at least fifty thousand POWs there – what a camp!' M130 replied:

'At Bergen?'

'Yes, Bergen in Germany, near Fallingbostel … You wouldn't believe what the camp was like! There was a high barbed wire fence, then the ground sloped down, and then there was another fence which was 2 metres high; there was one 1.25 metres high, and then another 1.5 metres high. They were all 1.5 to 3 metres and the spaces between them were filled with coils of barbed wire so nobody could get through. At each corner there was quite a high tower with machine guns and huge searchlights on all sides … the ones in Bergen can move about freely. There were a few sentries marching around the camp – it was a poor sort of camp.'

The subject of war crimes was raised in Kendrick's six-monthly survey at the end of 1941 where he wrote: 'A few prisoners have had some experience of, or heard about, the situation in Poland. Several spoke of crimes committed against the Poles.'[57] Intelligence officer and secret listener, Jan Weber, recalled:

I remember listening to two fighter pilots, both sons of senior Luftwaffe commanders. One, [Hubert] von Greim, told his cellmate of an experience when he was going on leave from the Eastern Front. He spent a night with an extermination unit who invited him to watch the killing of Jews the following morning. His comment: 'it was unpleasant'.[58]

References to concentration camps would become more detailed within a year, and in 1942, would include an eye-witness account of the Warsaw Ghetto.[59]

WOMEN AND INTELLIGENCE AT TRENT PARK

At this stage of the war, there was only a handful of ATS women trying to cope with the volume of intelligence reports, typing up the recordings of bugged conversations. That would soon improve when Kendrick organised an increase in the complement of female ATS officers at his sites. On 22 January 1942, Catherine Townshend (whose later married name was Jestin) was asked to report to the War Office. She was a gifted linguist who was serving in the FANYs, the female auxiliary volunteer Corps, and had had roles as a batman, orderly and staff car driver. At the Metropole Building, Major John Back of MI9 impressed on her the need for strict security and 'I was told to proceed next day by underground train from my home in South Kensington to Cockfosters station; a car would meet me at the appointed time to take me to a most secret intelligence installation.'[60] Catherine was given a brief outline of her future duties. She wrote to her mother: 'I wish I could tell you about my work. I can only say that it sounds exciting and interesting.' She went on to write:

In sombre mood, I commuted every day by underground to Cockfosters as instructed ... I was met by car and driven to Trent Park. I was advised at once under the Official Secrets Act never to divulge our location or talk about our work.[61]

Her first day at Trent Park was noted in a brief diary entry of 23 January: 'First day at Cockfosters Camp, Barnet. Interview with Col. Kendrick. Signing papers. Seems most interesting work.'[62]

Townshend's work gave her an insight into just how much value enemy POWs were to the interrogators:

Each prisoner was questioned at length on German strategy, Hitler's domination of almost all of Europe, and the possible invasion of the British Isles. More important were subjects such as radar, scientific research, codes, spies, and troop movements. POWs were not maltreated, but were comfortably housed and fed according to rank. Tiny microphones were hidden in inconspicuous places where every word could be heard.[63]

She went on to write:

J.F. Doust at the Post Office Research Department developed tiny and sensitive microphones; he was far ahead of the Germans in this field of engineering. Soldiers in every army were warned that if captured they must beware of microphones in prison cells, but Doust's inventions were seldom, if ever, discovered by the enemy. On one occasion, after an extensive examination of the walls, floor and furniture of his room at Trent Park, a senior prisoner was heard to say to his cellmate: 'There are no microphones here.' But for safety's sake the two men decided that they could converse more freely if they leant far out of the window. Little did they suspect that in addition to a minute microphone attached to the ceiling light fixture, another was hidden in the outside wall beneath the window sill, and that their faintest whispers, even in the open air, were being recorded for subsequent typing and distribution to all branches of Intelligence.[64]

Townshend's typing proved far too slow for interrogator Marsh, so she was moved across to the map room at Trent Park where she was responsible for 'charting the enemy's army divisions on land and his ships at sea.'[65] Her work led to the day-to-day plotting of key German battle-ships, the *Scharnhorst* and the *Gneisenau*, and in March 1942, she would plot the British Commando raid at St Nazaire. Her privately published memoirs also provide a unique snapshot into life for the female staff:

> During our lunch hour, on fine spring days, six of us women walked across the fields of daffodils to a rifle range in the park where a corporal guardsman taught us how to shoot … We were amused to see, when censoring a prisoner's letter to his headquarters in Berlin, that he had observed us from his window and written: 'Churchill is training women to fight'.[66]

Working in key administrative and organisational roles were Dawn Rockingham-Gill (later Mrs Doble), and J/Commander Elizabeth Angas who spoke French and German. Angas went on to serve most of the war with CSDIC Mediterranean, gaining some knowledge of the situation in Greece.[67] Captain L. Landsberg had knowledge of German and Afrikaans, and carried out the translation of X reports (bugged conversations). She was responsible for the whole of the main Italian series of transcripts coming out of the CSDIC posts in the Mediterranean.[68] J/Commander K.H. Phillips was at ease with French, German and Portuguese, had excellent secretarial qualifications, and became personal assistant to the commander in chief of CSDIC Mediterranean. She 'knew the work of CSDIC thoroughly'.[69]

WAAF officer, Elizabeth Bruegger (née Rees-Mogg) worked in Air Intelligence as Felkin's assistant.[70] Her role was to categorise the intelligence coming out of the M Room and decide who needed to see it. It was a hugely responsible job, and any failure to send it to the right commanders or branches of military intelligence could have real consequences. It required a wide understanding of what was significant, especially the technological material, and sound judgement. She was one of the few women who were privy to such an array of top secret intelligence material. Important figures came from Bletchley Park for regular meetings, one of whom was a liaison officer called Hans Vischer.[71] Bruegger confirmed that the sharing of classified intelligence between CSDIC and Bletchley only occurred at the highest level. She also recalled clandestine wartime missions involving courageous men of the Dutch Resistance Movement who risked their lives to row the English Channel at night bearing crucial information about German battle positions and military manoeuvres.

'Their reports were brought post-haste by bikers and couriers to Kendrick's centre and used by MI9,' she said.[72] On a few occasions, a dispatch rider took a report straight to Churchill.[73]

NAVAL INTELLIGENCE

During the first six months of 1942, Trent Park dealt with a total of 122 POWs from 6 U-boats and 2 E-boats, including prisoners taken during the raids by the Small-scale Raiding Forces into parts of Norway. The intelligence gained from these particular prisoners provided details on the German Order of Battle and new naval construction work.[74] It came from prisoners taken during the Vågsøy Raid on German positions in Norway on 27 December 1941 and a second raid on the Lofoten islands in January 1942.[75] Twenty-six German army prisoners were taken during the Vågsøy Raid and two from the Bruneval Raid in northern France in February 1942.[76] In this same period, the number of German air force personnel totalled twenty-seven, some of whom had also been captured in the Bruneval Raid. With the exception of two officers, they were all ordinary ranks. Although the number of POWs could be deemed relatively small, the secret listeners generated 936 reports from them.[77] Such a volume of bugged conversations is unusual in that (apart from the German generals later) so many transcripts were not usually generated pro rata. The intelligence gleaned from these particular bugged conversations, and its significance, is outlined below.

The secret listeners picked up details that the new German battleship *Tirpitz* was ready for action and that damage had been successfully inflicted by the Allies on warships *Gneisenau*, *Scharnhorst* and *Prinz Eugen*. The most detailed reports in the first months of 1942 came from E-boat crews speaking about German ships under construction, especially a new kind of E-boat that could travel half-submerged; information also came forth on the operations of E-boats in the Channel, Baltic and Mediterranean. E-boat tactics in torpedo attacks and mine-laying were also described. British intelligence learned that new E-boat shelters were being built at St Nazaire and other French ports. Other prisoners spoke about the difficulties of recruiting new officers to serve on U-boats, largely due to conditions in the German navy. They spoke about a major new programme of U-boat construction at a number of locations in Germany. Some sites were already known, others were new.

Prisoners claimed that U-boats were being constructed at Blohm & Voss, Hamburg, at a rate of three a fortnight. Other places of construction included the ports of Danzig, Kiel, Wilhelmshaven, Rostock, Lübeck and Flensburg.[78] The concern for Allied commanders was whether Germany's new construction programme was keeping up with U-boat losses which would only intensify the Battle of the Atlantic. Through the Special Reports, British intelligence gained knowledge of the extent of U-boat losses which the Admiralty could not otherwise have obtained. Losses were placed at as many as forty-seven by one prisoner and sixty-five by another.

An overall picture of U-boat tactics and areas of operation in the Arctic, Azores and the Mediterranean was emerging, as well as how U-boats were being restocked with new supplies from a German supply ship based at Vigo.[79] The most significant strategic discovery came from details of a major change in U-boat tactics. It was revealed that the protection of British convoys had become so highly successful that U-boat crews were undergoing a period of re-training in preparation for mass attacks.[80] Without the bugging operation, the British navy would have been less prepared for the new 'wolfpacks' whereby Germany planned to attack British supply convoys with between twenty and thirty U-boats en masse.

GERMAN AIR FORCE

Luftwaffe prisoners captured in early 1942 provided tactical information, especially on the 'Baedeker air raids' – when Germany began to bomb sites in Britain listed in the famous Baedeker tourist guide books. The secret listeners overheard details of the number of aircraft and units employed on the raids, and the strain being placed by the raids on an already depleted German air force. It confirmed to the Air Ministry that the German air force continued to be in decline.

Prisoners talked about the flying routes employed by the Luftwaffe, the heights they used when approaching England, and the impact of RAF bombing on the major German cities of Hamburg, Cologne, Lübeck, Essen and Münster.[81] It was learned that on the Eastern Front the Germans had dropped hundreds of Russian-speaking German parachutists behind the Russian lines to bring back information on the disposition of Russian troops. The Special Reports helped to understand the strength of the German air force in Russia, Finland and Italy and described the training of 5,000 German air force officers to be attached to an aerodrome in France. The flow of intelligence about new German technology continued, including the discovery that Germany was trying to develop a navigational beam that was not subject to British interference. There were several references during 1941 and 1942 to gas warfare that would be instigated on Hitler's order.[82]

ARMY INTELLIGENCE

Prisoners captured in the raids on Norway and France spoke about the operations in great detail. Defenders of the Vågsøy district (Norway) agreed that the British attack had taken them by complete surprise. References to the situation in North Africa were made and there was 'no wavering of confidence in Rommel and the belief expressed that he would in a short time be in Cairo'.[83] Details were forthcoming on the deployment of German troops on the Bulgarian–Turkish border which would break through to Palestine and the Suez Canal to link up with Rommel's forces, and also of tank reinforcements being sent by special aircraft to Rommel in North Africa.

A recurrent theme in the discussions was related to the Second Front and speculation of when and where the Allies would mount an invasion of Europe. They expressed the view that German forces in the West were inadequate to prevent defeat and should be reinforced by troops serving on the Eastern Front. Prisoners were divided on whether the threat of a Second Front was merely bluff on the part of the Allies. Conversely, talk of a German invasion of Britain declined during 1942.

Reports from Trent Park enabled commanders to gain a wider picture of the war. In particular, they brought information about resistance and acts of sabotage by the French civilian population against the German occupation. It included action by inhabitants of northern France who displayed lights to help British night-fighters. POWs taken during the Lofoten and Vågsøy raids were depressed by the hostility of the Norwegian people who carried out attacks on German troops. Kendrick's report stated: 'In Trondheim it was said that soldiers were found with their throats cut and a hidden arms dump discovered. In Bergen German troops fired on Norwegians who made the V sign. In Oslo, the leaders of a disturbance in a factory were shot.'[84]

One of the primary areas where intelligence was needed concerned conditions within Germany itself: how were ordinary Germans coping with the war? Was morale high or low? Was the nation on the brink of starvation or not? Such information enabled British intelligence to assess how far the war was affecting everyday life within Germany, and its continued fighting capability. Neither the Nazi regime nor the Allies would ever admit any weakness publicly in the media, because that could be used by the enemy to find effective strategies to further weaken the country. A number of references were made by prisoners to the use of Allied POWs and foreign workers for labour. Hitler used the SS to tighten his grip on power, with Gestapo guards stationed at key factories. Food was short in some of the larger German towns but areas that had been subjected to heavy Allied bombing were issued with a liberal amount of supplies, which were normally restricted under rationing, as a way of keeping up civilian morale. Sporadic outbursts from Communist sympathisers occurred. Although there was some resistance in Germany to the Nazi regime, there was no strong leader who could organise and activate opposition.

Special Reports during this period revealed a shift in attitude amongst the German POWs as they began to question the infallibility of Hitler. This was a marked difference from the previous six months as they began to express concern over the Russian campaign and pessimism increased over the outcome of the war. German airmen were becoming the most outspoken against the regime.

Carefully selected information from CSDIC reports was passed to the Foreign Office and used in propaganda by the Political Warfare Executive (PWE).[85] This propaganda work was based at Milton Bryan, not far from Bletchley Park, under the directorship of former journalist and fluent German speaker, Denis Sefton Delmer. Regular and reliable information gained from prisoners' conversations, via the M Room, provided gossip and rumour about the personal lives and salacious habits of Nazi functionaries and Wehrmacht officers that could be utilised to great effect by the PWE as a powerful propaganda tool.[86] One particular clandestine radio station called Gustav Siegfried Eins, actually operated by the PWE, purported to be run by a disaffected German army officer. It revelled in berating named Nazi Party leaders for their debauched and corrupt lifestyles. Details of lavish parties in Gauleiters' palatial country estates, paid for through profits made from the war effort, were often angrily denounced by the radio station.

British intelligence had no idea how effective this propaganda campaign was until the recordings from Trent Park confirmed that the programmes were being widely listened to by German forces. German airmen were tuning in to receive news about comrades missing in action because the PWE radio station announced their names as a hook to increase its listeners among all those eager for news of friends and loved ones at a time when news was scarce.[87] British intelligence had the confirmation it needed: that via radio broadcasts it had an extremely powerful tool at its disposal. It meant that phoney radio stations could be set up, masked as German radio stations broadcasting within Germany.[88]

CHAPTER 5

The Spider

In July 1942, Kendrick moved the headquarters from Trent Park to Latimer House. Former interrogator Dr John Whitten described Latimer House as: 'a very secret place. The prisoners entered and left in closed vans, so they never knew where they were.'[1] It became officially known as Camp 30 or No.1 Distribution Centre (No.1 DC). The prisoners were told that they were being held in 'Camp 7' – a fictitious title for Latimer House. After capture and transfer to England, the prisoners were processed via one of the 'cages' (slang for interrogation quarters) at Lingfield, Kempton Park or the London Cage.[2] These cages were part of the Prisoner of War Interrogation Section (PWIS) under Colonel Alexander Scotland – who had established interrogation quarters at Cockfosters at the outbreak of war.[3] At the 'cages', the prisoners were assessed and swiftly interrogated. If deemed to have special intelligence or knowledge (especially on technology or secret weapons), they were transferred to Kendrick's sites for detailed interrogation and were subject to the eavesdropping operation. MI9 had expanded to such an extent that in 1942 it divided, with Kendrick's unit and PWIS becoming the newly-formed MI19.[4]

When prisoners first arrived at Latimer House, they were taken to a green building in Ley Hill Road which housed the fumigation plant. Rumours of a plague on the Eastern Front necessitated fumigation precautions to be taken. The Latimer estate was enclosed by a barbed wire perimeter fence and two checkpoint entrances. Photography was strictly forbidden and no one could enter without a special permit. The main entrance was guarded by a security barrier across Ley Hill Road, with a second gated entrance located further up the road to the north.

Wilton Park, now No.2 Distribution Centre, opened in December 1942, under commandant Lieutenant Colonel Leo St Clare Grondona. Prisoners at Latimer House and Wilton Park usually stayed for only a few days or a week depending on their intelligence value, maybe longer if necessary. The lower-rank prisoners now also went through these two estates. When CSDIC felt they could provide no further useful intelligence they were transferred to one of the numerous regular prisoner-of-war camps around Britain where they spent the rest of the war, often working the land or carrying out forestry duties until repatriation at the end of hostilities.

Ten thousand lower-rank prisoners passed through Kendrick's bugging sites up to 1945. Their personal files or index cards either no longer exist or have not been declassified for the National Archives. As these prisoners came from lower military grades, information on their backgrounds is fairly limited in MI19 files. This is not the case for the individual files of those generals who were held at Trent Park; a personal profile was compiled for each general and senior German officer held by MI19. Kendrick increased the staff across the three CSDIC sites to 967 personnel, of which 167 were ATS.[5] The sheer volume of intelligence necessitated this increase in ATS officers to maintain continuity and cope with the workload. He was supported by two assistant commandants: Lieutenant Colonel Charles Corner (Intelligence) and Lieutenant Colonel F. Huband (Administration).

A VERY SECRET PLACE

The main mock-Tudor red brick house served as the Officers' Mess for all three services. Except for its slender chimneys, the house could not be seen from the wartime complex at the back of the King's Walk. The comings and goings in the mansion house remained largely secret from personnel working on the other side of the site. Kendrick held regular meetings there with intelligence chiefs and commanders without the knowledge of any of the other staff or non-commissioned officers. On one side of the house, a temporary wartime building was constructed as living quarters for the female Naval Intelligence officers. A room on the first floor of the country house became Kendrick's office, while the other rooms were used by female staff for typing up classified reports.

Wartime buildings which housed the interrogation block, M Room and cells, were built within a walled area at the far end of the estate. In this complex of buildings, cell blocks were constructed parallel to a long north-south corridor, divided down the centre by a breeze block wall, making the corridors rather narrow. At each end was a telescopic, steel-slatted security grille. A central watchtower with gun slits overlooked the whole complex. Prisoners were kept two to a cell, to enable the secret listeners to distinguish between their voices during the recording of conversations. They were usually from different services, in the hope that they would confide to each other about what they failed to tell British officers during interrogation.

Secret listener Jan Weber had less glamorous recollections of Latimer House as

> ... a dilapidated, rat infested building with outhouses, some of them added by the Military to house the guard troops commanded by a fierce looking Sergeant Major. There were officers, male and female from all three services, but mainly army. The women were typists. Their principal job was to transcribe recordings of conversations between prisoners, and between prisoners and stool pigeons.[6]

Denys Felkin relocated to Latimer with Kendrick to continue as head of the Air Intelligence section. The prisoners knew Felkin only by his cover name, 'Oberst King' (Colonel King). He was as much a part of the softening-up process as Kendrick: 'He [Felkin] knew his Germans and he would supplement friendly persuasion by leaning forward to give a touch on an arm or leg. His technical interrogations were often crucial in the "battle of the Boffins".[7] Former Air Intelligence officer, Joan

Stansfield, who worked in an office next to Felkin, wrote: 'POWs were seen from time to time crossing from the compound under escort. We had right of way and ignored their presence. If one had to cross through the grilles inside the building, the warders did not open them if there were POWs in the corridors.'[8] The clocks and calendars on site were changed to cause some disorientation for the prisoners.

A section called Marshland was run by Captain (later Major) Norman Marsh, and located in an annexe below the windows of the Editorial Section. It issued papers on prisoners' attitudes on matters political, religious, moral and professional. Attached to Marshland was the army psychologist, Lieutenant Colonel Henry Dicks, who was engaged in psychological studies of the prisoners at the site.[9] All this was located just at the top of the King's Walk, named after a tradition that King Charles I once hid on the estate before his execution. During the Second World War this charming secluded walkway (which still exists today) was used by Kendrick's intelligence officers to take a German general for a walk to befriend him and chat before his transfer to Trent Park. It was hoped that a mutual understanding might lead to him inadvertently giving something away about Nazi Germany. Individual profiles held by MI9/MI19 for each general list whether he was first brought to Latimer House or Wilton Park before long-term transfer to Trent Park's 'special quarters'.

By now, the unit required its own photographic section after an urgent request was received for an enlargement of operational maps.[10] The section was given the necessary facilities to enlarge maps and photographs, as well as equipment for the development and quick drying of film.[11] It was also equipped with cameras and copying equipment to take photographs of POWs for the records, copy documents, maps and plans and to photograph captured documents, maps and people.

The section enabled the swift copying of sea-stained and damaged photographs found on POWs – items which could provide clues for intelligence purposes. These could be enlarged and introduced during interrogation, so a prisoner would give up trying to hide information, believing that the British already knew everything there was to know.

The section also treated and cleaned films that had been exposed to the sea – found floating on the water or retrieved from U-boat survivors who were pulled out of the sea.[12]

Kendrick's unit may have shifted vast amounts of paperwork, but one of his most important jobs – and one that he was exceedingly good at – was hosting lunches and dinners. In the comfortable surroundings of the library and dining room he frequently wined and dined his guests as if they were at a gentleman's club, but one where the nation's secret operations could be discussed in total privacy. Pink gin was reputedly one of the favourite cocktails on the terrace – a habit acquired from the Naval Intelligence section. Over a fine luncheon and alcohol, Kendrick discussed the progress of the war and the latest intelligence gathered from his prisoners. In turn, the intelligence chiefs primed him on the kind of information that they needed, especially to confirm rumours of new technology being used on U-boats or German aircraft, or the latest German developments in weaponry. After a visit by General James Marshall-Cornwall, the head of MI9, Brigadier Norman Crockatt received a letter which praised 'the excellent lunch'. Marshall-Cornwall told him: 'I thought that you and Kendrick had organised a marvellously good show ... Kendrick is an old-stager on our side of the house.'[13]

After another visit, Commodore Edmund Rushbrooke (the then Director of Naval Intelligence) told Kendrick:

I was very much impressed with all I saw. You obviously have a most efficient organisation, and the inter-team work is of the highest order. I only hope my visit did not throw your busy machine out of order for half a day. Anyway, I assure you that I much appreciate the kindness of yourself and your staff. If at any time there is anything I can do to help in regard to the Naval side of your organisation, you may be sure of my best efforts.[14]

Kendrick continued to hold regular briefing meetings with Bletchley Park to share intelligence and corroborate material which the code-breakers were gathering.[15] Only a few personnel at the CSDIC sites knew about the existence of Bletchley and vice versa.[16] Kendrick facilitated the interrogation of special Axis prisoners at the CSDIC sites by using interrogators sent from MI8/Bletchley Park.[17] These prisoners were divisional intelligence officers, wireless station officers and officers dealing with German cyphers and high-grade cryptographic communications.[18] The reports which were generated from these interrogations were highly classified and only shared initially with Kendrick's unit; a special note on them read: 'This report is Most Secret and should not be passed beyond the list distribution without previous reference to MI8.'[19]

A lengthy interrogation of Gefreiter Pzuiara by Captain Heller of MI8 produced information on German traffic and codes.[20] He was shown an Enigma machine by Heller and asked how it differed from the one he had used in Hanover.[21] Pzuiara replied that there were some variations.[22] He also described how to encode a message on it and how a daily code was changed. A copy of the interrogation was sent to Commander Travis, Harold Fletcher and other key figures at Bletchley Park.[23]

WILTON PARK

By December 1942, the site at Wilton Park was finally ready for operations. It too masked as a supply depot and was known as No.2 Distribution Centre. Its commandant, Lieutenant Colonel Leo St Clare Grondona, was an Australian, born in 1890, who had studied at St Patrick's College.[24] He left Australia in 1916 to serve in France, and was wounded in action with a fracture to the left leg and gunshot wound to the right leg. In 1923, he was appointed a delegate to the Imperial (Economic) Conference in London and stayed on in the capital as a journalist and writer for the *Sydney Bulletin*. In 1940, he was given an emergency commission and joined Kendrick's team at MI9.

Major Le Bosquet headed the interrogation section. Wilton Park's adjutant, Kenneth Morgan, carried out interrogation duties from time to time and later at the London Cage in Kensington under Kendrick's colleague, Colonel Alexander Scotland.[25] Captain Victor Lang was the Intelligence Liaison Officer in charge of the German generals at the White House at Wilton Park.[26] Born Ludwig Victor Langstein (c.1885), he had served in the First World War, fighting with the 63rd (Royal Naval) Division on one of the bitterest battlefields at Gallipoli. Listed as wounded in 1915 in the Dardanelles, shrapnel in his left eye led to its removal in Dreadnought Hospital – hence the patch over the eye in later photographs.[27] At the outbreak of the Second World War he was given an emergency commission and attached to Kendrick's unit.

Wilton Park initially held captured Italian generals and some lower-rank German POWs. Later, principally after D-Day, it housed German generals before their transfer to Trent Park. Wilton Park had a block of cells and interrogation rooms in a format similar to its sister site. St Clare Grondona described it:

> Our troop's hutments were spaced amid tall trees within a few hundred yards of a Georgian mansion – the White House – which was our officers' mess and, at the outset, our living quarters, although it was subsequently to be put to very different use. The prisoners' compound, with its four long intersecting corridors leading to brick-and-cement cells, had been built within a 14ft brick wall that had enclosed a two-acre vegetable garden and orchard; and its low roofs were so camouflaged as to merge into the surrounding landscape and be invisible to other than low-flying aircraft. Cells were centrally heated and each had ample space for four spring-mattressed beds.[28]

The first prisoners there were a cocky lot, confident and hardened, believing that Hitler would still win the war. St Clare Grondona wrote that: 'It was our job to extract from them as much as possible of this – always with proper regard to the Geneva Convention.'[29]

It was not only the German generals who, unbeknown to themselves, were under the surveillance of British intelligence, but a number of captured Italian generals and senior officers. They included Field Marshal Giovanni Messe captured in North Africa after the fall of Tunis in

May 1943. On the morning of 17 May, Lieutenant Colonel Leo St Clare Grondona received a telephone call from the War Office informing him that the Italian Field Marshal and several of his generals were arriving at Hendon airport from North Africa that same afternoon.[30] The Italian commanders arrived at 3 o'clock. St Clare Grondona described the scene:

> A small group of British officers were waiting when staff cars – led by two jeeps bristling with armed sergeants – came through the gate. The party was under the escort of an Italian-speaking Colonel from the War Office. Out stepped the Marshal of Italy – a jaunty little man, not unlike Franco – with about 15 of his colleagues. Most were Generals, but they included two Admirals, a Colonel and a very tall subaltern. The contents of our guests' baggage made it evident that they had campaigned with no shortage of such minor solaces as liquor and cigars. The lists of their personal effects – all in sealed packages – revealed that the Marshal had £1,000 in £5 Bank of England notes, all apparently genuine, and that almost all the others had been carrying from £200 to £500. Their personal accounts were duly credited and they were allowed a limited weekly expenditure.[31]

The Italian commanders were taken to Camp No.4, an annexe at Wilton Park. The following month, they were joined by Italian Admiral Gino Pavesi who had surrendered on 11 June 1943 after heavy Allied bombing of Italy prior to the invasion of Sicily.[32] They would be joined a few days later by Italian Generals Guido Boselli, Giuseppe Falugi, Francesco La Ferla and Arturo Scattini. Messe remained at Wilton Park until 5 November 1943 when he was released because of the Italian Armistice a few weeks earlier.[33]

Whether dealing with German generals or prisoners of other ranks, the M Room could only work to full efficiency with a combination of interrogation, bugged conversations and befriending 'the guests'. Interrogators took turns to accompany a prisoner on the 'depression trip' around London, as Matthew Sullivan recalled:

We went by car and the driver was always an ATS girl who was fair, buxom and pretty with a large beauty spot on her cheek. She was known to us just as 'Carmichael' and was part of the treatment. She never spoke to, or answered, the prisoner who was always aware of her and whose confidence was being undermined as he was driven through large areas of London without any bomb-damage at all, totally belying Goebbels' propaganda. The carefully chosen route always led to Harrods. A stroll through the elegant and still well-stocked store – especially the food halls – was well calculated to shake morale. London life looked astonishingly normal and the sight of all the different Allied uniforms in the street and a table for two at a good restaurant or at thé dansant at the Piccadilly Hotel (though not for dancing) continued the softening-up process. Carmichael was waiting to take us back. When next day the prisoner was faced with his tough-type interrogator, it was reckoned he would be more malleable.[34]

Prisoners at Wilton Park and Latimer House were taken on walks around the Buckinghamshire countryside and 'befriended' by the British officer accompanying them. Over beer and tobacco, friendships developed which led to the exchange of information and ideas.[35]

M ROOM TECH AND LOGISTICS

MI19(e) was the section of MI19 that was responsible for the setting up of M Room sites (whether in Britain or abroad), the technical equipment, accommodation, personnel and gaining security clearance from MI5 for new staff members.[36] The section was headed by Major John Back and run efficiently with the help of Subaltern Winifred Felce.

In 1942, twenty-one-year-old Catherine Townshend was transferred to MI19(e): 'I was chosen because none of the efficient German-speaking women officers at Trent Park could be spared from the daily pressure of typing reports.'[37] When Townshend arrived, she was greeted by Lieutenant Colonel Rawlinson (head of MI19) and introduced to his immediate staff: Major John Back, Major Rait, Captain Bellamy and two members of the ATS, Subaltern Dawn Rockingham-Gill and Subaltern Winifred Felce. She was assigned to Major Back's office:

> I was much in awe of Major Back, an efficient administrator with a cold blue eye. For security reasons, he kept no records and expected Felce and me to cultivate an encyclopaedic memory like his own. All the reports from Trent Park were circulated in English and German for our information, so that I did not feel cut off from the gathering of intelligence, as I feared I would be in my new position. On the contrary, I was more involved than ever as a witness to the making of policy decisions, and privy to urgent operational questions, answers to which the Chief of the Imperial General Staff hoped MI19 would provide … Most secret of all were the negotiations with the inventors and suppliers of microphones. 'The work is more important and varied than at Cockfosters,' I wrote to my mother, and added with relief: 'Felce and I can call upon three clerks – we ourselves never use a typewriter.'[38]

On 5 October 1942, Major Back and Winifred Felce left Wilton Park and Townshend found herself in charge of MI19(e). Before he left, Major Back called Townshend into his office. He explained that she was the only person who knew the work and could take on the responsibility of MI19(e). Now, the highly classified work of overseeing all the technology for the M Rooms – and one of the most sensitive and hush-hush roles within MI9/MI19 – was taken on by a young female officer. Townshend went on to send listening equipment and recording machines to interrogation centres in England, the Middle East, India and Australia. She recalled the moment she walked into Major Back's empty office:

> It was alarming to find an 'IN' basket piled high, but I was determined not to disappoint Lieutenant Colonel Rawlinson – or confirm the opinion of some of my colleagues that he had made a mistake in

asking me to carry on – and so, nervously, I tackled one memorandum at a time … After drafting replies, I took them across
the hall for Lieutenant Colonel Rawlinson's approval. Rawli, as he
invited us to call him, was a big man in his early fifties. His skill in
delegating work to his subordinates left him free to make policy deci-
sions and to be welcoming if we needed help. He kept nothing on his
desk but a blotter and two telephones, a black one and a red – the red
one was for scrambling and unscrambling messages of extreme
secrecy.[39]

It highlights an important point – that the intelligence services were
often decades ahead of civilian life in appointing the right person for the
job, irrespective of gender. Consequently, during the Second World
War, women played vital roles within the intelligence world because
they developed the necessary skills for a particular job. Townshend was
also responsible for keeping the operations map in Rawlinson's office
updated.

With the benefit of Townshend's memoirs, it has been possible to
piece together links between MI9/MI19 and Latchmere House – MI5's
secret interrogation centre at Ham, near Richmond. It was known as
Camp 020, not to be confused with Wilton Park's Camp 20. Latchmere
House played a crucial role in the Double Cross System, where captured
German spies and agents were interrogated in attempts to 'turn' them to
work for the Allies as double agents.[40] MI19(e) supplied microphones
and trained personnel to a highly secret installation rarely mentioned,
except in hushed tones. The commandant, Lieutenant Colonel Stephens,
supervised the interrogation, trial, imprisonment – even the execution
– of enemy agents. Townshend recalled:

We knew little about him; consequently, alarming stories grew up
concerning his past and methods of operation … Communication
between 020 and MI19(e) was conducted by scrambler telephone or
correspondence. For months, everything went smoothly until I
received a request from the commandant for permission from the War

Office to promote members of his staff. Rawli ordered me to refuse with a polite explanation that the establishment of 020 did not permit higher ranks. Lieutenant Colonel Stephens was adamant. Again I explained. Exchanges became tense. 'I will come to Beaconsfield in person,' he said. I made an appointment for him to see Rawli, but on the day of the meeting Rawli was called to Whitehall on an urgent matter, leaving me to talk to the irate and formidable head of 020. Tall, with a black patch over one eye, he strode along the corridors of Camp 20, flung open the door of my office, and stood for a moment in amazement before bursting into a loud laugh. 'Are you Junior Commander Townshend?' he asked, 'I thought you were going to be a fierce bureaucrat in her fifties!'[41]

ANGLO-AMERICAN COOPERATION

The bombing of Pearl Harbor by the Japanese on 7 December 1941 finally brought America into the war. Within a matter of weeks, American personnel began to arrive at Kendrick's unit to receive training in specialist intelligence and interrogation.[42] American intelligence was now copied into the Special Reports and information being generated at Kendrick's sites.

Cooperation between British and American intelligence over the handling of Axis prisoners of war was already under way during autumn 1941, nearly two months before Pearl Harbor.[43] In October 1941, the Director of Naval Intelligence in Washington dispatched Lieutenant H. T. Gherardi of the United States Naval Reserve to the United Kingdom to 'get an idea of the types of personnel required for work in connection with prisoners'.[44] He visited Trent Park to understand the background of the bugging operation as preparation to setting up parallel sites in the United States. A secret memo of 28 October 1941 noted that Gherardi had been 'attached to our Prisoners of War Section ... Presumably you would not wish to hold back on any technical methods as in actual equipment the US is undoubtedly as well versed as we are. The line we have taken all along over the subject of prisoners generally is such as it is hoped will encourage the Americans to use our background, and facilities rather than start their own.'[45]

Over the course of the next three years, Kendrick and his officers oversaw the training of a number of American intelligence personnel and, from 1942, worked closely with the newly-formed US intelligence agency, the Office of Strategic Services (the OSS, forerunner of the Central Intelligence Agency – CIA). Based in the Rockefeller Center in New York, the OSS was established on 13 June 1942 by Major General William Joseph Donovan with the express aim of coordinating operations behind enemy lines in Europe, and subversion operations in liaison with the Special Operations Executive (SOE). Kendrick and Felkin's involvement in the training of American intelligence officers placed them at the highest level of Anglo-American relations; a contribution for which they would later be rewarded with a Legion of Merit from the White House. Major Frank Cassels, who oversaw the M Room and its personnel on a daily basis, was awarded the Bronze Star for assuming 'the burden of directly supervising the training of American intelligence personnel in a highly specialized branch of interrogation'.[46] Several hundred American officers received instruction from him, and went on to serve in American mobile intelligence units.[47]

That same month, Lieutenant Colonel W. Stull Holt of the United States Army Air Force (USAAF) was appointed to command the American presence at MI9 and MI19,[48] located at both Latimer House and Wilton Park. Other US personnel, including from the FBI in Washington, passed through these sites for special intelligence training by Kendrick's officers, for anything from two weeks to two months. Close cooperation had already existed between the Americans and Bletchley Park and the work with CSDIC was an extension of that.

On 15 August 1942, Mr Witney Shepardson and Mr Maddox of the OSS visited Latimer House from America. The Joint Intelligence Committee (JIC) ruled that copies of transcripts emanating from the M Room should now also be circulated to American intelligence, including copies to Washington.

The following month, Mr H.M. Kimball of the FBI made a transatlantic visit to Latimer to see the operations at work. Kendrick impressed Kimball with the highly efficient nature of the covert work. A grateful Edgar Hoover, head of the FBI, wrote a personal letter of thanks to Kendrick afterwards:

> My dear Colonel, I am writing to express to you my deep appreciation for the assistance which you rendered to Mr H.M. Kimball of this Bureau during his recent visit to London. It was very good of you to be so helpful, and you may be sure that your kindness is sincerely appreciated by me.[49]

The following months saw a number of site visits from personnel of the US army to Latimer and Wilton Park. These included Colonel Conrad, Captain Grimmel, Major Settle and Major Yudelson.[50] In the coming year, Kendrick accompanied other top officials from the United States on visits, including Brigadier-General Kroner (Chief of Military Intelligence Section),[51] Commander Riheldaffer (US Navy, CSDIC section) from Fort Hunt,[52] Colonel Catesby-Jones (Military Intelligence Section, POW department, Washington) and members of US intelligence G-2 ETOUSA. Commander Charles Herbert Little, Director of Naval Intelligence, Ottawa, also visited in order to cement the Canadian intelligence cooperation.[53]

In October 1942, the US Air Force joined with AI1(K), the latter still under the command of Felkin and now based at Latimer House, with a small presence at the other sites. Felkin later wrote: 'A successful fusion of the RAF and USAAF air interrogation was founded. This cooperation was maintained with the highest measure of success until well after the closure of the war.'[54]

One American intelligence officer at Latimer House was Heimwarth Jestin who, after initial training in the United States, had originally been attached to the 169th Infantry Regiment, 43rd Division.[55] After several other training postings within the US, he was sent to Camp Ritchie where officers received in-depth training in interrogation and intelligence work. In February 1943, he received orders for an overseas transfer to England for top secret work. One of his first assignments was to the London Cage in Kensington Palace Gardens where he first met Colonel Alexander Scotland. There, Scotland insisted that German was spoken at all times, to enable the interrogators to learn the dialect and inflections of the language. Jestin commented: 'We interrogated special prisoners and were vetted in regard to language usage, technique, and ability to understand the prisoners we talked to. It was a thorough and careful training.'[56] After a short posting to Glasgow to interrogate POWs of the Afrika Korps, captured in North Africa, Jestin was sent back to London and soon was posted to Latimer House where, 'the interrogation was more exacting, for these prisoners were, on the whole, intelligent and unwilling to disclose information'.[57]

From Latimer, Jestin was posted for the remainder of the war to Wilton Park where the prisoners knew him as 'Lieutenant Colonel Jenkins'. Here, he interrogated captured German generals before their transfer to Trent Park.

Thousands of lower-rank prisoners from all three services – the German navy, air force and army – would pass through Latimer House and Wilton Park before the end of the war. The tens of thousands of transcripts of their interrogations and bugged conversations survive in the National Archives, revealing an extraordinary volume and breadth of intelligence which warrants detailed analysis by historians.

Trent Park at Cockfosters was now reserved for a very special 'guest'. The stage was set to receive the first captured German generals and some of the most prized prisoners ever held by British intelligence. Much drama would unfold in the stately house in the coming years, more astonishing than fiction, in scenarios that kept Kendrick's staff busy for the duration of the war.

CHAPTER 6

Battle of the Generals

May 1942 saw the capture of the first German general in North Africa.[1] Infantry General Ludwig Crüwell's plane was shot down over British lines in North Africa after his pilot lost his way.[2] For British intelligence this was just the beginning of what would become the saga of the German generals. University-educated, Crüwell (b.1892) had served in the First World War, then during the Second World War had commanded the 11th Armoured Division in the Balkan campaign (1939–40) and the Russian campaign, which began a year later.[3] During the latter, he had seen fighting around Rowno and Kiev, and was decorated with the Oakleaves to the Knight's Cross of the Iron Cross. In October 1941, he succeeded Rommel as German Officer Commander of the Afrika Korps, then was taken prisoner on 29 May 1942. At the time of his capture near Cairo, he hastened to defend himself against rumours that he was responsible for massacres in the neighbourhood of Kragujevac, in Serbia.

Crüwell was finally brought to Trent Park on 22 August 1942. His personal file does not mention where he was held prior to that. Crüwell's character was summed up by British intelligence: 'He tried to impress everyone with his own importance and knowledge, a trouble-maker and a bore.'[4]

In October 1942, the second Battle of El Alamein pushed surviving members of Field Marshal Rommel's Afrika Korps back into Tunisia. The campaign led to the second German general to be taken into British captivity. He was 51-year-old General Ritter von Thoma, commander of a Panzer tank division, who was captured on 4 November 1942 at Tel-el-Mapsra, west of El Alamein.[5] Four days later, British and American forces landed in North Africa in Operation Torch that took place between 8 and 11 November. Under the leadership of American commander Dwight D. Eisenhower, Allied forces successfully re-took Morocco and Algeria in an effective liberation of North Africa. Von Thoma had served in the First World War and in 1937–38, before the Second War broke out, he had been based in Spain as experimenter-in-chief of the technical and tactical aspects of tank warfare,[6] often accompanying Field Marshal Brauchitsch on visits to tank factories. In 1940, von Thoma was tank commander at Dunkirk and had been assigned as a key commander for the invasion of Britain. Like Crüwell, he had seen action on the Eastern Front and, in September 1942, was transferred to Africa as a commander.

After capture, von Thoma was transferred straight to Trent Park. In British intelligence files, he is described as 'very intelligent and exceedingly well read, a cultured man whose hobbies included the study of art, history and politics'.[7] It was noted that: 'he has a striking personality and is violently anti-Nazi, a man who does not suffer fools gladly. He could have been a great leader if he had possessed the ability to coordinate his ideas with action.'[8] Von Thoma preferred to spend time alone in his room reading books on art, politics and history than playing cards. British intelligence noted: 'His reminiscences are as interesting as his political views and he has had many and varied contacts with all sorts of eminent people from New York, from actresses to Balkan monarchs – not to speak of the Führer!' Von Thoma could read English well, but in conversation spoke little English.

His conversations with Crüwell were recorded by the secret listeners and transcripts made.[9] The copy of a conversation between von Thoma, Crüwell and Major Burckhardt on 18 January 1943 landed on the desk of Edward Travis, the new commander at Bletchley Park who had taken over from Denniston.[10] Crüwell commented, 'I am always worried in case they [the English] should crack our code.' Burckhardt asked, 'For diplomatic messages?' to which Crüwell replied, 'All our communications with Japan are by W/T. All the things we hear when the English are using their W/T are startling when they are worked out. They don't worry about it at all. Of course they may be doing it purposely.'

On 4 February 1943, reflecting on the fall of Stalingrad and after hearing about the capture of Field Marshal von Paulus, Crüwell told von Thoma: 'I should have blown my brains out. I am bitterly disappointed!'[11]

THE AFRIKA KORPS

During early 1943, the Allies continued their slow advance towards Tunisia. By early April, Axis forces found themselves outflanked and outmanned in Tunisia and by mid-month they were clearly in an intense squeeze. Finally, on 12 May 1943, the Afrika Korps collapsed and commander General Hans-Jürgen von Arnim surrendered with a staggering 350,000 men. The war in North Africa was effectively over. Also captured were all the commanders of North Africa, including Hans Cramer and Gerhard Bassenge.[12] Before transfer to Britain, they were held at either 208 POW camp at Constantine, north-eastern Algeria, or in a tented camp at Boufarik. Even at these sites their conversations were bugged and copies of the transcripts sent via CSDIC Algiers to Kendrick's headquarters.[13]

After the first hours of capture, the senior officers discussed how they had suffered an honourable defeat and stated that the German air force in Tunisia had been in a sad plight.[14] They believed that the Allies would invade southern Europe, but felt that they would be unable to maintain military superiority after the landings.[15]

The softening-up and befriending of senior German generals and officers, so characteristic of their treatment in captivity, began already in North Africa. They were taken on a three-hour excursion and tea party at a private house.[16] Only then did the generals relax and open up in conversation with their escorting officers. They discussed how the Allied barrage before the final breakthrough had been overwhelming and worse than at El Alamein[17] and expressed amazement at the amount of equipment and ammunition behind Allied lines. Bassenge, an officer amongst the group on the excursion, was described as a 'voluble talker and extremely self-confident'.[18]

On 16 May, nine German generals were flown to England and landed at Hendon aerodrome.[19] They were transferred straight to Trent Park with their batmen to join Generals Crüwell and von Thoma. Shown honour and dignity immediately, they were greeted in front of the country mansion by Major General Sir Ernest Gepp (1879–1964), Permanent Under-Secretary of State War Office and the director of Prisoners of War (Administration).[20] Gepp was a career soldier who had joined the British army in 1900 and had four decades of distinguished military service. Standing next to him, to greet the generals, was Major Charles Corner.

In the coming months, the generals and their batmen would become key characters in a series of disputes and personal rivalries, yielding at the same time excellent intelligence for the British. The house was run along military lines in which the batmen, whose duties included making the beds and polishing the boots of the generals, were also expected to dine separately.

A week later, two more captured generals and a colonel joined the prisoners.[21] On 30 May, four more generals arrived from North Africa by sea at Plymouth, Devon. They were temporarily housed at Wilton Park, before being transferred to Trent Park on 2 June.[22]

In their conversations, the generals speculated on the course of the war and tried to analyse the next Allied military plans. Crüwell, von Thoma, Cramer and von Vaerst discussed together the consequences of the Allies overrunning the Romanian oilfields which, in their opinion, would mean that Germany could not last a year. General Fritz von Broich expounded the view that the British would not invade Italy because the only benefit would be gaining access to the airfields in southern Germany and the British would be left to deal with the logistics of supplies and feeding the Italian population.[23] Others discussed a possible Allied invasion via Spain and southern Greece, raising the question of whether they knew about the deception of Operation Mincemeat – in which British intelligence had floated a dead body off the coast of Spain in June 1943 with fake invasion plans to make the Germans think the invasion would occur in Greece.

Whilst at Trent Park, General von Arnim received a letter from his wife in Germany in which she reassured him how no one at home blamed him for the failure of the Tunisian campaign.[24] Von Arnim was often found playing cards or chess with Crüwell or Krause. He was a keen gardener and asked his minders if he could have a window box to plant seeds from the walks around the grounds. As these defeated but proud military men discussed politics and military strategy, little did they know that they were about to receive some very special treatment at the hand of British intelligence.

Lower-rank German prisoners captured in North Africa were taken to Latimer House or Wilton Park where they too were subjected to the special bugging treatment. The intelligence files note that these particular prisoners took time to recover from the first shock of their defeat and the depression that followed capture.[25] They watched events in Russia with growing interest, with many voicing their belief that Germany's victory would soon be won and the war would be over. The listeners also noted: 'The Afrika Korps men have been greatly impressed by the fairness both of our fighting and of our and the Americans' treatment of them as prisoners of war.'[26]

The overall impression was of a war-weary army. After hard fighting in Tunisia, many prisoners admitted relief that the war was over in Africa. One prisoner, Willi Liebig, was overheard saying: 'May the time come when we get over these days of terror; not hatred and discord, but a common creative effort can alone lead to sound reconstruction.'[27] Many of their letters home to Germany expressed how hard the last days were in Tunisia, fighting against superior Allied forces. Prisoner Karl Stiglbauer wrote to his wife: 'You can have no idea how glad I am that I have not to see Africa again. I know how you worried, but anyhow now you have the certainty of seeing me again and the anxiety that I might be killed is now over.'[28] For the senior officers, Trent Park with its park and surroundings, offered 'a haven of retreat to weary, disillusioned men who have suffered bitter defeats.'[29]

'A GENTLEMAN'S CLUB'

Bringing the generals to Trent Park began one of British intelligence's most cunning deceptions of the war. The generals expected to be held in a rudimentary prisoner-of-war camp with Nissen huts and barbed wire, exactly the kind of surroundings that would lead the generals to behave like prisoners and give very little away. British intelligence knew that direct interrogation of them would not be feasible because of their status.[30] Instead, the generals found themselves living a life of relative luxury at, they believed, the generous behest of the King and according to their status as military commanders – and this played right into their sense of self-importance. Their every need was catered for and they began to relax into their surroundings. Trent Park could be likened to a traditional privileged, exclusive gentleman's club in central London. The three most senior generals, Crüwell, von Thoma and Cramer, were given a bedroom and adjoining sitting room. Cramer was allocated a particularly large room. Other generals were allocated a single room with no sitting room, and the batmen were accommodated two to a room.[31]

A room was set aside for creative activities – for painting and drawing, playing cards, table-tennis and billiards.[32] The generals devoted time to learning languages and studying other subjects. They had freedom to roam the house and grounds, they received newspapers and were able to listen to BBC radio broadcasts. One officer wrote home to his wife that he would love his family to stay there with him, but without the barbed wire.[33] Little did they suspect that even the billiard table had a bugging device hidden in it. Kurt Köhncke commented: 'Our involuntary hosts are thoroughly gentlemanlike.'[34]

The Director of Military Intelligence wrote to Colonel Gatesby (Chief of Prisoners at the war branch MIS-X – the American equivalent of MI9 in Washington) and told him:

The camp is a large country house in a fine park of its own. The fact that it happens to be 'fitted' by us is just too bad ... We are, unfortunately, having lovely weather and these blasted generals will spend a lot of their time out of doors instead of in their rooms. It makes our job much more difficult, and I pray nightly for rain.[35]

One German general was enamoured of the gardens and parkland with its beautiful old woods, ancient oak trees and lime tree avenue, but he was not so polite about the house: 'The old manor house with its high gabled roof constructed in the Lower Saxony style, lends itself better to the countryside than the showy, tasteless stone box which passes for a castle.'[36]

The generals did not realise that everything that could be bugged was – from the light fittings to the fireplaces, plant pots, behind the skirting boards, under floorboards of the bedrooms, and even the trees in the gardens. The hidden microphones were wired back to the M Room in the basement where teams of secret listeners worked from the time the generals woke until the time they went to sleep. A British officer would even sit on a bench outside for a chat with a general, carefully placed near a hidden microphone so their conversations could be recorded.

The secret listeners never saw the generals; they only heard their voices through the headphones and came to recognise their individual voices so they could distinguish who was speaking. The listeners were able to record the raw, unadulterated opinions of the generals on a range of political, technical and strategic information. It also gave an insight into the mind-set of the enemy, enabling British intelligence to understand them and fool them into a false sense of complacency. A secret staircase led down from Kendrick's office into the basement, which was sealed at each end of the house by a clever use of false walls and panels to prevent any of the generals taking a wander down there.

During the first week, there was a feeling of constraint, but soon they began to reflect on whether they were in any way responsible for the defeat in Tunisia and North Africa. Some blamed the Italians for not using their fleet; others felt the responsibility lay with German High Command. Von Arnim expressed the opinion that reports of the true military situation had been withheld from Hitler. His real allegiance was somewhat of a mystery to British intelligence as he continued to profess a belief in a German victory, was fervently anti-Jewish and anti-Bolshevik, but with no overt evidence of strong Nazi views while at Trent Park. Bülowius and Krause were depressed by the turn of events and their capture, but soon became resigned to their situation. The intelligence summary for this period reported:

> Their present abode, with its park and lovely surroundings, appears to afford a haven of retreat to weary, disillusioned men who have suffered bitter defeats. They are devoting their time largely to learning or perfecting their English. Reading newspapers or entering into conversation with the English officers who accompany them on walks, helps them in this.[37]

Perhaps in a gesture to lift their spirits, the generals were offered the opportunity of having their portraits painted by an official war artist. They discussed the matter amongst themselves. Von Arnim, who had been appointed camp leader by the other generals, told the British army officers that permission would not be given for it.

General von Thoma took another approach. Interested in art, he suggested that the artist may be glad of a model and that he, von Thoma, had all the time in the world and would welcome the entertainment. He was the most highly decorated general in the camp, and although entitled to wear his medals, he declined. He had received decorations from Spain (Franco), Bulgaria and Romania, as well as the Knight's Cross of the Military Order of Max Joseph and the Knight's Cross of the Iron Cross, awarded for bravery and meritorious leadership in battle. When the question arose of what he would wear for the portrait, he said he preferred to be painted in his bush shirt without badges of rank or decorations, just as when captured in the desert.[38] Von Arnim disapproved strongly of von Thoma sitting for the artist.

The most important dimension of the scenario created at Trent Park was that it provided British intelligence with the unguarded conversations of Hitler's top military commanders. The place was, in essence, nothing more than a location to garner secrets – everything else was a façade, a theatrical stage set created by Kendrick and his immediate boss, Major Arthur Rawlinson. The personal mannerisms of the generals were noted by MI19 on their personal files to build a physical and psychological profile of each of them. Understanding their characters would enable British intelligence to make the most of 'the guests' (as they were called in intelligence reports) and create scenarios which would facilitate unwitting disclosure of the closely protected secrets of the Third Reich.

THE FAKE ARISTOCRAT

On arrival at Trent Park, the generals were escorted by military vehicle through the beautiful parkland with their first glimpse of the impressive country house that Sir Philip Sassoon had remodelled in the 1920s using red bricks from the dismantled Devonshire House in Mayfair. How could they not fail but be impressed by it? Standing in front of the imposing black door to greet them was a certain Lord Aberfeldy.[39] He was, they were told, their welfare officer – an aristocrat of distinguished Scottish ancestry and a second cousin of the King. His role was to gain the generals' confidence and raise questions without arousing suspicion.[40]

The generals were led to believe that the King had instructed him to look after their every need and to ensure they were treated according to their status as military commanders. Lord Aberfeldy was, in fact, a fictional character whose true identity was never discovered by the generals. They genuinely believed him to be of distinguished Scottish ancestry, but he was no aristocrat. He was one of Kendrick's intelligence officers, Ian Thomson Munro, who was exceedingly good at acting.[41]

The small market town of Aberfeldy lies on the river Tay, home to Aberfeldy Whisky and in a remote part of the Scottish Highlands. The town is not far from Castle Menzies which once belonged to the ancient

Menzies clan. From 1939 to 1952, Sir Stewart Menzies was the head of MI6, and, although there was no obvious connection between him and Menzies Castle, Stewart Menzies's grandfather was a whisky distiller. Was this pure coincidence or deliberate humorous name-play on the part of British intelligence?

Munro was born in Dundee in 1913, educated at a Gymnasium in Kassel, Germany, and graduated with an MA (hons) in French Language and Literature from St Andrews University in 1934. He spoke fluent German and French, with some knowledge of Spanish and Italian, and attained a postgraduate diploma in Business, Economics and Administration. His childhood had not been without tragedy: his father died when he was two years old, two siblings died in childhood and his mother never remarried. Whatever his background, Munro clearly enjoyed and was extremely good at his role as an aristocrat.

When he enlisted in April 1939 at the age of 26, Munro was working as a bank clerk in London. His enlistment form states that he had lived and worked extensively in Europe. In October 1940, he was badly injured in an air raid and had to have a leg amputated. Perhaps his wooden leg gave him ample excuse for a rest during the frequent walks with the generals, and always sitting close to a hidden microphone.

After being wounded, he was drafted into the Intelligence Corps and served initially in the Prisoner of War Interrogation Section (PWIS) of MI9, under the command of Colonel Alexander Scotland.[42] In August 1941, he was promoted to Captain and two years later, on 18 January 1943, was posted to CSDIC (UK). He first appeared at Trent Park as the generals' welfare officer, Lord Aberfeldy, in May that same year.[43]

Interrogator Matthew Sullivan knew Ian Munro/Lord Aberfeldy and wrote of him: 'A delightfully outgoing and intelligent Scot, he was the prototype of the officer and gentleman and his contribution to the war was to act this out to the full. He took his guests on walks, to restaurants, galleries and shops in London, disarming not a few with his snob appeal and his assumed title.'[44]

As Lord Aberfeldy, Munro provided a sympathetic ear for the generals and made trips into central London once a fortnight to buy extra items that they requested, including shaving cream, chocolates, sweets and cigarettes. He arranged for a tailor from Savile Row to come out to Trent Park to provide new clothes for them. The generals were permitted to run their own small canteen for extra items they wished to purchase from an allowance given to them by MI19. Catherine Townshend mentioned him in her memoirs:

> He masqueraded as a Scottish peer with a secret admiration of Hitler. Dressed in a kilt and provided with snapshots of 'his' castle in Scotland, he frequently visited the imprisoned generals and played on the Nazis' snobbery. Soon confidences were shared, and these led to discussions of Hitler's secret strategies. There was a twist to this story. The young interrogator refused to drop his role when off duty in our officers' Mess. He became too grand to talk to any of us, expected orderlies to address him as 'your lordship', and broke his girlfriend's heart, for he considered that she was no longer good enough for him.[45]

Occasionally Lord Aberfeldy was given instruction on particular information required by other services or military departments.[46] For example, in July 1943, MI14 wanted to know whether there was a genuine rift between the generals and the Nazis. It was Lord Aberfeldy's job to find out. In 1965, a three-part radio play based on Trent Park, Lord Aberfeldy, Kendrick and the German generals was broadcast as 'faction', entitled *Lord Glenaldy*.[47] It was written by none other than playwright, and former head of MI19, (then) Lieutenant Colonel Arthur Rawlinson. The original names of intelligence officers were changed to hide their real identity.

BATTLE LINES: PRO-NAZI V. ANTI-NAZI

On 16 June 1943, Lieutenant Colonel Wolters and Colonels Buhse, Reimann and Drange arrived in captivity at Trent Park along with German air force prisoners Dr Carius, von Glasow and Bock, Colonel

Schmidt, Colonel Heym and Lieutenant Colonel Köhncke.[48] Also joining the 'guests' was 52-year-old Captain Paul Hermann Meixner of the German navy who was captured at Tunis on 11 May 1943. He was taken first to Latimer House before being transferred to Trent Park on 16 June where he shared a room with General von Hülsen. He seemed to be well liked by his fellow prisoners and generals.

Meixner had served in the Austrian navy during the First World War and offered his services to the German navy in the Second. First impressions of him were of a benevolent rosy-faced man whose white hair seemed to heighten this perception. Described by British intelligence as 'too polite and too gushing … a supporter of Crüwell in his nagging of von Arnim', Meixner's jovial behaviour masked him as 'an Austrian Nazi and a dangerous man'.[49]

Colonels Egersdorff and Borcherdt soon followed. The first priority for Egersdorff was to suggest improvements to life at Trent Park by asking if they could have parole for pheasant shooting and 'a plentiful supply of whisky'.[50] Not unsurprisingly, his requests were denied. The fact that the captured officers thought the British might actually give them these extra comforts, and even went so far as to ask for them, says much about just how relaxed they were in their surroundings.

As the generals and senior officers settled into their life of captivity, they began to form into two distinct groups: pro-Nazi and anti-Nazi.[51] Crüwell headed the vehemently pro-Nazi group which consisted of Gotthard Frantz, von Hülsen and Meixner. They considered Trent Park 'a sanatorium for tired generals'. General von Thoma became a pillar of the anti-Nazi clique that consisted of Cramer, Sponeck, Bassenge, Neuffer, von Liebenstein and von Broich.

Heading the pro-Nazi group, Crüwell continued his allegiance to Hitler whom he had only met in person twice. His MI19 file described him as 'an ignorant, stupid, sentimental, narrow-minded, conceited, vain and self-satisfied type of Prussian senior officer'.[52] Crüwell was supported by the tall, slim figure of General von Hülsen who constantly urged him to cause as much trouble for the British as possible. Crüwell listened readily to von Hülsen who busied himself trying to persuade the others to cause trouble. Von Hülsen, 'a hanger-on of the worst type and always trying to be with Arnim',[53] perpetually moaned about something, legitimate or not, and every letter or card written home to his wife contained some sly dig at conditions in the camp. His complaints, usually pure fabrication, were always delivered in a polite yet petty way.

The 55-year-old Lieutenant General Gotthard Frantz was of medium height, slim, with a beak nose, wrinkled face and thin lips, and an ally of the pro-Nazi group.[54] Somewhat neurotic and described as suffering from 'barbed wire psychosis', he was 'a stage caricature of a Prussian general and never without his monocle which had deformed his eye. Only once had he been seen without his monocle, and that was when he took it out to wipe it after an emotional moment.'[55] British officers noticed that he even wore it under sunglasses and seemed to sleep in it because it was always in place when he was counted in bed in the morning. Having heard the news that he had been awarded the Ritterkreuz [Knight's Cross] while in British custody, he could not wait to receive the medal from Germany. His puffed-up ego was so impatient that he borrowed a Ritterkreuz from one of the other generals and always wore it around his neck.[56]

While at Trent Park, Frantz wore so many decorations from the Great War that he had to 'button up his tunic and then fasten them on over his buttons'.[57] Bizarrely, he even went to bed with them on. In a clipped voice, he moaned constantly to British officers and fellow prisoners and even tried to lay down the law with the British officers, but gradually learned that this was futile. Bluntness was deemed the only way to deal with him. It took three weeks for Frantz to learn that it was not the duty of Lord Aberfeldy to search the London shops for red-brown boot polish, even for a German general.

Frantz made himself the most unpopular prisoner and was especially disliked by the batmen. It was noted: 'He spends practically all his time alone in his room and has even been seen walking alone in the after-dinner parade round the courtyard.'[58] His personal file concluded with the assessment: 'This man is the most difficult to get on with in the camp.'

Amongst Crüwell's ardent supporters was Paul Meixner who tried to please his fellow officers, but when in the company of the anti-Nazi camp, was much less the ranting politician. MI19 were surprised to find that his colleagues thought him a man of fine character. In spite of his pro-Nazi beliefs, Meixner was spotted one evening by a British officer who entered his room, reading a copy of Lord Vansittart's virulently anti-German book, *Lessons of my Life* which he had borrowed from von Thoma. Meixner's English was considered very good, and on two evenings he translated material for the other generals; most evenings, however, he spent playing bridge with a group formed by von Arnim.

After Meixner's arrival at the 'special quarters', Crüwell began to canvass the anti-Nazis to change allegiance. Lieutenant General Schnarrenberger and Krause took no part in the political battles in the communal rooms of the country mansion. Krause preferred cultural activities and engaged his time in playing chess, table tennis and bridge. He was an enthusiastic member of the Camp 11 String Quartet.

The anti-Nazis around General von Thoma quickly outnumbered the pro-Nazi clique and gained the upper hand. Their diverse characters soon became obvious. Amongst the anti-Nazis was General Hans Cramer whose file showed him to be an 'anti-Nazi and a monarchist who detested the Nazi Party and wanted the Hohenzollern dynasty restored to the Throne'.[59] He had English blood on his mother's side, as she was descended from an old county Somerset family. He admired England, was tired of the war and yearned for peace between Britain and Germany. Forty-seven-year-old Cramer had been decorated with the Iron Cross during the First World War having served in an infantry regiment. During the Second World War, he served as a commander of the German Afrika Korps.

Whilst at Trent Park, Cramer preferred to isolate himself from the other generals by often remaining quietly in his room. His outward appearance was somewhat deceptive; of medium height, his sparse hair was plastered tightly back and he always wore a monocle. A neat and straightforward figure, he gave the impression of being a typical Prussian officer, yet despite immediate appearances, British intelligence officers found him to be 'a pleasant and interesting conversationalist who talked too fast such that no one could get a word in'.[60] Throughout his time in captivity, he suffered a number of asthma attacks and would be repatriated to Germany in 1944.[61]

General Gerhard Bassenge, also a veteran of the First World War, offered to collaborate with the British in getting rid of Nazism and ending the war. He tried to convince the British officers that no selfish motives lay behind his offer. He shared a room with Neuffer and they frequently talked politics together. His personal file provides something of the colourful life at Trent Park:

> This POW looks much younger than his age. This may, of course, be due to his enormous consumption of face cream. He is very proud of his person and is often to be found with his sleek fair hair controlled by a hair net. A frequent sight is Bassenge strolling nonchalantly along the corridor, dressed in a miniature silk cache-sexe and his hair net.[62]

Bavarian-born Georg Neuffer made no secret of his anti-Nazi views. He was found to be good-natured, well read, intelligent and exuded a certain charm. He was the only senior officer who had a good word to say for the Russians and understood what democracy stood for.[63] Another German veteran of the First World War was Lieutenant General Sponeck who had been recognised by Field Marshal Rommel as fine leader material. Sponeck had led his division in difficult defensive actions and retreats in North Africa with 'prudence, skill and determination'.[64] Whilst at Trent Park, he was prone to be neurotic, moody on the one hand, and exceedingly talkative on the other. A talented painter, he spent most of his time on his art. Described as a defeatist, monarchist and anti-Nazi, one report of him said he sometimes 'snoops around the place like a dog with his tail between his legs'.[65]

Fritz von Broich was the son of a general, and was described as 'a jolly ex-cavalry man with a twinkle in his eye'.[66] Having transferred from the German cavalry to command the 10th Panzer Division, von Broich also surrendered with the German army in Tunisia. He was not particularly intelligent, but always seemed amusing and charming. Widely travelled in Europe, he displayed a pride in his aristocratic blood. From Trent Park, he wrote strong anti-Nazi letters home to his wife which caused her no small amount of aggravation from the Gestapo. MI19 noted that he had a weak will and 'a horror of Communism only equalled by his horror of Nazism'. In captivity, von Broich envied the English political system and sought to understand democracy and its significance. In that respect, he was not dissimilar to von Liebenstein who admired both English democracy and French culture.

General Kurt Freiherr von Liebenstein, aged 44, was a talented artist who painted credit-worthy watercolours during his time at Trent Park.[67] Von Arnim appointed him deputy camp leader. Although Liebenstein was inclined to read very little, he began to support the anti-Nazi cause by taking up the reading of anti-Nazi literature supplied by the British; politically, he declared himself a monarchist who detested dictatorship in all its forms. A great lover of horses, he expressed gratitude when hunting scenes were provided for the walls of his bedroom.

The anti-Nazis were summarised by MI19 as 'the most intelligent, widely-travelled and cultured officers who looked eagerly to a restoration of the Monarchy in Germany'. Von Thoma petitioned to be allowed to read books that had been banned in Germany under the Third Reich, a request which was granted. Once the books were available he tried to entice the pro-Nazi group to read them as well. The anti-Nazi group never complained about life at Trent Park and told their captors how grateful they were for their excellent treatment. The pro-Nazi faction had no interest in literature, and frequently complained about their conditions. Carius and Bock left on 11 June, both considered 'unpleasant specimens'.

Most of the generals now believed that Germany had little chance of victory,[68] and therefore seemed uninterested in military advances made by the Russians. For them, the war was as good as lost and they spent their time discussing how the complete collapse of Germany could be avoided. Of course, they themselves were powerless to do anything as 'guests' of His Majesty's government in England. A minority, that included von Arnim, expressed the opinion that reports of the true military situation had been withheld from Hitler. Crüwell and von Arnim were horrified by the defeatist attitude and suggested that the disloyal generals should be shot when they were repatriated. The other generals isolated these two characters as 'windbags who refused to engage in reasonable debate'.

British officers monitoring the transcripts of conversations felt that behind the defeatist exterior the generals really still harboured the idea of world domination and were planning for the next war while also speculating about their own role after the end of hostilities. The anti-Nazis naively believed that they could still hold on to power in post-war Germany. Comments in the British intelligence reports make it quite clear that Britain was not going to entertain any such notion – the generals would not be granted any power in post-war Germany. The pro-Nazis suggested that they themselves might be forced to retire in disgust and 'take up bee-keeping, poultry-farming or work as estate agents'.

In spite of its numerous defeats, von Thoma believed that Germany would nevertheless recover ground in the war. Of all the generals, he was the one who engaged readily on politics with British officers at Trent Park. British intelligence saw straight through his two-pronged propaganda: that as soon as possible Britain should make a statement of intention for Germany, and second that they should reach Berlin before the Russians so that 'Germany may be saved from Bolshevism'. Fear of Russia became one of the most persistent themes of their political discussions. One of the Lieutenant Colonels commented: 'As long as our Army is intact, the English with us, would be in a position to march against the Russians.'[69]

The generals discussed the belief that the next world struggle would be between Communist Russia and the western capitalist powers. History would, of course, prove them right. It was only a matter of years before Western Europe and America were thrown into the Cold War. Bassenge and von Thoma believed that in the next struggle Germany would side with Russia against the West – and of course in that, they would be proved wrong.

THE LIFE OF GENTLEMEN

The numbers of the anti-Nazis swelled with the arrival of Colonels Schmidt and Reimann, and Lieutenant Colonels Köhncke and Wolters. Reimann, however, seemed not to have the moral courage to stand up for his views against the opposition. He insisted to those around him that as a Silesian, he must not be mistaken for a Prussian. He became an excellent manager of the prisoners' canteen. The arrival of Colonels Drange and Heym again added to the anti-Nazi numbers, although it was initially assumed that they were pro-Nazi.

At noon on 25 June 1943, the new commandant at Trent Park, Major Denis Bevan Topham, summoned Generals von Arnim and von Liebenstein to his office to announce two major changes. Because of the number of German officers being housed there, those below the rank of Lieutenant General would be required to share bedrooms; and there would be a reduction in rations.[70] Von Arnim and Liebenstein had already drawn up a list of complaints for commandant Major Topham, but this news completely took them by surprise. They were visibly shocked by the announcement and asked for time to think about it. They left after requesting to see an interpreter later that afternoon.

During the afternoon, von Arnim and some of the senior generals tried to bully the warders into giving them empty rooms in another part of the house, but their request was refused.[71] They continued to plot together and because their conversations were secretly recorded, when one of the camp interpreters, Captain E. Hamley, entered the common room later, he already knew what they were going to say.[72] They had worked themselves up into quite a frenzy. An enraged von Arnim, who was seated with fellow generals, laid down their demands and concluded uncompromisingly:

'We will sleep in the corridor rather than share rooms!'

'Do you really mean it?' said the interpreter.

'Yes!' Arnim replied indignantly.[73]

The interpreter left the room briefly. On his return, he made the situation perfectly clear. 'You must remember,' he told them, as they hung onto his every word, 'as prisoners of war in Germany our own generals are not treated in the same excellent way that you are treated here. Some of ours are still in shackles. We are in a democracy here where Parliament still has a say. Questions are being asked already in Parliament about the comfortable lifestyle which you enjoy here. So gentlemen, if you prefer to sleep in the corridor, you may do so. But, you will not be permitted to remove any furniture from the rooms.'

He turned to von Arnim directly and said: 'Remember that as a prisoner of war you must submit to British military discipline.' With a cursory nod, he left the room.

With the interpreter gone, the generals engaged in an intense discussion and decided that they had better give in. Later during the evening, probably in an unofficial discussion with Lord Aberfeldy, they were given friendly advice that it would be wise to accept the situation. Most of the generals agreed again that they were receiving excellent treatment. The pro-Nazis continued to grumble in letters written home to their families and made sarcastic remarks to their British minders about the reduction in food rations. They saw the rationing as an admission that things were in a bad way in England. Amongst themselves, not realising they were being eavesdropped on, they admitted the food was still good and ample.[74] Krause even conceded that the food was better than anything they had had in Germany since 1914 and added: 'There is good coffee and tea at all meals.'[75]

The battle of the generals left a sour and strained atmosphere for a few days but it was soon forgotten. They had little, after all, to complain about.

THE DAY TRIPS

Regular walks around the grounds of Trent Park were permitted and the generals understood that this was a privilege granted by the commandant. It was Lord Aberfeldy's job to relay the following message to them from the commandant:

The commandant would like me to explain ... he can no longer permit the officers to go out for walks improperly dressed. It is irregular for the officers to go out in just a shirt and shorts ... they must wear a proper uniform ... He has no objection to the officers wearing shorts ... but they must wear a tunic [with them].[76]

The generals were taken on special trips to central London, something they particularly looked forward to. On occasion, they dined with Kendrick or Felkin at Simpsons on the Strand where they were served a plate of meat and heaps of vegetables, followed by a pudding.[77] Did the generals never suspect that their conversations were being bugged and that their life of comfort was a bit odd as prisoners of war? It was noted in the intelligence reports: 'Von Thoma is of the opinion that the British don't need to listen to what "small fry" like the POWs here say, as their Intelligence Service is so good.'[78]

The intelligence report went on to comment: 'Von Arnim and Crüwell are themselves amongst the biggest careless talk offenders here.'[79] Secret listener Eric Mark, who accompanied the generals on a lunch trip to Simpsons, explained: 'They thought we were being so nice to them because, they believed, we were trying to seek favours with them so that when they won the war, we would be well treated too. It did not occur to them that it was all part of the bugging deception plan.'[80]

When Churchill found out about the lunches at Simpsons, he was furious. The belligerent Prime Minister banned the 'pampering of the generals'. But MI19 knew that the treatment of the generals was reaping intelligence results that could not be obtained in interrogation. Kendrick and Felkin relocated lunch with their 'guests' to the Ritz instead, and it appears Churchill never found out.

The generals were even occasionally taken on a three-hour excursion which ended in tea at Kendrick's house in the secluded village of Oxshott in Surrey.[81] Their stiffness soon began to melt as the day progressed and they finally relaxed in the company of their escorting officers. Kendrick's granddaughter Barbara and grandson Ken sang songs from the First

World War whilst the generals enjoyed sandwiches and tea.[82] Kendrick's wife, Norah, did not ask any questions when her husband arrived in an army chauffeured car with an accompanying car of German generals.

Other ranks of German officers were also periodically taken on trips into London or further afield. On one occasion, they were treated to a day out in Whitby on the coast. It did not quite turn out as planned because some of them consumed too much beer causing a near crisis when a U-boat captain and his First Lieutenant started shouting firing orders for torpedoes when they saw ships sailing by in the bay.

In spite of the occasional glitch, by all accounts the trips were deemed a success. Puzzled by Germany's continued military defeats, Bassenge was overheard saying to Neuffer, and recorded by the secret listeners: 'We have the best generals and are losing the war!'[83] Clearly, talking too much within earshot of the hidden microphones may have had something to do with that.

CHAPTER 7

Mad Hatter's Tea Party

Life at Trent Park continued along the drawn battle lines of pro-Nazi and anti-Nazi and British officers were faced with an almost farcical scenario on a daily basis. The generals provided no small amount of entertainment as they continued to battle over their political leanings and preen the feathers of their egos like peacocks strutting around the grounds of a stately home. After dinner on 9 July 1943, von Arnim gave a rather long-winded talk directed against the anti-Nazis who were seen as defeatists. His speech was noted by British intelligence for its absence of any reference to Hitler.[1] Afterwards, von Thoma added his opinion that 'old men blind themselves before the blatant facts'. Shortly before von Arnim's speech, General Cramer had been discussing politics with a British army officer about possible leaders for a revolution in Germany. After von Arnim's speech, Cramer shouted loudly from the corridor outside the dining room: 'I look forward to continuing this discussion!'[2] Von Arnim and Cramer had become noticeably closer that last week and Cramer had been invited with some other 'defeatists' to play bridge in Von Arnim's room. There was speculation that von Arnim might be moving across to the anti-Nazi camp.

Rather than deterring the anti-Nazis, von Arnim's speech had the effect of drawing them out. Anti-Nazi literature was no longer read secretly behind the closed doors of bedrooms. Colonel Borcherdt openly read Braun's *Von Weimar zu Hitler* in the courtyard in full view of the other generals. The following day, von Liebenstein read the book and quoted chunks of it to a British army officer in front of his batman – a great crime according to von Arnim's speech the previous evening. The colonels all appeared to have joined the anti-Nazi camp.[3]

BATMEN'S REVOLT

Trouble with the batmen had been simmering for a while. Each general had his own batman, captured from the battlefields with the general. The batman was a personal servant, in uniform and of lower rank, who was responsible for making the general's bed each morning, polishing his boots, laying out his uniform and attending to any other needs. He usually walked a few steps behind the general, carrying his bags and a ceremonial baton in his right hand.

During the week of von Arnim's after-dinner speech, the batmen at Trent Park began to grumble that they should receive the same comforts as the generals because they were all equal as POWs.[4] The situation came to a head over the distribution of cigars from the German-run tuck-shop. The generals discussed the behaviour of the batmen and made a written request to their British minders, asking for the removal of three batmen: Schmidt, Dittmar and Wodtke. Erich Schmidt was the most disliked of the batmen. His personal file is not flattering. A Nazi and a rather odd character, he frequently found something to complain about, and had innumerable physical complaints:

> The first being caused by being hit in the stomach by a medicine ball. This caused him to lie on the ground groaning. He was taken to hospital where after an X-ray examination it was ascertained that he had merely been winded and the groans immediately ceased. Next he decided that rheumatism was killing him. The English climate was to blame. He retired semi-permanently to bed. When talk of repatriation arose he became permanently incapacitated. He only got up to draw nudes.[5]

The batmen had another go at persuading Crüwell to make things unpleasant for the British minders. Although Crüwell had already agreed to get rid of the three batmen, he petitioned von Arnim to make out that the British were riding roughshod over the generals and forcibly trying to remove their batmen. He suggested to von Arnim that he should put his foot down. Von Arnim was wise enough to keep quiet about the whole affair, and began to tire of Crüwell's nagging.

Von Arnim had long talks with Cramer and Crüwell about the war situation.[6] In spite of their disagreements, they agreed not to give in to defeatism, but to support the regime to the bitter end. Von Arnim continued to sign his letters home, 'always your old optimist'.[7]

During the summer months of 1943, Meixner too began to show leanings towards the anti-Nazi defeatists. Von Broich had an interesting defeatist talk with his batman who happened to be head batman at the camp. Von Hülsen revealed his hand as a monarchist, adamantly against Nazi figures like Hermann Goering, although publicly he still professed to be in the pro-Nazi group. All the generals were concerned about possible roles after the war and the anti-Nazis in particular believed they would still hold on to their military positions. Political literature continued to be circulated and provided for them by their British minders.[8] A few German newspapers were circulated, designed to enable the generals to relax further into camp life, be totally off-guard in their conversations and to think that the British were stupid. So great was the ego of the generals that they could not entertain the idea that British intelligence was pulling the strings of their stage-set in a situation where the melodrama turned into an almost comical charade.

On the afternoon of 15 July 1943, von Hülsen was taken by army truck to the dentist.[9] His military escorts expected him to comment on the journey, but instead he offered absurd comments about how badly local people were dressed and how decrepit the houses looked – all due, in his opinion, to the war. To add to his smug confidence, that day was early closing and the shops had already pulled down their blinds. He believed that the closed shops were a sign that the war was going badly wrong for the British. When he saw a trolley-bus, he declared it had been electrified because Britain had a serious shortage of petrol.

Frustrations were running high at Trent Park. Crüwell displayed an outburst to a British officer over his treatment in the camp, telling him he knew that life for many German prisoners was much better in Allied POW camps in Canada. The British officer offered to request a transfer, at which Crüwell quickly rescinded and complained that the lack of food was making him thin. He received the response that he looked less flabby and much healthier for it.[10]

On 20 July, von Arnim requested a meeting with the new administrative camp commandant at Trent Park, Major Denis Topham. (Kendrick was based at new headquarters at Latimer House). In the meeting, von Arnim made further requests on behalf of the generals, asking Major Topham for a German cook on site, a German tailor and German dentist. He considered British methods of dentistry old-fashioned. Complaints were made about the quantity of rations, until it was pointed out to him that the other POWs had already expressed approval of the rations. This still did not prevent him asking for more cigarettes, cigars and tobacco until he was promptly told that such rations for British prisoners in Germany were far less.

The following day, von Arnim was escorted to hospital for a problem with his feet. There he was allowed to visit Lieutenant General Frantz who had been hospitalised for an unknown complaint. Von Arnim expressed disgust at the methods of medical treatment which he considered old-fashioned. He objected to being treated by a female doctor over which, according to intelligence files, he almost collapsed into a fit of shock.[11]

Following several severe defeats, the generals began to criticise the higher command of the German air force, especially Hermann Goering as its commander in chief.[12] General Neuffer said that every time he had met Goering, he had thought to himself: 'My God, if that's all the brain power there is!' Goering was largely felt to have been responsible for the Stalingrad disaster as, according to the recorded conversations, Germany's generals had advised Hitler that Stalingrad could no longer be held, but Goering maintained that it could – and Hitler listened to him, rather than his generals.[13]

On the afternoon of 23 July, the generals received a visit from Mr Barwick of the British YMCA and Tracy Strong of the American YMCA.[14] No secret was made of the existence of Trent Park as a prisoner-of-war camp, but the bugging side of the operation was completely hushed up. Access to the site was still strictly controlled. The YMCA representatives promised to ameliorate life for the prisoners by offering to provide a grand piano, gramophone, golf clubs and a range of literature from Liverpool University.[15]

News of Mussolini's resignation on the night of 25 July 1943 rendered the generals speechless. It shattered them and was clearly unexpected.[16] Even the defeatists were seriously affected. In response, von Hülsen declared that Germany's position was precarious and von Arnim and Crüwell had to agree. During the first few hours after the news, Crüwell despaired and declared: 'I am no Nazi!' This quick change of heart was typical of him. The British intelligence report the following morning read:

> It would have been difficult to have found a gloomier collection of people than our guests here. The only smiling face was von Thoma's and he went about with an 'I told you so' air, much to the annoyance of the anti-defeatists. Thoma told a British officer he had discussed the news with Crüwell and said to him 'which of us has made a fool of himself, you or I?' Which of course must have poured salt into Crüwell's already smarting wounds.[17]

That same day, the General Officer Commanding (G.O.C) London District, was due to inspect Trent Park. As the generals' camp leader, the previous evening von Arnim had been advised by commandant Major Topham that he and the other generals might like to remain in their rooms because the G.O.C would probably wish to see their rooms and would also inspect the guard in the courtyard. Von Arnim reacted badly to the news as a restriction on their freedom of movement. He was politely reminded that the last time the guard had been inspected he had requested advance notice so the generals could choose to stay in their rooms out of the way.

The reaction of the other generals to the impending visit was not without its humour. Von Hülsen and Meixner, who shared a room, decided to hide their cigarettes in the hope that the G.O.C would think they were badly treated and had been given none. The G.O.C did visit the upstairs rooms but, much to von Arnim's disgust, did not stay to talk with him. That evening, von Arnim complained to every British officer he saw that the G.O.C had not given him the time of day – all this on the same day that one of the batmen gave a Nazi salute to a British officer in the corridor, then swiftly apologised.

Von Arnim and Cramer requested a walk that evening in the grounds with a British officer. It was described as a gloomy affair. Von Arnim appeared to have drastically aged and all he wanted to do was sit and dig holes in the grass with his stick.[18] They were in no mood to discuss Mussolini, in spite of much prompting by the British officer. Meanwhile, the other generals sat alone in their rooms to contemplate the latest news and day's events.

During the week of 7 August, von Thoma discussed the developing political and military situation in greater length with Lord Aberfeldy than with his own fellow officers. The intelligence report for that week noted: 'At meals, he [von Thoma] makes a point of sitting with the anti-defeatists as he takes pleasure in baiting them.'[19] The report went on to say that the British officer 'had his usual Sunday talk with von Thoma, who warned him not to discuss politics with von Arnim and Crüwell. He advised him that it would be a thankless task'.[20]

General Neuffer heard on a news broadcast at 5 p.m. on 7 August that he had been awarded the Ritterkreuz.[21] Bassenge got hold of Neuffer's Iron Cross and asked a British army officer to have a silver ring put on it so it could be worn on a ribbon round his neck. The intelligence report noted: 'This was done – the silver ring being replaced by a paperclip.'[22]

Sunday 23 August was the first anniversary of Crüwell's arrival at Trent Park. Von Liebenstein asked the (unnamed) interpreter if they could 'do anything to mark the occasion and brighten the day for Crüwell'.[23] An arrangement was made for Crüwell and von Arnim to go to the British army officer's room for a drink but von Arnim insisted that, as a senior German officer, the drink should be in his room and that the British army officer should bring the whisky, soda water and a glass so the generals would not have to use their own rations. The generals received a range of items, such as tins of cheese, milk, butter and fish regularly in parcels from the German Red Cross.

APPEALING TO THE SWISS

On the morning of 29 August, the commandant gave the generals a few hours' notice of a visit to Trent Park by Dr Preiswerk, a Swiss representative – Switzerland being officially a neutral country. The news sent the generals into a frenzy of preparatory activities. Nothing focused their attention better than being motivated by their own cause. They began to work on a plan to bring various complaints before Dr Preiswerk. Every bit of their privately-planned strategy was recorded by the secret listeners.

The generals agreed amongst themselves to complain about the major generals being assigned two to a room. Also on their agenda were: the question of parole and taking walks outside the wire fence, provision of a German doctor and dentist to be found from amongst German POWs being held in camps around Britain, and specialist officers to come to Trent Park to provide lectures on a range of subjects. They raised the issue of the unequal treatment of the batmen who were given beer at meals (rather than wine) and were only allowed to write two letters and four cards to Germany a month, whereas the generals were allowed to write three letters and four cards. They asked why only one lower-rank German officer was permitted to go for a walk at any one time, whereas two generals could go.

The generals agreed not to offer the Swiss representative any cigarettes so he would think that the British were not giving them any. Crüwell suggested that they should ask Dr Preiswerk to tea in one of their rooms if he was proving helpful to them and told von Arnim that he should wear full uniform and decorations so the special visitor would be impressed. It was urged on von Arnim that Dr Preiswerk should be steered clear of those generals and officers who did not approve of the grumbling campaign. Behind the scenes, British intelligence was monitoring their plan via the secret listeners and decided to intervene by ensuring that Dr Preiswerk visited von Thoma who was guaranteed to be much more appreciative of life in the camp.

Von Arnim kept to the plan and brought up the list of complaints with Dr Preiswerk who proved unhelpful. He advised von Arnim not to press matters too much because it might provoke an investigation which could turn out unfavourably for the generals. The issue of parole was raised by von Arnim, as he asked 'Why should we be accompanied by a British officer at all if we have signed a parole form and the whole park is surrounded by barbed wire?'

'You are mistaken,' replied Dr Preiswerk. 'It is a normal peacetime fence and under the Geneva Convention the power holding the prisoner has to protect them from hostile demonstrations. It is in your interests to be accompanied by a British officer.'

Von Arnim had nothing to say in response. Dr Preiswerk asked to see the other generals, but von Arnim swiftly assured him that they had nothing to discuss with him. Dr Preiswerk was not deterred and managed to see General von Thoma.

At the end of the month, Lieutenant General Frantz was discharged from hospital and brought back to Trent Park. The nurses told the British officer that they had tried to discharge Frantz earlier and they had never come across 'such an unpleasant, domineering and thick-skinned patient'. On his return, Frantz seemed happy with the medical treatment but complained bitterly that he had been insulted by having a sentry posted outside his room at all times. He complained about the quality of the food, which for him was an indication that the war was not going well for the British.

SNAKE IN THE GRASS ACTIVITIES

During August 1943, the generals seemed as disunited as when they first arrived. After Sunday lunch on 15 August, von Arnim gave another of his 'pep talks' and warned the others against defeatist talk. He announced that he suspected a British army officer of listening into their talk from his window – why else had he moved to a room in the middle of the first floor? He also declared suspicions that their conversations might be overheard by the establishment. The speech created uproar amongst the other generals who thought him mad to believe the British could be listening in to their conversations. Even the pro-Nazis objected to the tone and language of von Arnim's rhetoric.

The following day, von Arnim added more fuel to the fire when he said that all he was trying to do was save the defeatists from court-martial when they finally returned to 'the glorious Fatherland'. The other senior officers objected strongly to what they termed 'the Gestapo-style methods' contained in von Arnim's speech which resulted in them suspecting von Arnim of suffering from psychosis.[24] Crüwell too was deemed to be unbalanced. They speculated whether the British army officer assigned to talk to them was in fact part of the British secret service, but concluded that he could not possibly be engaged in intelligence because his manner was not subtle enough.

Crüwell began to work against von Liebenstein to have him deposed as deputy camp leader, perhaps hoping that he himself would be selected.[25] When this did not happen he was bitterly disappointed and continued to vent anger and to harbour a hatred of von Thoma, but the other officers no longer showed any interest.

The generals continued to be supplied with literature. Crüwell complained that the anti-Nazi books had been supplied by the British authorities and should in no way be distributed in wartime without being censored by the German authorities.[26] The other generals quickly responded – who did he mean by the 'German authorities'? British intelligence commented in a report, 'He [Crüwell] probably meant himself!'

General von Arnim tried to veto listening to broadcasts in German as being secret British propaganda. Bassenge, for one, threatened to ignore von Arnim's veto, and von Thoma questioned whether, under the terms of the Geneva Convention, it was legal for von Arnim to ban listening to radio broadcasts.

On 20 August, Frantz, Schnarrenberger, Heym and Drange were informed that they were being transferred the following day to an American camp.[27] The other generals could not resist commenting on the reasons for the unexpected transfer. Frantz bizarrely decided he was being exchanged for some American machinery and that he had been chosen because he was the senior Luftwaffe general in the camp and the Americans wanted him for reasons of prestige. Heym decided he was being exchanged for forty old destroyers. Drange suggested that he and Heym were on the American 'Black List' and shouldn't be transferred. Then the M Room listeners overheard an extraordinary comment which gives an insight into the brain-washing of the Nazi regime: four senior officers feared that they were victims who might fall into the hands of the Jews in America and be paraded through the streets of New York.[28]

Intelligence reports occasionally mentioned mail that the generals received from Germany – all censored by MI9. On 29 August, von Thoma received a letter from a retired general in Germany who wrote at length about the marvellous morale of the German home front. Von Thoma's reply was short: 'Please write only about personal matters and nothing else!'[29] Another intelligence report narrated how Colonels Reimann, Köhncke and Wolters had a drink in their room and invited a British army officer. 'A very pleasant evening was in progress when von Arnim appeared with six bottles of beer and asked if he could join the party,' it reported.[30] Von Arnim was accepted by the others, but with the firm suspicion that he was only there to spy on them.

That autumn of 1943, the generals reacted with concern to news about the Moscow Conference in which Allied leaders discussed ways to shorten the war and how to deal with justice and war crimes.[31] The Moscow Agreement provided for the trial and punishment of individuals suspected of war crimes in the country where the atrocities had taken place. The intelligence reports at the time mentioned: 'Our guests are still all very worried by the war criminal clause in the Moscow Agreement. Vain and violent efforts at counter propaganda are being made by our guests to a British army officer.'[32]

By November 1943, General Cramer's health was sufficiently bad that MI19 considered repatriating him before the end of hostilities. After his medical examination, he was quite open with a British army officer and discussed how he would be interrogated by Hitler on his return. He assured the British officer that he would tell Hitler how confident the British were of a victory, and that he had been well treated as a POW. He planned to tell Hitler, 'There is no hope of peace as long as he [Hitler] and his gang form the government'.[33] The subsequent MI19 report stated that on his return, Cramer would 'try to find out what is being done to overthrow the Nazi regime. We can rest assured that any attempt will have his full support and that of his friends.'[34]

Cramer believed he would still have significant influence in Germany as a 'kommandierende General'. He reassured the British officer that he had a good friend in General Korten, the German air force Chief of Staff, whom he would tell after his repatriation that the recent raids on London were a waste of time and petrol.[35]

During this period, the generals enjoyed raised morale, largely due (in their minds) to the German offensive towards Kiev, the slow and difficult progress of the Allied advance through Italy, and the belief that much of November had passed without any crack in Germany's home front. There were comments, too, about the bombing of Berlin which von Thoma and Reimann believed 'served the Berliners right, as they were not sympathetic enough when the Ruhr and Rhineland were being bombed'. British intelligence noted: 'On the majority of our guests, the raids on Berlin have not had as great an effect as expected.'[36]

WINTER FESTIVITIES

As Christmas approached, British army officers turned to plans for festivities at Trent Park. On 9 November, the 'guests', as the generals were politely referred to in intelligence reports, had group photographs taken, sitting on a bench in the grounds. The photograph was to be sent to their wives and families in Germany as a Christmas card.[37] In a move which surprised intelligence staff, the generals organised themselves along political lines for the official photograph. Clustered in one group were von Arnim, Crüwell, von Hülsen, Meixner, Schmidt, Buhse, Egersdorff, Borcherdt, Boes, Glasow and Hubbuch. The other group was composed of Sponeck, Broich, Liebenstein, Bassenge, Neuffer, Krause, Reimann, Wolters and Köhncke. Von Thoma refused to have his photograph taken at all because he did not want a reminder of his time in a prisoner-of-war camp or to be seen with 'old Blimps' as he termed his colleagues.

A short time later, a British army officer stumbled across an advertisement for Trent Park written by one of the generals. Its tongue-in-cheek humour perhaps brought a smile to British minders and reads in translation:[38]

PARK SANATORIUM
First class accommodation, running hot and cold water at all hours of the day, also baths on the premises. Four generous meals daily, first class English cuisine.
Regular walks under expert guidance.
Large library of carefully chosen literature of all countries.
Table-tennis tournaments, billiards, chess and bridge circles.
Instruction in art and handicrafts.
Alcoholism cured without extra charge.
Moderate terms, varying according to social position.
Best society assured at all times!

Internal rivalry continued unabated. Crüwell endeavoured again to have the deputy camp leader von Liebenstein removed from post, proposing to have him replaced by Bassenge in the hope of bridging the rift between the pro-Nazis and defeatists (anti-Nazis). His strategy was aimed at isolating von Thoma and giving the Nazis more influence in the camp.

Towards the end of November, Generals von Broich, Sponeck and von Liebenstein were informed by a British army officer that the Führer was sending a gift of money to all prisoners. Their response to Hitler's generosity was, according to the intelligence files, 'uncomplimentary and unprintable'.[39]

Christmas celebrations began after afternoon tea on Christmas Eve. That evening, the generals and senior German officers sat down to Christmas dinner. Afterwards, the various groups retired to their rooms to celebrate quietly. Only von Thoma spent the remainder of the evening alone. Major Boes, one of the most violently pro-Nazi officers in the Camp, received news from his wife by letter that he had been promoted to Lieutenant Colonel. The intelligence report for that week noted that his 'Anglo-phobia gets more marked each day'.[40] The festivities were marred only by von Arnim who, even on Christmas Eve, felt it his duty to annoy British officers by raising complaints about their treatment of prisoners. However, Bassenge took a firm stand and told the British that the others were only too grateful for what had been done for them in their 'Park Sanatorium'.

On Christmas Day, the generals gathered around a wireless set to listen to the King's Speech.[41] Cramer commented to a British army officer how impressed he was with the speech and how the King was a figurehead which a nation could rally around in times of crisis. He blamed the removal of the Kaiser for all Germany's subsequent ills. The other generals said little.

The pampered generals were rather profligate with electric light and water and at last the British minders brought this to the attention of von Arnim who discussed the matter with Cramer. Both agreed it would be better to limit consumption than have the British retaliate by cutting rations.[42]

New Year's Eve saw no particular celebrations in the house. The generals gathered in the common room to listen to the German wireless broadcast at midnight. Goebbels's speech and Hitler's proclamation did nothing to lift their sombre mood, except inspire a rare unified agreement, even amongst the defeatists, that they would support their motherland to the bitter end. The generals were wished a happy new year by their British minders, which elicited the response from General von Thoma: 'It might be a happy new year for you, but it's not for us!'[43]

CHAPTER 8

Secret Listeners

By 1943, a vast volume of intelligence had been amassed through the M Room. What emerges from reading the transcripts and reports today is the sheer amount of information that was gathered about Nazi Germany. Events were taking a dramatic turn on the Eastern Front, too. At the end of January 1943, German Field Marshal von Paulus, in charge of the German 6th Army trying to take Stalingrad, had surrendered to the Soviets. The city of Stalingrad finally fell on 2 February 1943. The tide began to turn for the Allies and would soon bring with it more prisoners of war. The RAF and US Air Force continued to hammer the enemy's industrial centres in successful air raids across Germany. At Latimer House, Kendrick faced a problem. He needed to urgently increase the number of secret listeners to cope with the extra workload, influx of prisoners and the technical nature of the conversations.

Until 1943, the majority of the secret listeners were British-born men who had fluency in German. There were exceptions, like Jan Weber, who was born in Berlin but had fled to England prior to the war and submitted an application for British nationality, which he finally secured in August 1942. He was able to gain a commission and enlisted into CSDIC through the 'old boys' network' – in this case, via a cousin by marriage. Weber later described his experience as a listener:

> My job, and that of the junior army officers at the time, was to listen
> to and record conversations between inmates of possible intelligence

interest. By the time of my arrival, most German army prisoners caught in North Africa had been dealt with, but to my amazement I saw the name of Wolf Breitling on the list of prisoners for interrogation. He had been the driver batman of a Luftwaffe officer, and I was convinced that he knew nothing. His own rank was that of a corporal but he was sent for interrogation because he spoke several languages and was used as an interpreter by the British. I told Wing Commander Felkin (the head of our air force wing) of my acquaintance with Wolf and went to see him in his cell. He plainly knew nothing but it was an enjoyable experience to speak to him – the only German friend I met during the war, other than fellow refugees.[1]

By early 1943, the German dialect and specialist technical information being picked up via the microphones was too difficult for British-born linguists. The listeners needed to have an extensive knowledge of service slang, conditions and technical gadgets. In a memo to intelligence chiefs, Kendrick wrote: 'The difficulty of finding suitable M Room personnel cannot be overstressed.'[2] He needed native German speakers to monitor the thirty bugged rooms at each of the sites, and turned to the German-speaking refugees serving in the Pioneer Corps.[3] They had fled Nazi Germany and Austria prior to the outbreak of war and wanted to make a difference to the outcome. For some of them, their chance came in 1943.

From her office at MI19(e) at Wilton Park, Catherine Townshend spent much of her time during the autumn of 1942 and 1943 arranging interviews at the War Office in London for Kendrick's recruitment drive for new secret listeners.[4] She processed the paperwork for new intelligence staff, whom Rawlinson then appointed officially as officers, but lower ranks were recruited direct by her and she coordinated all clearances from MI5. It meant travelling to London several times a week for the interviews, but the other office work needed attention during her absence. She was given an assistant, ATS officer Margaret Morley, and they became firm friends. They shared an office with ATS officer 'Tigger'

Agar-Robartes whose job was to censor prisoners' letters and search for any small clues or information that could be useful for intelligence.

The demand for new secret listeners was pressing. Townshend wrote:

> German linguists were in greater demand than ever for listening posts in the various M Rooms. Rawli suggested that I investigate a source that had not yet been tapped: Jewish refugees in the Pioneer Corps. Sons of bankers, lawyers, doctors, and other professions, well educated, hounded from the country in the 1930's, these young men had found sanctuary in England.[5]

Kendrick ran the recruitment interviews with Major Corner, Major Le Bosquet and Townshend. She recalled:

> I attended the interviews, sought security clearances through MI5 afterwards, and in the weeks that followed, sent successful candidates their instructions to report to Beaconsfield or Latimer. The long and careful questioning by Lt. Col. Kendrick prepared me for the role of interviewer, a task that I had to assume in the year ahead.[6]

Around a hundred male German-speaking refugees were eventually transferred to CSDIC as secret listeners. One of them, Frank Stevens, wrote to a fellow 'alien' Pioneer Hans Francken after his interview and told him: 'I only want to tell you that I had my interview yesterday and I think I passed it alright. Anyway, out of 14 we were only three who were asked to come back in the afternoon, when we had our interview with MI5. I guess that it will be the same sort of job as yours. Of course I don't know anything about it, and shall not ask you either.'[7] Their respect for secrecy is clear, and neither did Stevens know what special duties he was being interviewed for. That would be revealed eventually by Kendrick, who became his new commanding officer.

It is ironic that many of these ex-refugees were once mistrusted by the British government as 'enemy aliens' and not even permitted to carry a camera at the outbreak of war, and had spent several months behind barbed wire in internment camps on the Isle of Man in the summer of 1940. Then they had sworn allegiance to George VI and enlisted in the Pioneer Corps where they carried out manual jobs for the war effort.

FRITZ LUSTIG

One such secret listener was Fritz Lustig. Lustig's background was quite typical of the émigrés who went on to work for MI9 and MI19. After Kristallnacht (the 'Night of Broken Glass') in November 1938, when the Nazis smashed Jewish businesses and shop windows across the country, Lustig had to find a way to flee Nazi Germany. The SS and Gestapo were rounding up male Jews and sending them to concentration camps. The city of Berlin where he had been born in 1919 had become an alien place. Securing visas to leave was difficult, but he finally succeeded in emigrating to England in April 1939. His parents later fled to Portugal and his elder brother Ted had already left for America where he fought in the US forces.

Lustig was in England on temporary work when war broke out. In the summer of 1940, as an 'enemy alien', he was arrested and interned on the Isle of Man in Churchill's policy of 'Collar the Lot!' that saw the mass internment of nearly 30,000 German refugees behind barbed wire.[8] On one level, life in internment could have seemed idyllic, far removed from the dangers of war. But many of the internees like Lustig felt a deep resentment at being unable to fight. This was their war and they did not want to sit back while others did the fighting.

In September 1940, he was released from internment to join the Pioneer Corps. As an amateur cellist, he was posted to its orchestra and commented, 'It was not my idea of fighting the Nazis'.[9] A bitter-sweet revelation was the discovery that the only unit open to him as an enemy alien was the Auxiliary Military Pioneer Corps – essentially an unskilled labour corps. Still without British nationality, Fritz donned British army uniform, swore allegiance to George VI and received the King's Shilling. He was one of around 6,500 German-speaking refugees to enlist in the Pioneer Corps between 1940 and the end of 1941. They became affectionately known as 'The King's Most Loyal Enemy Aliens' and, as their individual war records show, they served Britain with total loyalty and were prepared to die for the country that had saved them.[10]

In early March 1943, Lustig was on leave and staying in London. His mother's cousin had introduced him to two friends in the city, Norman and Christel Marsh. Christel was of German origin and her husband, a barrister by profession, was a captain in the Intelligence Corps. Lustig visited them several times during his army leave and often expressed frustration at not being able to do something worthwhile for the war effort. Norman listened patiently but gave nothing away. He asked Lustig if he would be willing to transfer to a special unit that was looking for fluent German speakers. Behind the scenes, Norman put his name forward.

On 18 March 1943, Lustig arrived outside the Metropole Building in Northumberland Avenue, London for an interview. Inside were about a dozen other candidates waiting for interview, all ex-refugees from Germany or Austria. Some of them had already transferred to other units and were no longer serving in the Pioneer Corps. He was ushered into an interview room where a board of six officers that included one woman (now known to have been Catherine Townshend) sat around a horseshoe-shaped table. He made a sufficiently good impression to be asked for a second interview after the lunch break. He recalled:

The second interview was with two civilians who I am convinced were from MI5. There was little they did not know about me – they knew for instance that I had corresponded with my parents while they were still in Germany, and that they were now in Portugal. As far as I can recall, I was not interrogated about my political views at all.[11]

Lustig left that afternoon with no idea whether he had been accepted. He returned to the Pioneer Corps and life carried on as before. Two months later, on 17 May 1943, he received a telegram asking him to report again to the Metropole Building. The following day, he arrived there to be informed by intelligence staff that he was to take the Metropolitan Line to Chalfont & Latimer where he would be met at the station. Having been handed the necessary train ticket, he left the building none the wiser about his new unit. That same day, he penned a letter to his parents, uplifted by new military successes in North Africa after Montgomery's 8th Army had taken Tunis:

> We have been reading the reports of English journalists about Germans streaming into captivity, who this time – for the first time – have not been fighting to the bitter end, as if they were fairy tales – too good to be true. Let's hope that German morale will soon start to break in other places as well.

The next day, 19 May, Lustig took the underground to Chalfont & Latimer. At the railway station, he was met by a driver in military uniform and driven to nearby Latimer House. On arrival, he discovered that the unit was a special prisoner-of-war camp. He was immediately issued with three stripes – the sleeve insignia of a sergeant – and told to report to Colonel Kendrick the following day. 'I was stunned,' he said, 'by the fact that I had been promoted from private to sergeant – three ranks in one go!'

The contrast to life in the Pioneer Corps could not have been more stark. Sergeants and sergeant-majors had their own Mess with easy chairs for relaxation and a wireless to listen to radio broadcasts. Sergeants of the intelligence staff had their own Mess and did not mix with staff not involved in intelligence activities. Personnel were not allowed to discuss their work with each other.

Lustig vividly remembered his first meeting with his new commanding officer. Colonel Kendrick explained the nature of the work as a secret listener and impressed on Lustig the importance of not telling anyone about it, not even family or close friends. Kendrick passed him a form and asked him to sign the Official Secrets Act. Before dismissing him, Kendrick said something which Lustig never forgot: 'Your work here is as important as firing a gun in action or joining a fighting unit.'

The irony was not lost on Lustig. Back in November 1938 when the Nazis had unleashed Kristallnacht, he and his family had feared for their lives and, like many Jews, had gone into hiding. That terrifying night they were expecting a telephone call from Lustig's brother who had already escaped to America. The Gestapo were known to tap the telephones of Jews and political opponents of the regime. Fritz recalled:

> Many people even suspected that secret microphones had been attached to their telephones which would enable the Gestapo to listen in to conversations while the receiver was on the hook, and therefore piled several cushions on top of their telephones in order to muffle the sound reaching the supposed microphone.

At the height of the terror being inflicted on the Jews of Germany that fateful night in 1938, Lustig's family managed to get a telegram to his brother warning him not to telephone them for fear of the consequences. Nearly five years later, Fritz found himself working for British intelligence against the Nazis. His loyalty to the country which had saved him was never in doubt, but now his adopted country finally trusted him with their most closely guarded secrets. In a twist of fate, the man who once feared being bugged by the Gestapo was himself about to bug the conversations of Nazis.

How did Lustig feel about bugging German prisoners and spying on his country of birth? He replied: 'They were no longer our compatriots.'

ÉMIGRÉ LISTENERS

The secret listeners had similar backgrounds and tales of how they fled Nazi Germany. Fritz's friend, Peter Ganz, was originally from Mainz. The 20-year-old Ganz was firmly agnostic, but this did not save him from the Nazi threat, even though his grandparents had converted from Judaism to the Lutheran Church. Ganz was arrested by the Gestapo as a 'non-Aryan' and transported to Buchenwald concentration camp.[12] It was six weeks before he was one of the lucky ones to be released after a guarantor came forward. He fled to England where, in 1939, he enrolled as a student of German and Spanish at King's College London. His studies were interrupted in 1940 when, as an enemy alien, he was arrested and interned on the Isle of Man from where he managed to enlist in the Pioneer Corps and eventually became a secret listener with MI19 at Trent Park.

John Gay (born Hans Ludwig Göhler) finally escaped Nazi Germany after spending time in Sachsenhausen concentration camp. Like the other secret listeners, he joined the Pioneer Corps in 1943, then transferred to the Intelligence Corps and was based at Latimer House and Wilton Park. He later became a renowned photographer and wartime scenes of the Wilton Park estate are amongst some of his photographic works.

Also at Latimer were Hans Stern (an eminent professor of linguistics) and Hans Francken (Hannen Geoffrey Francken) who transferred there in August 1943. At the end of the war, like the other secret listeners, Francken was given an exemplary reference from the Intelligence Corps which stated:

This Sergeant has been doing work of great secrecy and has shown all those qualities of tact and discretion that were required. He has a wide experience in handling difficult people and situations and possesses an agreeable personality. He speaks fluent French and German and seems well suited for a position of trust and responsibility.[13]

Secret listener Herbert Newhouse (born Herbert Heinrich Neuhaus in Berlin in 1908) also received high recommendation: 'This NCO has been in the Intelligence Corps for more than two years and has been engaged on special and highly secret duties with absolute integrity.'[14] Herbert had fled to England with his father in 1933 and set up an import/export company. He went on to marry Ilse Frank, a refugee and the daughter of Theodore Frank, a director of the Deutsche Bank.

Herbert was interned on the Isle of Man in 1940, from where he enlisted in the Pioneer Corps, and then transferred to the Royal Army Service Corps. He began working for British intelligence in January 1944, most probably first at Trent Park before being transferred to Latimer House.

Another listener was Rudi Oppenheimer, a lawyer, who had fled Nuremberg with his wife in 1934. After a brief spell in internment, Rudi joined the Pioneer Corps and trained in Ilfracombe, North Devon. He served from 10 September 1940 until May 1942 when he joined the Royal Army Service Corps (RASC). Then from 18 March 1944, he transferred to the Intelligence Corps and was based in the M Room at Wilton Park. He remained with MI19 until 28 December 1945.

Some émigré listeners were sent to Trent Park to listen in to the conversations of the German generals. They rarely crossed between the CSDIC sites because they would learn to recognise the individual voices of the generals. This included Eric Mark who was born in Magdeburg, Germany as Erich (Meyer) Mark, and fled the Nazi regime in January 1935. During the war, Eric enlisted in the Pioneer Corps and transferred to the Intelligence Corps on 1 March 1944. He was posted first to Wilton Park and then Trent Park where he eavesdropped on the generals' conversations. He remembers the generals talking about the V-2 at Peenemünde, and their reaction to the failed assassination attempt on Hitler's life in July 1944. Nine months later he was promoted to sergeant major.

Secret listener Alfred Fleiss was born in 1903 in Czernowitz at the eastern end of the Austro-Hungarian Empire. His father was in the textile trade and eventually moved the family to Chemnitz. Alfred studied law in Berlin, Leipzig and Heidelberg, receiving a doctorate in 1926. He became a successful lawyer in Chemnitz, but lost his job when the Nazis came to power in 1933. Because of business connections in England, Alfred was able to leave Germany and start again in London. In 1942, he volunteered for the British forces and joined the Royal Army Service Corps, then transferred to the Intelligence Corps. Fleiss never spoke about his work, but next to wartime photographs in an album, he wrote: 'Hush Hush job … The rest is silence.'[15]

Teddy Schächter, who anglicised his name to Teddy Chester, told his family that he had worked for MI5 but could never speak about the work.[16] They accepted that and only after his death, as a result of this research, did his wife and family finally discover that he had been one of the secret listeners. He appeared in a photograph with other secret listeners outside Latimer House.

George Pulay was born in Vienna on 5 March 1923, the son of eminent skin specialist Dr Erwin Pulay and Ida Pulay. After Hitler's annexation of Austria in March 1938, George's father was immediately at risk because of the Gestapo round-up of Jewish intellectuals and professionals. Dr Pulay came to England during 1938 ahead of his wife and children, aided by Kendrick, who was then acting as the British Passport Officer in Vienna. By 1939, Ida managed to come to England with son George and daughter Uli. At the outbreak of war, George Pulay was not old enough to enlist in the British forces and therefore did not come to MI19 via the usual route. In 1943, possibly as a result of voluntarily enlisting in the British forces, George was drafted straight into the Intelligence Corps and posted to Latimer House where he became close friends with Fritz Lustig.

Secret listener Paul Douglas, who had anglicised his name from Konrad Paul Korn, remembered Kendrick as: 'A fair man, discreet and the right man for the job. He understood our situation – the situation of the refugees who worked for him.'[17] Douglas joined the unit in May 1943 and served in it until the end of the war. He recalled:

Unlike other intelligence staff on the site, we never saw the prisoners and they never saw us. We were never bored. It was a highly interesting job and most of the prisoners were cooperative. I remember on one occasion I overheard a prisoner saying in his cell, 'the buggers know everything.' The prisoner was referring to his British captors. We needed confirmation of facts. If something was mentioned 2 or 3 times, or more, from different POWs, then we knew it to be true. Our work was secret and very isolated.[18]

How did he feel about bugging the conversations of his former countrymen? Douglas replied: 'I never felt I was betraying Germany. Germany betrayed me.'

Prisoners were not permitted to leave their rooms for any length of time to avoid discussing critical information out of range of the hidden microphones. Apart from half an hour in the exercise yard and visits to the toilet, they remained in their rooms. The environment was always geared towards encouraging the prisoners to talk and therefore they were only permitted one newspaper a day – enough to stimulate conversation between each other. Literature was kept to a minimum so the prisoners spent time talking rather than reading. An exception to this was at Trent Park where the German generals were given newspapers and books, also complete freedom and access to the house and immediate grounds. But not a single moment of the prisoners' waking day was left unmonitored, as Lustig recalled:

We were organised into squads of up to twelve operators; each squad divided into two shifts of 6 operators and an officer in charge. We worked in two shifts: early and late. The early shift started after breakfast at 8 am and ended at 4 pm. The late shift began at 4 pm and finished whenever the prisoners stopped talking and had gone to sleep. This could be as late as 11 pm or midnight.

A night duty officer always slept in the M Room overnight in case of an emergency.[19] Weekends were treated as normal working days but operators were given one day off a week which had to be booked in advance so that there was always sufficient cover in the M Room. Access to the M Room remained highly restricted – the key to it only given to staff working there. Other intelligence staff did not know of its existence.

There were roles too for other émigrés who had fled Nazism. Unbeknown to the family until decades later, Czech refugee Ernst Lederer, grandfather of comedian Helen Lederer, worked at Trent Park for British intelligence. Ernst was originally from Teplice, Sudetenland, and spoke fluent German and Czech.[20] He fled in the 1930s and came to England. Having contacts in Britain, he began rebuilding his business and then in 1941 was conscripted into the Home Guard where he was purportedly tasked with guarding Hampstead Heath. It was believed he kept in touch with people from the Czech resistance, which brought him to the attention of the British intelligence service. Granddaughter Helen Lederer recalls:

> Little did my Grandmother know that when she waved him off to guard the Heath that Big Baba, as I called him, was heading for Trent Park to take up a very different role. Only letters and medals have since revealed what he did. His job, as an officer, was to oversee the 'tapping of Hitler's Generals'. This role was highly secret – and having been recruited by M19, he kept his secret to the grave. Big Baba was known for his charm and I can see that his infamous 'affability' would have been most expedient when it came to leading and goading information out of the incarcerated generals, where he was tasked with assessing their character and interviewing them personally in German. They must have wondered who he was in Home Guard uniform with fluent German! In fact, the work he did was vital in working out who the German prisoners were, where they fitted into the Nazi hierarchy and what intelligence they could be coerced to give up. This not only gave an indication into attitudes towards Hitler, but also crucial information on weapons, tactics and vital evidence into the Holocaust. However, I know this opportunity would have been especially bitter sweet for him – given his memories of the country he had to leave behind. He saw his own mother drop dead in the street from shock and many close family members perished in concentration camps.[21]

In the family's possession is a letter addressed to Captain Lederer from Major General J.A. Sinclair (the then Director of Military Intelligence):

I wish to convey my real gratitude for and appreciation of the assistance you have given to my interrogation organisation in respect of POWs captured during recent operations on the Continent. Your keenness and self-sacrifice in volunteering to assist in this work, and the efficiency shown in its execution, have materially contributed to these satisfactory results. Thank you again for what you have done.[22]

Such a personal letter from the Director of Military Intelligence is rare. The secret listeners and other intelligence personnel did not routinely receive a personal letter. It is now believed that Lederer aided the interrogation teams by posing as a stool pigeon, discarding his Home Guard uniform for that of a fellow German officer.[23]

LAYERS OF DECEPTION

The deception plan was multi-layered and included not only surreptitiously recording the private conversations of the prisoners, but also their formal interrogations. The main reason for emphasising the camp's function as an interrogation centre was all part of MI19's complex gambit. German prisoners expected to be interrogated after capture, and British intelligence believed that if the POWs underwent extensive interrogation they would not suspect their informal conversations too were being bugged in their cells. The interrogation rooms were 'miked' back to the M Room where the secret listeners monitored and recorded information which the intelligence officer was gaining from a particular POW. The interrogator could not take notes during questioning without running the risk of a prisoner clamming up, thus a fairly relaxed but prolonged interrogation was carried out to enable the prisoner to feel less inhibited. At their sets in the M Room, the secret listeners quietly recorded aspects of the interrogation which they had been primed to listen for. Today, the reports of interrogations also survive in the National Archives.[24]

There was yet another dimension to this. Having heard the interrogation through the earpieces, the secret listener knew what aspects were likely to come up in conversation once the prisoner had returned to his cell. 'All prisoners were interrogated several times,' recalled Lustig. 'Always by officers not working in our monitoring section. We never dealt with any of them face-to-face. Their reaction to interrogation was often particularly fruitful. They would tell their cell-mate what they had been asked about, what they had managed to conceal from the interrogator and how much we (the British) already knew.'

Lustig commented: 'The prisoners never complained about their conditions, so they must have been reasonably comfortable.' British-born Cynthia Turner (née Crew), who worked in the Air Intelligence section, corroborates this and adds: 'I certainly never saw any written complaints about accommodation from the prisoners. I saw a few complaints from German Prussian officers about the way Hitler was conducting the war.'[25]

The secret listeners were briefed in advance about the kind of information that British intelligence needed.[26] They had to be able to pick out certain topics to record, including a knowledge of military, U-boat and Luftwaffe terminology. Ahead of D-Day, they were picking up a vast array of information, including details of the German coastal defences, bunkers and the camouflage of gun emplacements at Calais.[27] This kind of information enabled Allied planners and strategists to build a comprehensive picture of what needed to be penetrated.

Secret listener Peter Hart (born Peter Klaus Herz in 1914) commented on the skills needed by the listeners to do their job:

Not only was it necessary to have a complete mastery of the German language, but often prisoners coming from regions where dialects were spoken were extremely difficult to understand, unless one knew the dialect well. In addition, we not only had to be knowledgeable about the whole arsenal of German weapons in all three services – Army, Navy and Luftwaffe – but also know about the ranks of personnel, including the infamous SS. Furthermore we had to be well informed about what was going on militarily and look out for any gossip and information which our High Command wanted to pick up.[28]

1. The Tower of London where the British intelligence services opened their secret bugging operation at the outbreak of war. A special area was reserved for enemy prisoners of war who in the early years of the conflict were mainly captured German U-boat and air force prisoners.

2. Inside the Salt Tower at the Tower of London. This is one of the rooms where two to three German prisoners were held together and their unguarded conversations picked up by microphones hidden in the light fittings and the stone fireplace.

3. Trent Park at Cockfosters, North London, the former home of the Bevan and Sassoon families. The estate was requisitioned by British intelligence in 1939 and 'wired for sound'. Prisoners began arriving there in mid-December 1939.

4. Colonel Thomas Joseph Kendrick, a longstanding MI6 spymaster and commanding officer of the unit. Kendrick was the mastermind behind the wartime bugging operation on behalf of military intelligence branch MI9.

5. A commercial 88A pressure microphone made by the Radio Corporation of America (RCA). Fifteen of these were shipped to Kendrick at Trent Park. The metal casing was too big and heavy to hide inside light fittings, fireplaces or plant pots, so a team from the Post Office Research Station at Dollis Hill dismantled it and used only the components inside.

6. The tiny microphone that was taken out of the RCA's 88A. This was hidden behind skirting boards and inside light fittings, 'wired' to a small porcelain junction box, from which hundreds of metres of wires fed under the floorboards in the living quarters all the way down to one of three M Rooms in the basement. Here the teams of secret listeners sat at special equipment.

7. Catherine Townshend, the 21-year-old British intelligence officer who took sole responsibility for acquiring the Top Secret sensitive bugging equipment and setting up new M Rooms after her immediate boss, Major Back, was posted to another job. She also interviewed and selected the secret listeners with Colonel Kendrick.

8. General Hans-Jürgen von Arnim and other high-ranking German officers arriving at Trent Park with their batmen on 16 May 1943 after surrendering to the Allies in North Africa. Greeting them is Colonel Richardson with Major Spencer of the United States Eighth Army Air Force (in the foreground) and Major General Sir Ernest Gepp.

9. German generals walk in the grounds of Trent Park with their British 'minders', noticeably relaxed in their surroundings in captivity.

10. 'Lord Aberfeldy', the fake aristocrat created by British intelligence as a welfare officer to pamper to the needs of the generals, designed to soften them up and encourage their indiscreet conversations. He was in fact a senior intelligence officer, Ian Munro.

11. An official photograph at Trent Park, November 1943. This was the generals' Christmas card to their families. From left to right (standing): von Glasow, Boes, Hubbuch, Buhse, Schmidt, Borcherdt. From left to right (seated): Egersdorff, Crüwell, von Arnim (camp leader), Meixner, von Hülsen.

12. Samuel Denys Felkin, head of the Air Intelligence section AI1(K). His team interrogated thousands of air force prisoners and U-boat crews and amassed volumes of intelligence on new German technology as well as U-boat tactics. They were responsible for the discovery of X-Gerät and Knickebein in February 1940 – the new German equipment that enabled precision bombing. Without this discovery, Felkin later wrote, Britain would have lost the Battle of Britain.

13. A secret listener using special equipment in the basement of one of the secret sites.

14. The M Room area as it looks today in the basement at Trent Park before renovation. It is directly below both the Blue Room (ground floor) and the largest bedroom (first floor). The latter was thought to have been allocated to General von Arnim and was the most heavily bugged sleeping quarters in the house.

15. Ernst Lederer, a Jewish émigré who fled Nazi-occupied Czechoslovakia. He enlisted in the Home Guard and told his family he was defending Hampstead Heath. Instead, he had been taken up by British intelligence to help the interrogation teams at Trent Park as a 'stool pigeon': he was disguised as a senior German officer and encouraged the generals to speak about what the British needed to know.

16. An aerial view of Latimer House near Chesham in Buckinghamshire, requisitioned by Kendrick for lower-rank German prisoners so that from 1942 Trent Park could be reserved exclusively for Hitler's captured generals. It became the new headquarters of Kendrick's unit, now known as Combined Services Detailed Interrogation Centre (CSDIC). To the left of the house (adjoining) is the wartime Naval intelligence block and in the immediate foreground, almost hidden by trees, is Block B.

17. An aerial view of 'the spider' at the rear of the Latimer estate, a central part of the bugging operation on site. Here are the newly constructed interrogation rooms, cells, an administration block, Air Intelligence section, and an M Room which housed the secret listeners.

18. Intelligence Officers with Kendrick, outside Latimer House.

19. The Naval Intelligence team outside Latimer House, c.1943. Ralph Izzard (tall man standing at the back, alone). From left to right (standing): unknown, unknown, Ian Fleming, Commander Burton Cope, Richard Weatherby, Donald Welbourn, unknown. From left to right (seated): Jean Flower, Evelyn Barron, George Blake, Esme Mackenzie, unknown.

20. The Naval Intelligence team interrogated thousands of U-boat crews throughout the war and gained intelligence on U-boat tactics, new weapons and technology, and U-boat loss and production to enable the Allies to assess Germany's ongoing fighting capability.

21. Block D at Bletchley Park, Buckinghamshire. The close intelligence cooperation between MI9/ CSDIC and Bletchley Park began as early as 1939 and continued throughout the war.

22. Some of the female intelligence staff who worked across Kendrick's sites. They translated the transcripts from the M Room, kept POW records and typed intelligence reports.

23. Non-commissioned officers working across Kendrick's sites, pictured outside Latimer House. The men are émigré secret listeners; the women (also émigrés) carried out vital translation and related intelligence duties.

24. German Jewish secret listeners.

a. Freddie Benson.

b. George Pulay.

c. Fritz Lustig.

d. Eric Mark.

25. The White House at Wilton Park, Beaconsfield in Buckinghamshire. For a short time, the house was used for captured Italian generals and later for occasional German generals before their transfer to Trent Park. Within the grounds was a specially constructed complex with cells, interrogation rooms and an M Room, similar to 'the spider' at Latimer House.

26. American interrogator, Heimwarth Jestin, who questioned German generals and senior officers at Wilton Park before their transfer to Trent Park.

27. Some of the émigré women and secret listeners who worked across Kendrick's sites, photographed here at Latimer House.

28. The launch of a German V-2 rocket at the experimental test site at Peenemünde on the Baltic coast.

29. Peenemünde, site of Hitler's secret weapon programme of V-1 and V-2 rockets. The site's true identity was first confirmed from the bugged conversations of the generals at Trent Park and those of lower-ranked prisoners at Latimer House and Wilton Park. From mid-1943 the RAF flew over the site and photographed it, and their film footage was analysed at RAF Medmenham. The site was rendered inactive by the RAF bombing in Operation Crossbow in August 1943.

30. An example transcript of a bugged conversation from Trent Park between General Kreipe (kidnapped by SOE in Crete in April 1944) and General Bassenge (captured in North Africa in May 1943), discussing Hitler's secret weapon programme. SR denotes 'Special Report' and 'GG' denotes 'German General'.

31. Prime Minister Sir Winston Churchill, a great supporter of the bugging operation, wrote that the records of conversations between enemy prisoners of war 'afford an excellent insight into the German character and the results of the Nazi regime'. His wish for a play to be written after the war was denied by Sam Derry, the new head of MI9. Britain had entered the Cold War and was eavesdropping on a new enemy. The tens of thousands of transcripts were locked away for almost sixty-five years before the secrets of the M Room were released into the public domain.

Access to the M Room remained highly restricted and only staff working there were given the key. The vast majority of other intelligence staff did not know of its existence. Cynthia Turner, who transferred to Latimer in 1944 from the 102 Halifax aircraft base at Pocklington (south of York), recalled:

> One day, I was given privileged access to the M Room by senior WAAF officer, Olga Sieveking. Olga took me to the end of the passage to our offices and unlocked the door, taking me inside. I then saw several Jewish sergeants listening to telephones, which obviously explained the origin of the SD/SR reports. I had signed the Official Secrets Act and did not speak of this until a few years ago.[29]

Cynthia's own work had involved going through the reports of conversations to mark important information for intelligence purposes; for example, where the Germans were constructing the V weapons at Peenemünde. She passed information on to relevant departments of the Air Force, Army and Navy. ATS officer Lucy Fielding Addey worked first at Latimer House, but also spent time with CSDIC (Mediterranean) as an intelligence officer in the Information Room.[30]

WOMEN AND INTELLIGENCE DUTIES

Once Latimer House and Wilton Park were fully functioning from 1942, an increase in staff became necessary, particularly to deal with the influx of prisoners. Kendrick received authorisation to increase the quota of ATS women working across his sites[31] which enabled him to draft in German women who had been forced to flee Nazi Germany. As native German speakers, they proved invaluable for carrying out vital clerical duties, typing, translation work, keeping prisoners' records and sifting the intelligence for its level of importance. Amongst them was Gerda Engel (born Breslau, 1921) whose father was a dentist in Breslau. Her family was forced to flee to England in 1935 after the Nazi regime forbade Jews to hold professional jobs. During the war, Gerda was based at Latimer House and Wilton Park where she became close friends with Susan Cohn (also from Breslau and born the same year).

Susan had emigrated to England on a domestic permit in July 1939 and obtained work in North London. On the day war broke out her employer dismissed her, 'not wanting a German living in her house', so Susan joined the Engel family and trained as assistant in the Engel dental practice.[32] During 1943, Susan joined the ATS, with a posting to Fenham Barracks in Newcastle-upon-Tyne. After a number of other postings, while on leave in London she caught up with Gerda Engel, now a sergeant in the Intelligence Corps, who recommended Susan for a transfer to the same unit.

In December 1943, Susan was invited for a selection interview at the War Office where she underwent various aptitude tests. Four weeks later, she received a letter for transfer to Latimer House to join Kendrick's unit:

It was all very exciting. I had a railway ticket to Chalfont and Latimer station and was told that I would be met there. A very smart naval officer and his driver waited for me in a jeep outside. As I got into the car the driver said to me, 'I bet you a packet of cigarettes that you'll be a sergeant by tonight.' I didn't believe him. That evening, I was unexpectedly promoted to sergeant and I owed him a packet of cigarettes![33]

Susan was allocated to a typing pool, but since her typing was rather poor she soon found herself transferred to a department for checking prisoners' documents. The work was highly classified and she spoke to no one else in the camp about it; nor did she have any idea what the other intelligence staff were doing on site. At one point, she was surprised to come across documents for her former English teacher from Breslau, whom she knew was not a Nazi. He was being held at Latimer House. 'I put in a good word for him,' she said. 'And he was soon transferred.' During her time at Latimer House and Wilton Park, she met secret listener, Fritz Lustig.[34] They married on 6 June 1945 with Kendrick's blessing as a commanding officer's permission to marry was necessary at the time for those still serving in the army.

The role of women in intelligence is often a hidden story of wartime, and is difficult to recover. Many were modest about what they did, and believed it was not worth talking about. There was also the matter of secrecy – the oath that bound all intelligence ranks across Kendrick's sites. Having signed the Official Secrets Act, the émigré women and secret listeners were bound by oath to withhold whatever classified information came their way. The unit's existence had to be protected at all costs. As they carried out their daily duties, they could not discuss their work, even with other intelligence staff in the camp.

It would be at least sixty years before some of them broke their silence – and only after they were sure that the official files had been declassified. The majority went to their graves bearing British intelligence secrets. Most did not live to see their story become public knowledge.

CHAPTER 9

Rocket Science

The year of 1943 started well for Kendrick when his services to British intelligence were honoured with an OBE from the King. It recognised the success of his three centres, but most specially the discovery of X-Gerät at Trent Park. Norman Crockatt congratulated him on 'the best merited OBE of the war', and went on to say that the material emerging from CSDIC 'was of such vital importance and marked a credit to the staff who had worked hard and loyally to bring it about. Therefore the OBE was as much a tribute to their efforts as also being a personal triumph for you as their leader'.[1]

Kendrick had just returned from a transatlantic trip where he had attended meetings on behalf of MI6 with intelligence chiefs in New York and Washington, including officers at the FBI and the newly-formed Office of Strategic Services. His visit, in December 1942, was less than a month after the capture of General von Thoma and the success of Operation Torch, which marked the beginning of the end for German occupation of North Africa.

Whilst in America, Kendrick discussed matters of joint intelligence and the training of new American intelligence officers at his sites in England, thus forging closer Anglo-American cooperation. In New York he visited the MI6 headquarters of the US Operations, known as the British Security Coordination (BSC). It was based in Room 3603 of the Rockerfeller Center and headed by William Stephenson, a wealthy Canadian businessman. Stephenson was on the payroll of the British

Secret Intelligence Service and carried out operations with Allen Welsh Dulles (the first director of the Office of Strategic Services). Kendrick never spoke about his mission to America and no official documents of his meetings have yet come to light.

Within weeks of Kendrick's return, on 11 March 1943 in a cell at Latimer House, a paratrooper (A77) gave away information about projectiles to an infantry soldier (M11). He had told his cellmate: 'I was very amused yesterday when they [interrogation officers] showed me a drawing of the sloping ramp rocket projector.'[2] Their conversation revealed technical details about launch ramps. References to Hitler's secret weapon programme had been made by prisoners in the Tower of London as early as autumn 1939, but their comments were vague. The Oslo Report of November 1939 had mentioned Peenemünde, but British intelligence had nothing concrete to verify the references. Aerial reconnaissance missions in 1942 over Peenemünde had failed to identify anything unusual about the weapons site and the photographs were simply filed at RAF Medmenham.[3] By late 1942, the interrogating teams at Latimer knew about a possible German programme to develop long-range rockets because of information sent to British intelligence by two secret agents working behind enemy lines.[4] The warning about the first long-range rockets came from an untried source that could not be deemed totally reliable without further independent corroboration. It would take a revelation eleven days later from Hitler's top commanders held at Trent Park for the information from A77 and M11 to be taken seriously. It came in a bugged conversation on 22 March 1943 in which General von Thoma told Crüwell:

... but no progress whatsoever can have been made in this rocket business. I saw it once with Feldmarschall Brauchitsch, there is a special ground near Kunersdorf (?) ... They've got these huge things which they've brought up here ... They've always said they would go 15kms into the stratosphere and then ... You only aim at an area ... If one was to ... every few days ... frightful ... The Major there was full of hope – he said 'Wait until next year and then the fun will start!' ... There's no limit to the range.[5]

The two generals had inadvertently provided, arguably, one of the most important pieces of intelligence thus far. Their conversation was reproduced in the 1970s in a book by R.V. Jones, who had been head of the Scientific Section of MI6, but he was not able to specify that it had come from the bugged transcripts because they had not then been declassified. Instead, he merely made reference in his book to 'a remark by General von Thoma'.[6] The Chiefs of Staff were briefed;[7] it was concluded that von Thoma's rocket statement 'may seem slender evidence after this lapse of time [since the agents' reports of 1942], but it represented a crucial point in the intelligence picture at that date'.[8] Von Thoma's evidence was deemed reliable because it appeared to be an eye-witness account and it was unlikely that his information was a 'plant'; or 'chicken-feed' (to use espionage language).[9]

Air Intelligence officers once more turned their attention to the site at Peenemünde as the possible location. At RAF Medmenham at Danesfield House in Buckinghamshire, the aerial photographs of Peenemünde from 1942 were pulled from storage and re-examined in every minute detail. Looking at them again, it was possible to make out the launchers for the powerful new V-1 flying bomb (the 'vengeance weapon') and V-2 rocket.[10]

By April 1943, the Air Ministry was still trying to understand the nature of the site at Peenemünde on the Baltic coast of northern Germany. Declassified reports, maps and aerial photographs of the site are deposited in Air Intelligence files.[11] These include a report dated 29 April 1943, headed 'Extract from an Interpretation Report of the New Development at Peenemünde', in which it was still not clear that Air Intelligence knew of the site's exact purpose:

> The general appearance of the factory, which is situated in a clearing in the forest, suggests that it may be employed in the manufacture of explosives … The building near the centre of the works has the appearance of a gas plant. It has a chimney and dumps of coal or coke can be seen at either end of the building … Several low buildings in the areas 10, 11 and 12 have been erected since 15.5.42.[12]

On 26 May 1943, the secret listeners at Trent Park overheard a lengthy discussion between General von Arnim and a senior German officer whose voice they could not identify. They spoke about the V-2 rocket – the 'retribution weapon' – and the world's first long-range ballistic missile:

C: I wonder how the development of these rockets will turn out. You don't hear anything more about them …

A: Yes, this rocket business is all very well, there are all sorts of things, but you can't propel an aircraft all the time with it.

C: No, not aircraft, bombs – they just fire rockets.

A: Fire rockets?

C: Yes. I know the 'liquid rocket'. It can easily travel 200km but it has tremendous dispersal.

A: That doesn't matter.

C: It has a tremendous dispersal, but you need large copper boilers and precious metal for the burners and for the jets. It would be economically quite impossible to produce it in large quantities in order to keep up a continuous fire. I believe they are heated by means of pure alcohol which produces a steely blue flame 8 or 12 metres long which comes out at the back. The great … of liquid …

A: I have heard that they have a range of even 300km.

C: They can reach 300, there's no difficulty about that. You just need to make the fuel boiler longer. I saw one which we developed some time ago and was present at the first tests. It had a range of 150 or 200km.[13]

As a direct result of the conversations at Trent Park, Air Intelligence chiefs acted. RAF pilots were sent out again on secret reconnaissance missions to photograph the Peenemünde site.[14]

'The first discoveries in the M Room about Peenemünde caused great excitement,' recalled Fritz Lustig. 'It was quickly realized that a new rocket programme was underway. Picking up this kind of intelligence

for the British was very important to us because it could mean the difference between winning or losing the war.'[15]

OPERATION CROSSBOW

On 29 June 1943, Churchill's Cabinet Defence Committee met in the
Cabinet War Rooms. At that time, chief scientist Professor Frederick
Lindemann told Churchill that he believed the objects seen on the
aerial reconnaissance photographs of Peenemünde were either torpedoes
or fake dummies to divert attention away from the real weapon.[16]
Dr R.V. Jones believed that the accumulating evidence for the V-1
programme should be taken seriously. After considering Dr Jones's views
at the meeting, Churchill authorised an attack on Peenemünde.[17]
Because it was beyond British radio navigation beams, Churchill told
the Committee: 'We must bomb by moonlight ... we must attack on
the heaviest possible scale.'[18] The reasoning behind the mission was
straightforward: 'The destruction of this experimental station, large
factory workshops and the killing of scientific and technical experts
would retard the production of this new equipment and contribute
largely to increasing the effectiveness of the bomber offensive.'[19]A target
information sheet for aircrew was issued:

> The target is the Experimental Establishment at Peenemünde situ-
> ated on the tongue of land on the Baltic Coast about 60 miles N.W
> of Stettin, engaged upon the development and production of a new
> form of R.D.F equipment which promises to improve greatly the
> German night fighter air defence organization.[20]

The only information the air crews were given was a briefing before the
mission that if they failed, they would repeat the raid a second night,
and the following night, until the job was done, and regardless of casualties. Preparations began for the mission that would eventually take
place in mid-August 1943 under the wider name of Operation Crossbow.
In a meeting between Air Intelligence chiefs at Bomber Command on

7 July 1943, it was decided for security reasons that any reference to 'rockets' or 'Peenemünde' was to be eliminated in all reports. The meeting concluded that 'the plant is being called an Experimental Establishment'.[21]

On 8 August 1943, with only ten days until the operation to knock out Peenemünde, a conversation was picked up at Trent Park between Lieutenant Colonel Wolters (captured in Tunisia on 11 May) and General von Arnim (captured in Tunisia on 12 May):

WOLTERS: In his speech, Goebbels hinted at a new weapon – he was speaking of various things which we have in mind. I heard recently on good authority that there are great things afoot, which actually date back a long time. We are said to be building (?) enormous rockets. UDET (?) I believe, was working mainly on the things. These rockets –

VON ARNIM: Which go over England?

WOLTERS: Yes. They are supposed to be fired from the neighbourhood of Brussels.[22]

By full moon on the night of 17/18 August 1943, pilots of Bomber Command left their base and carried out the first attack on Peenemünde Army Research Centre in a mission codenamed Operation Hydra that included 324 Lancasters, 218 Halifaxes and 54 Stirlings. This was the start of the much larger Anglo-American operation aimed at destroying any sites connected to the V weapon programme and the production plant for hydrogen peroxide needed for the rockets. The first wave of bombers attacked the sleeping and living quarters, the second the factory workshops and the final wave the experimental station itself. The raid was deemed a success because it delayed Hitler's rocket test launches by at least four weeks to six months. But it came at a price. Two hundred and fifteen British aircrew were killed. Forty bomber aircraft were lost and hundreds of civilians in the nearby concentration camp, Trassenheide, also died. Two German V-2 rocket scientists, Dr Thiel and Chief Engineer Walther, were killed during the attack.[23] It was later confirmed that 720 people had been killed on the first raid on Peenemünde.[24]

The impact of the Allied bombing of Peenemünde cannot be over-emphasised. It bought extra time for the Allies and delayed Hitler's first launch of a V-1 on London until 13 June 1944, a week after the successful D-Day landings.[25] Without the intelligence from the M Room, it is doubtful that the Allies would have realised the full significance of Peenemünde until it was too late. Germany could have won the techno-logical war which would have made it difficult to mount the D-Day landings the following year. It was a major landmark in thwarting Germany's race for weapon superiority.

It was anticipated that Germany would not cease its weapon devel-opment programme but shift it elsewhere. The new launch sites for the V weapons in France and Holland were often first picked up in bugged conversations at Trent Park or via interrogations at the CSDIC sites.[26] Under the umbrella of Operation Crossbow, the Allies continued to bomb suspected V-1 and V-2 launch sites until the end of the war.[27]

Hitler's captured generals continued to talk about the secret weapon programme in their casual conversations, and explicitly about the new V-2 rocket that was being developed at Peenemünde.[28] Von Thoma spoke to his comrades again about how he had seen some of the early experiments with rocket apparatus before the war, but these had been nothing less than a disaster.[29] He claimed to know that the rockets would only go to about 10,000 metres and few would be able to reach London. He did not realise how far the technology had advanced and commented to Bassenge that the rockets were 'too expensive for the game to be worth the candle'.[30] Von Thoma was quite scornful of the presumed decisive effect of firing rockets on Britain and said:

If there really is something, it is only rocket stories. Of course that is rather laughable and does not decide the outcome of the war. It creates only uncomfortable disturbance here. Instead of perhaps a few aeroplanes coming over here in the evening, a rocket flies in.[31]

Bassenge added: 'Even if all London is reduced to rubble and ashes, it is unimportant for the outcome of the war because they (V-2s) can get to Glasgow or anywhere else at the time.'[32]

Within a week of the RAF attack on Peenemünde, the secret listeners overheard another conversation, this time between Neuffer and Bassenge, in which Peenemünde was specifically mentioned:

BASSENGE: This place Peenemünde was begun at a time when I
  left the technical office and therefore I never went to see it
NEUFFER: But for what purpose? Hadn't we already got Rechlin?
BASSENGE: Well, Peenemünde was not built by the German Air
  Force [G.A.F], but by the army and we had only one section built
  into it by the G.A.F which attracted my interest, and that was the
  rocket business.[33]

The conversation rambled on. Ironically, at the end of the discussion, the generals seemed quite dismissive.

'This business about a new weapon – I don't believe it. As a matter of fact – I mean as regards a new weapon – technology today is such a complicated affair – you can't just produce a new weapon out of a hat,' said Neuffer.

To which Bassenge replied, 'I consider it all bluff, nothing more.'

'Just one of those Jules Verne affairs,' Neuffer responded.

Bassenge agreed: 'Yes. In England they're joking about it.'[34]

Of course, nothing was further from the truth. British intelligence had taken the leaked information very seriously.

On 11 September 1943, Generals Neuffer and Bassenge discussed the secret weapon again, but this time with naval Captain Meixner:

NEUFFER: Perhaps there really is a secret weapon or –
BASSENGE: Yes. For instance there are the liquid rockets, 5 to 6
  metres long. They contain an explosive charge about the same as
  that of a good torpedo.

MEIXNER: Good, but that will penetrate one block of houses at the most.

BASSENGE: No, it doesn't penetrate that either. The effect is just like a 1,000kg bomb. You can fire the things and they can travel a comparatively long distance; you can use them for a sweeping fire on fleets here. The things are extremely complicated and have a frightful amount of copper and valuable metal in them … I know all about these things. I've seen them.[35]

In another discussion with Neuffer that day, Bassenge stated that the rockets were about 10 feet in height with the explosive power of a 1,000kg bomb but were expensive.[36] 'These things have an extremely complicated apparatus,' he said, 'a frightful lot of copper and very valuable metals inside because otherwise the jet or fuel injector – that is most certainly the most expensive and valuable steel – melts away with the colossal temperatures which are generated.'[37]

Bassenge made comments about the possibility of Hitler using gas because Goering wanted it as a reprisal weapon.[38] Bassenge maintained that no really serious preparations for gas warfare had been made by Germany. Von Thoma replied that if the Germans tried to use gas, they would be completely finished because the Allies were superior in chemical warfare.[39] He commented that the gas specialists were Jewish and most were working in London. The British intelligence report stated: 'Others [generals] have expressed similar views, though one or two are frightened of the Nazis using gas as a last desperate measure, and even bacilli have been mentioned.'[40]

In another conversation with Neuffer the following month, Bassenge said: 'Giant rocket guns … those enormous things are the rockets filled with liquid, they are twice as high as this room (note: height of room is 10ft), are this size in diameter (demonstrating) and it is a sort of aerial torpedo with rocket propulsion … in the air. It climbs pretty vertically, goes as high as this in a curve and drops like this.'[41] Although the rockets proved to be comparatively inaccurate, he commented that they would land somewhere within the London area.[42]

To which Neuffer responded: 'Then we'd better all go out into the trench!' At the end of the report, a comment has been added by MI19 that Bassenge's experience of the secret rocket programme was somewhat dated.[43]

The subject of secret weapons continued that day when Bassenge told Neuffer: 'I set up a department "D" for rocket development, together with a very good engineer by the name of Bender.'[44] He then proceeded to give technical details, referring to directional control by radio and the use of rockets to attack aircraft in formation.

Admiral Hennecke, commandant of sea defences in Normandy before being taken prisoner, was asked by a senior British naval officer (unnamed) about the use of chemical weapons.[45] He replied that the Germans widely believed that the British would use gas warfare and they had therefore taken considerable precautions along the frontline. He added that he did not think the Germans would use gas because the British were 'in a much better position to wage that type of warfare on account of their air superiority'.[46]

Captain Meixner posed the view that the secret weapons 'may force the British to make a premature landing.'[47] He was referring to the Second Front, an invasion of Europe which the German generals knew would come, but they had no idea when and where. The defeatist camp was pretty much agreed that the rockets would not win the war for Germany and would only cause bitterness amongst the Allies. Major General Sattler commented to Colonel Borcherdt that he believed the V-2 was to weigh ten times more than the V-1 and that it would 'require a colossal installation to launch the larger projectile'.

V-1 AND V-2

References to the V-1, V-2, Peenemünde, secret weapons and rockets continued to be picked up in subsequent conversations, not only from the German generals, but also lower-rank prisoners being held at Latimer House and Wilton Park.[48] One particularly important prisoner being held at Latimer House was Herbert [Peter] Cleff, a member of the

German army's scientific civil service. Cleff became disillusioned with the Nazi regime after his own brother died at Stalingrad and decided to help the Allies. He provided helpful information about the V-1 and V-2. Captured at the end of 1942, Cleff was valuable to British intelligence because he had first-hand experience in the field. Lieutenant Commander Donald Burkewood Welbourn, a Naval Intelligence interrogator at Latimer, described Cleff as:

> Probably the most brilliant all-round engineer I have ever known, being skilled with his hands at anything from watch-making to general fitting, and being certainly the most original kinematician of his generation. I soon was spending a lot of my time walking the fields round Latimer with him, talking both engineering and politics. I lent him a few books on theoretical engineering which I had with me, and he started to write for his younger brother the superb notebook on kinematics.[49]

Cleff told Felkin, head of Air Intelligence at Latimer, that he knew of a new type of aircraft engine working on the ram jet principle. Within a few months, this was identified as the V-1.

On 30 July 1943, a German pilot referenced Peenemünde and told his cellmate: 'The experimental flights were carried out up there in the Baltic from Peenemünde.'[50] Another conversation between two German bomber pilots came less than a week after the RAF had bombed the site. A pilot codenamed A713 asked: 'Is it all complete?' His cellmate, A130, replied: 'Yes, all completed ... now they are going to bring out the "Peter X 2" ... that is ... being tried out. They have it at Peenemünde at present.'[51]

Other prisoners discussed the destruction of Peenemünde.[52] On 27 October, two soldiers (one captured from Regimental Headquarters in Italy, the other in Tunisia) showed concern that they might find themselves under one of the rockets being fired on England:

> M238: It's hell being a POW and perhaps on top of it all, we'll get one of these new things dropped on us.

M304: The whole of the civilian population was evacuated from Rügen three years ago and from Peenemünde as well.

M238: They must got … somehow … under cover when they set a thing like this going.

M304: How do you mean? The thing is set up, it is ignited by remote control, electrically, and then it goes off.

M238: They get into shelters beforehand, below ground …

M304: Well of course. They may be something … it is ignited electrically by remote control and then it rises very slowly from the ground with mighty crashing, banging and hissing – it is frightful!

M238: And they fire over to –

M304: Over to England – they can fire it 500km. They fire up the whole length of the Norwegian coast … It is a pretty fine apparatus, it weighs eighty tons – eighty tons – the remaining sixty-five tons are just for propellant, for the rocket force … and fifteen tons of explosive is quite a nice lot![53]

In spite of the Allied bombing of Peenemünde, prisoners still believed that the new weapon would change the course of the war. They did not want to be in a camp in Britain when Hitler started using it because they might not survive the attacks.

SECRET WEAPONS: 1944

Peenemünde and the secret weapon programme was still being discussed by prisoners at all the bugging sites during 1944.[54] On 1 February 1944, sub-Lieutenant Schramm of T-25 described what the rockets looked like to two imprisoned pilots: 'As soon as it was released you could recognise this rocket bomb above the clouds owing to the fiery glow; once they were through the clouds you could see they had the typical rocket characteristics, on the tail piece the yellowish red.'[55] On 5 March 1944, the secret listeners recorded an unguarded conversation between two bomber gunners, codenamed A1441 and A1500. The lengthy conversation revealed that that they were both eye-witnesses to the new technology. An extract reads:

> A1441: At Peenemünde I saw a new fighter – a turbine-fighter; is that the 'Motte' (moth)?
>
> A1500: 'Kuckucksei' (cuckoo's egg) with a pressure cabin.
>
> A1441: Does it jettison its undercarriage after taking off?
>
> A1500: It has a skid.
>
> A1441: Yes, it lands on skids.
>
> A1500: It hasn't an undercarriage.
>
> A1441: The one at Peenemünde had an undercarriage. It jettisoned it immediately after take-off. It did nearly a thousand k.p.h. It flew for half an hour. First there were all sorts of rumours afloat about it. The men who fly them don't talk about them. He said it takes off once he has put out ['rausgemacht'] propellers (?).
>
> A1500: Then I must have seen it at our place. We were at the experimental station. It can reach a speed of sixteen hundred k.p.h.[56]

Two days later, on 7 March 1944, two German air force personnel (one a gunner, the other a fighter pilot) made a veiled reference to the V-2. The Messerschmitt fighter pilot (codenamed A1499 and captured in Italy in February 1944) explained to fellow airman (A1497): 'We were told that if one of those things came over here a few square … would be destroyed, and so it will be. The new weapon will decide the war.'[57]

At Trent Park on 10 June 1944, four days after the D-Day landings, a lengthy conversation took place between Generals Bassenge and Kreipe (captured in Crete on 26 April 1944),[58] part of which is reproduced here:

> KREIPE: I am very disappointed that they haven't started using the retaliation weapon yet.
>
> BASSENGE: I am interested in the rocket business. I know all about this great problem of the rockets with liquid propellant. I knew about them years ago in peace time. I was constantly at the experimental establishment at Kumersdorf. (?)

KREIPE: I know nothing about the liquid propellant.

BASSENGE: Rockets with a liquid propellant.

KREIPE: This isn't one of them. That's a very different thing. A rocket with a very long range and very high explosive material.

BASSENGE: Have you seen inside?

KREIPE: No, no. I heard that it had a very high explosive charge, but nothing about a liquid propellant.

BASSENGE: They are called rockets with a liquid propellant because this high explosive stuff is a mixture of liquids in the fuse container. This basis is alcohol and a high degree oxygen carrier with the addition of barium (?) – ammonia – perchlorate and such things. The difficulty is to obtain in that short time the required amount of oxygen for those high combustion temperatures ... There is a Dr Braun – the son of Dr von Braun. His son, a very nice fellow and above all a very talented engineer, has been responsible for the development of this whole affair.[59]

British intelligence had a clear result: not only information about the rocket programme, but mention of its key chief rocket scientist and development engineer, Wernher von Braun and his son.

In reaction to a V-1 coming over Trent Park in the early hours of the morning of 10 July 1944, that woke the generals, Admiral Hennecke commented: 'Greetings from Germany! Here of all places! If only these things could be intercepted.'[60]

Most of the generals in captivity did not really know what the V-2 was, or when it would come. The Allies were making progress in Europe after the landings. Paris was liberated on 25 August 1944. That same day, Lieutenant Generals Ludwig and Menny discussed the progress of the secret weapons. Ludwig commented: 'They [the Americans] are afraid we've got something which will fire 500km, from the Rhine to Cherbourg, or something. I believe we've got it too. That's the new thing. Long range and a terrific size. They are afraid of it because we shall then command the whole of France with it.'[61]

Within three days, Germany surrendered at Toulon and Marseilles in the south. The generals were still talking about the V-2.[62] With the Allied destruction of Peenemünde the previous year, it was a race to discover the mobile launch sites. Lieutenant General Menny told Badinsky: 'I know several sites south of Dieppe from which the V-1 and V-2 are launched, but of course I can't say whether there are more than that. It goes down as far as Rouen. There are also sites in the district of Rouen from where they are launched.'[63]

On 30 August 1944, the day that the Allied Canadian forces entered Rouen (in north-western France), the captive Generals Hans von Sponeck and Dietrich von Choltitz discussed air weapons.

'Surely V-2 is the flying torpedo?' asked von Sponeck.

Choltitz replied, 'V-2 is a gun … goes 10,000 metres into the air…'

To which Sponeck responded, 'Yes, the rocket bomb – and when is it supposed to be coming?'

'In September, but of course that is much too late. We can't fire them any longer because we haven't got the territory,' Cholitz told him.[64]

A brief conversation about the V-2 was recorded at the end of August 1944 between Generals Schlieben, Choltitz, Spang and Elfeldt:

SCHLIEBEN: When is the V-2 coming?

CHOLTITZ: Never!

SPANG: What are those enormous constructions then, which the English are always photographing? They are those enormous great concrete constructions which appear to be future launching ramps for the V-2.

CHOLTITZ: They are just the same as at Cherbourg.

ELFELDT: They maintain that they found some nearly ready by the Seine.

CHOLTITZ: I am absolutely certain of it.[65]

In a separate conversation between Elfeldt, von Choltitz and Broich, Elfeldt said, 'The V-2 hasn't arrived because the Allies have bombed and destroyed the launching sites.'

Von Choltitz asked, 'Did you ever see the things launched or fired?'

Broich replied, 'There was a picture of some huge installation at Cherbourg with a very wide launching ramp, which, one presumed, was for the very heavy things; they were gigantic concrete constructions which they had been building for six months and which still hadn't been completed yet.'

Elfeldt commented, 'No, because every time they had got to the point when the concrete was to be .... the enemy dropped a six-ton bomb and bang!'[66]

By the autumn of 1944, as the Allies were advancing towards Belgium and Holland, Major General Bock von Wuelfingen (surrendered at Liege on 8/9 September) was overheard talking to Generals Heyking and Seyffardt about the building of launch sites for the V-2 at Liege.

Heyking asked, 'But was that for the V-2?'

Wuelfingen replied, 'Yes. They have been working on it for four years.'

Seyffardt added, 'But then it can only reach as far as France – if it comes at all – and by that time the war will long have been over.'[67]

This snippet of information enabled British intelligence to keep ahead of the constantly moving launch sites. It also enabled Air Intelligence to coordinate their RAF bombing missions to take out the new sites before they became operational.

Meanwhile the V-1 pilot-less flying bombs continued to rain down on towns and cities, wreaking havoc across England. The German generals experienced the frightening effect of their country's weapons when a V-1 passed over Trent Park the following summer. However, Colonel von Aulock told Lieutenant General Spang that he had looked in vain in London on his way through for any signs of the effects of the V-1.[68] This kind of comment demonstrated to MI19 that the generals and senior officers were disconcerted by the lack of overt consequence of Hitler's war machine. It was a very strong tool of persuasion for the British.

Secret listener Peter Hart recalled that their reports about Peenemünde were 'given top-priority, as obviously there was something afoot which looked like a last desperate measure'.[69] The discovery of Peenemünde alone proved the value of the whole MI19 operation and more than justified the three sites.

DEVELOPMENT OF V-3

The range and importance of intelligence coming through the secret listeners' headphones could vary dramatically. At Trent Park, in the autumn of 1944, the generals began to make the first reference to V-3, otherwise known as the super gun or 'London gun', and information about which was not known at any other intelligence site. It transpired that Hitler was planning the construction of twenty-five gun installations at Mimoyecques, near Calais in northern France, to fire up to 300 shells an hour on London. Ultimately, this did not happen because the Allies bombed the site on 6 July 1944 when 617 Squadron of Bomber Command, the famous Dambusters, attacked with the 'Tallboy' deep penetration bombs. Between December 1944 and February 1945, the Germans only managed to fire two slightly smaller V-3 guns on the city of Luxembourg.

After hearing V-1 and V-2 explosions near Trent Park, Colonels Wilck and Wildermuth leaked references to the new V-3:

WILCK: The V-3 is also expected this month. Whether there's anything in it or not, at least they still keep on achieving more and more in that line, even in our case.
WILDERMUTH: At any rate there must still be huge stores which we shall now fire off.
WILCK: Desperation measures![70]

General Eberbach spoke about the V-3 to fellow officer, Major General Gutknecht (captured at Soissons-Rheims on 29 August 1944). Their conversation was recorded on 1 September 1944:

EBERBACH: Above all they are counting on the V-3.

GUTKNECHT: The V-2.

EBERBACH: No, the V-3.

GUTKNECHT: V-3, what's that supposed to be?

EBERBACH: The V-2 is only a small affair. It is a V-1 remotely controlled from an aircraft; and V-3 is that large rocket which flies through the stratosphere, and which is said to have several times the effect of the V-1, but apparently we need special launching ramps for it which are no longer there. They have been lost to the enemy.[71]

Three days later, Eberbach spoke again about the V-3. Within a couple of hours of the recording, Eberbach found himself in discussion with a British army officer (below, BAO) who asked him about reprisal weapons. The officer gave no hint of how he knew about the V-3 and Eberbach appeared not to be suspicious about the source:

BAO: Have you ever heard of the V-3?

EBERBACH: Yes, there was talk about the V-2 and the V-3. V-2 is supposed to be the remote controlled aircraft filled with explosives which is controlled from another aircraft. And then V-3 was supposed to be that rocket business which is supposed to climb very high, right into the stratosphere, and then also to be controlled some way. I don't know any more about it.

BAO: How is it supposed to be controlled, by a pilot?

EBERBACH: No, by wireless or something.[72]

Eberbach went on to tell the British officer that he had as much knowledge of the reprisal weapons as any average soldier. He said he thought the V-3 was a long-range radio-controlled rocket which had a longer range than the V-1 and could be fired at England from western Germany. The only difficulty in his opinion was that it needed the necessary firing ramps, which was a challenge for Germany. With uninterrupted and undetected work day and night, he said that it would be possible to complete such a ramp in eight days – by which time he felt it would be too late.[73]

If the conversations at Trent Park had not uncovered the V-3, and Eberbach's latter piece of information proved in fact to be true, then Hitler could have fired this new deadly weapon from as far away as Germany, with little hope of the Allies finding the launch sites. The launch sites were mainly underground and difficult to detect on aerial reconnaissance without clues from the bugged conversations as to their location. Even surface installations may not have been discovered in time and could only have been overpowered once the Allies had invaded Germany.

ATOMIC BOMB

Throughout the war, the Allies sought to assess how much progress Hitler was making towards realising an atomic weapon. The stakes were high. The atomic programme had to be disrupted wherever possible and any intelligence on it was like gold dust.[74] The Allies mounted a number of special operations against facilities in Norway that were aiding that programme, one of which was Operation Freshman. Using a small airborne force composed of sappers from the Royal Engineers, an assault mission was mounted on 19 November 1942 to destroy the Vemork heavy water plant outside Rjukan in Nazi-occupied Norway.[75] The plant was producing heavy water necessary for the development of Germany's nuclear weapons.[76] Operation Freshman was known to be extremely risky, with a high probability that the sappers would be captured. Two Horsa gliders headed for the site at Vemork with thirty-one men on board.[77] The weather was against them and high winds had separated the gliders.[78] The first glider crashed on cliffs above Lysefjord, near Stavanger after the tow rope snapped. Five survivors, all Royal Engineers, were captured by the Germans and taken to Grini concentration camp in Baerum near Oslo.[79] On 18 January 1943, the men were marched into nearby woods and executed on the orders of a Colonel Probst (Chief of Staff to Lieutenant-General Karl von Behrens of 280th Infantry Division).[80] The second glider crashed near Egersund. Fourteen survivors were picked up by German patrols also under the command of Colonel Probst. However, their execution in cold blood after capture was quite unexpected. The men were shot by members of the German 355 Infantry Regiment – a war crime that was eventually investigated at the London Cage.[81]

Allied intelligence needed to keep abreast of developments in the enemy's atomic bomb programme. This is where the unguarded conversations of Hitler's top commanders at Trent Park proved most valuable.[82] General Kittel declared that he already knew about the development of the secret weapon from as early as 1931.[83] He named Generals Dornberger, Sturm and Zansen as playing a large part in its development, but he too affirmed that the chief character involved was Professor Wernher von Braun, along with his son.[84] In conversation with von Thoma, Kittel referred to the weapon:

KITTEL: It's an –
THOMA: Atom business (sarcastically).
KITTEL: Yes, yes – but it really does exist.
THOMA: Yes, so does the V-2, but it doesn't trouble anyone.[85]

Von Thoma doubted the idea that the Germans had already split the atom. Kittel insisted that they had and were testing the 'atom bomb' at Bornholm.[86] In the same conversation, he told Kittel that the regime had been experimenting with spraying chemicals in the air.

Other senior officers appeared scathing of the idea of an atom bomb. In conversation with a British army officer, General Eberbach said: 'Senior German officers visited the frontline and told the troops about the wonders of the secret weapons, if only they could hold out and fight a little longer. The V-1 and V-2 had both proved useless and there was nothing more behind talk of the atom bomb.'[87]

General Dornberger, mentioned by Kittel in relation to the weapon, ended up in captivity at Trent Park in August 1945, where he talked about Germany's attempts to split the atom.[88] He told Lieutenant General Heim and SS Obergruppenführer Herff:

Our people tried to split the atom by means of higher tension current. About 50 million volts are needed to get the pitchblende, mixed with heavy water, to disintegrate. But the amount of energy released was only as much as that put in. We haven't yet got it to the stage where the process will continue independently ... I wanted Professor Braun to give us a lecture on the atom bomb, as the results of the research work could have materially influenced the development of V weapons.[89]

Dornberger also confirmed that Hitler intended to send 300 rockets a month to destroy London – a terrifying prospect if it had succeeded.[90]

General Röhricht discussed the atomic bomb with von Thoma and revealed: 'We carried out our big experiments in splitting the atom on the Monte Generoso in Switzerland. The energy from lightning was harnessed to carry out the first atom-splitting experiments. A whole lot of people were involved in the business of splitting the atom.'[91] Von Thoma replied philosophically: 'But I don't know, all these discoveries seem to me to be no blessing for mankind.'

Information about the nature and progress of the Germans' work on the atomic bomb continued to be passed to British intelligence. Hitler's secret weapon programme had far-reaching consequences that went beyond the Second World War: whoever gained this technological knowledge would have an advantage in the new tensions of the Cold War. Thus, in 1945, Britain and America raced to hunt down Hitler's atomic scientists in Germany, to avoid them coming into the hands of the Russians, and the Russians thereby developing the first atomic bomb.[92] Key German scientists were 'snatched' from their places of work or found in hiding and taken eventually to America to work on the atomic and hydrogen bombs.[93] German scientists, such as Wernher von Braun who worked for the American aerospace programme, went on to help the United States develop advanced rocket technology that enabled it to land the first man on the moon in 1969.

CHAPTER 10

'Our Guests'

The end of January 1944 marked the eleventh anniversary of Hitler coming to power in Germany. The generals gathered around the wireless to listen to the Führer's radio speech. None of the generals appeared impressed by it, and Reimann summed it up as 'a worn-out gramophone record'.[1] One German officer (unnamed) was recorded saying: 'If we entertain the possibility that we may lose the war, then we have already lost it.'[2]

Whilst Allied commanders made the final preparations for the largest invasion in history, the mammoth task of collecting intelligence ahead of D-Day continued at Kendrick's sites.[3] German prisoners were escorted from the battlefields of Sicily and Italy to temporary holding camps before being brought to England for processing. Fritz Lustig recalled: 'Most of our prisoners were initially either shot-down Luftwaffe-pilots or members of U-boat crews who had been rescued when their boat was sunk. There might have been a few army prisoners captured in North Africa, but a major influx of those only started after D-Day in June 1944.'[4]

On 11 January 1944, M Room operators overheard the generals in the anti-Nazi clique debating whether they should set up their own official political council at Trent Park.[5] Sicily and Italy had already fallen the previous summer and the war was clearly not going Germany's way. Bassenge commented: 'It's quite possible that within the next few months the Nazi regime will collapse.' To which Neuffer replied: 'Do you want to have a military council here? Crüwell might even collect the batmen as witnesses and set up a government or something (laughter).'[6]

This led to discussions on what should happen to the Nazi leaders back in Germany. On 15 January, Cramer, Reimann and Köhncke were overheard discussing how the main leaders of the Nazi regime must go:

CRAMER: It is high time to get rid of these people.
REIMANN: Those hot air merchants like Hermann Goering.
CRAMER: These people must go, and that Jew-baiter too.
REIMANN: Yes, but Streicher really doesn't count any more.
CRAMER: Those people must disappear for good. They are …
REIMANN: Criminals.
CRAMER: Yes criminals. We must be governed by decent men again.[7]

The generals believed that they could achieve political change in Germany if they united and stood up to Hitler. Cramer pointed out that they were being governed by the SS (whom he termed the 'peacetime army') and that the combined numbers of SS and police outnumbered the military. Köhncke considered that a 'very great risk'. To which Cramer replied: 'We can't get around the fact that we started it. That's the bad thing about it.' Cramer admitted: 'I too am in favour of fighting to the last ditch, but I don't want to find Goebbels sitting in the last ditch. It is a pity that the idea of fatherland and country have been lost.'[8]

In monitoring and recording these conversations, British intelligence tried to ascertain whether the military men would rise up again after the war, with their old aspirations for world domination. Reimann, Köhncke and Cramer all agreed that the First World War was 'an honourable, chivalrous one – we all knew what we were fighting for'. Cramer continued, 'In this war, when everyone is being killed, and all the things the army is made to do, the shooting of prisoners and commissars and Jews, etc., it's so vile. And it really was the limit when I came across the case of a General who was suddenly degraded to the rank of private.' Cramer's comments were quite extraordinary – he was more outraged by the downgrading of a general than the mass murder of innocent people.

That same week, Dr Haccius of the International Red Cross visited Trent Park to report on conditions there.[9] He was received by General Bassenge on behalf of the other generals. The secret listeners were primed to record their conversations. Haccius was overheard expressing mild criticism of American methods and lack of understanding at an American camp which he had visited at Oxford. Bassenge gave a description of the Christmas festivities at Trent Park and told Haccius: 'The British made a great effort to ensure our celebrations were a success.'[10]

Haccius suggested that there ought to be a vegetable garden on site.[11] Bassenge seemed unenthusiastic and said the food was ample. They discussed long delays in prisoners' mail and censorship. Haccius asked about the two interpreters in the camp and received assurance that they were excellent and had arranged English and mathematics lessons. Haccius promised to send more cigarettes for the batmen.

A separate conversation took place between Haccius, von Arnim and Bassenge in which they discussed the possibility of an exchange of German internees and prisoners.[12] Von Arnim continued his complaint about English dentistry and insisted on having a German dentist and doctor.[13] Over coffee, von Arnim thanked Haccius for the Red Cross parcels and asked if it was possible to buy wrist-watches from Switzerland.[14] A discussion about the difficulties of obtaining such items ensued during which Haccius seemed to become quite chatty and over-sympathetic with the Germans. Two days after his visit, MI19 compiled a summary report:

> The general impression made on the M Room operators was that Dr Haccius did not observe a strictly neutral attitude. His remarks on other camps, censorship and exchange of POW gave the impression of being more pro-German than neutral.[15]

One of the positive outcomes of the visit was that the batmen were given the opportunity to work in a vegetable garden on the estate, for which they received payment.[16] Five pro-Nazi batmen refused, saying it helped the British war effort. Deputy camp leader, General Bassenge pointed out that, if they rejected work in the vegetable gardens, logically they should refuse to receive English cigarettes which helped the British war effort through taxation. Neuffer and Bassenge dismissed the attitude of the pro-Nazi batmen as pure stupidity.[17]

DISCONTENT IN 'SPECIAL QUARTERS'

Discontent continued amongst the batmen who, like the generals, had formed into two distinct groups of pro-Nazi and anti-Nazi. The British officers had difficulty with General von Hülsen who, according to the camp diary: 'Seems to think that camp orders do not refer to him.'[18] Instead of arranging an afternoon walk with his minders, he just turned up at the allotted time and expected to be accommodated. Neuffer was already irritated by von Hülsen and 'gave him a piece of his mind', leading to a very public row in front of the batmen. Von Hülsen went so far as to call Neuffer an 'imprudent fellow'.[19] The intelligence report for this period commented: 'The fat was in the fire and the whole camp buzzed with excitement.'[20]

Major Topham, camp commandant, warned von Hülsen that if he carried on as before, he would be subject to 'special treatment'. The generals speculated on the meaning of his words and concluded it might mean transportation to Russia.

Suspicions ran high with the arrival on 22 January 1944 of Lieutenant Colonel Müller-Rienzburg of the German air force. Not understanding the politics in the camp, Müller-Rienzburg made the mistake of airing his defeatist and pro-British views to some members of the pro-Nazi group who consequently suspected him of being a British Secret Service agent – which was not the case.[21] Ironically on the other hand, they had failed to suspect that most of the British officers in the camp were from British intelligence.

Crüwell began to realise that he had become the most unpopular man in the camp. The others avoided sitting with him at mealtimes and the dejected Crüwell only came downstairs for dinner, taking other meals in his room, becoming more and more isolated. British officers found him mainly in his room, staring into the distance or playing a game of patience. The British intelligence report noted that he and von Arnim were 'heading for mental disaster if they don't change their attitudes'.[22]

Lieutenant Hubbuch and the ardent Nazi Lieutenant Colonel Boes left for a POW camp in Canada.[23] This caused a stir amongst the generals who feared they too might be sent to Canada, something which they saw as a backward step. In spite of their grumblings, life in Trent Park was comfortable, and they now petitioned British officers against leaving. With the departure of Hubbuch and Boes, the bedrooms were slightly rearranged. Neuffer was given a room on his own; Müller-Rienzburg and Bassenge shared a room, and so did Reimann and von Glasow.

The generals enjoyed a timetable of wireless broadcasts that included all German news bulletins from Germany, BBC concerts and the daily 10 a.m. BBC news broadcasts. Towards the end of the first week of February 1944, the 'guests' were shown the film *Christmas Carol*, during which 'God Save the King' was played. The pro-Nazis were furious and considered it an insult that they should be shown a film with this in it.[24]

NAVAL SUCCESSES

Information continued to be forthcoming on the U-boat war, details of which enabled the Allies to keep ahead of the battle at sea. General von Broich (codenamed M159 in the transcripts) gave a British army officer (below, BAO) detailed descriptions about the U-boat shelters at St Nazaire.[25] The U-boat pens were not visible from the air and, without this conversation, could not have been found by RAF aerial reconnaissance missions. Von Broich had visited the site himself and was able to give an extraordinary eye-witness account:

> M159: The most interesting sight will be these U-boat shelters at St Nazaire. There are large underground shelters there with a covering of cement the depth of this room.

BAO: Have you seen them?

M159: Yes, they're terrific. You simply can't imagine what these vaults are like. As in an engine shed where there's a turntable in the middle and engines can go in from every direction, in the same way here there's a large basin and on all sides these –

BAO: How many U-boats can get in there at one time?

M159: Oh, dozens of them. They just laugh at this bombing of St. Nazaire. I myself saw the effect of one of the heavy bombs on one of those things; it's made of special cement, not the normal kind, and it knocked out a piece this size.

BAO: Ten centimetres?

M159: Yes.[26]

References to St Nazaire and Lorient came up frequently in conversations between lower ranks. These prisoners provided details of the extent of damage to U-boat pens after Allied bombing campaigns and were sources of valuable eye-witness material. In one such conversation, two naval prisoners discussed the aftermath:

N15: At St. Nazaire everything has been damaged. Only the shelters are still standing and they have been partially damaged.

N1584: Then it isn't a proper base any longer?

N15: Oh yes, the base as such – the U-boat shelters are still standing, they can't destroy them. To do that they would have to fire torpedoes into them from aircraft, but they can't destroy them from above.[27]

The same conversation revealed details of the complex living quarters in the U-boat shelters which also had female personnel: 'They were smart women and they really made the U-boat hostel look very nice and smart.'[28] The complex of deep bunkers had a lounge, ladies' room, swimming bath, dance hall and facilities for playing golf and billiards. Everything was catered for the men, who even decorated their shelter with flowers picked when they went ashore in the evenings. If beer was plentiful, they drank well into the early hours of the morning. Prisoner N15 even admitted: 'At Lorient we lived in the shelter. We had a wonderful officers' mess. The chief petty officer had a mess, which made you feel you were in a country mansion.'[29]

SCHARNHORST

News of the sinking of the German battleship *Scharnhorst* in the Battle of the North Cape, off Norway, on 26 December 1943 caused surprise amongst the generals, who speculated that Hitler had intentionally sent her to her doom because all was not well with the German navy.[30] The *Scharnhorst* had been attacking Britain's Arctic convoys and its sinking was a priority for the Allies. The thirty-six survivors, out of a total crew of 1,968, were brought to Wilton Park and Latimer House.[31] Their arrival made news in the M Room at Wilton Park where secret listener Fritz Lustig was then working: 'We were quite excited when we heard that the few survivors of the *Scharnhorst* had arrived at our unit. We felt privileged when we were told to cover the cell which was holding one of them. We were very conscious of the fact that they required special attention.'

For Kendrick, events had come full circle. During the 1930s, his spy network, which he ran from Vienna, had carried out espionage missions into Nazi Germany to penetrate the dockyard at Wilhelmshaven where the *Scharnhorst* was then being constructed.[32] For him, there must have been a great sense of satisfaction to see part of that military might of Germany being 'dismantled' during the war.

Information from the survivors of the *Scharnhorst* was widely discussed in naval intelligence circles. Edmund Rushbrooke (head of Naval Intelligence) wrote to Lieutenant Commander Cope at Latimer:

> The heavy simultaneous influx of nearly 250 prisoners from *Scharnhorst*, T.25, *Alsterufer*, U.593 and U.73 threw a greater strain than ever before on your section. The results have nevertheless maintained the high standard to which I have been accustomed, and the

speed with which they have been produced has been very creditable. You and all those concerned are to be congratulated on this very good effort. Please convey my thanks to those officers who were responsible for these satisfactory results.[33]

However, the formidable German battleship *Tirpitz* still plagued the seas. Two surviving able seamen from the *Scharnhorst* spoke about the *Tirpitz*:

> N2145: The *Tirpitz* was lucky; the adhesive charges only adhered to her for a moment and then fell off again. There was too much sea-weed and too many mussels on the ship, she had been lying there too long. They [the charges] fell to the bottom of the sea, where they exploded; otherwise the *Tirpitz* would no longer be there, she would have been split in two.
>
> N2133: The whole thing is said not to have been so serious. They [the English] are supposed to have come on board and [one of them] said: 'I report having carried out the King of England's orders – the *Tirpitz* will blow up in so-and-so many minutes time.' Then everybody left the quarterdeck.
>
> N2133: I suppose the *Scharnhorst* made off pretty quickly then?
>
> N2145: No, the *Scharnhorst* had been making a trial trip that night. She was sailing about in the fjord. The captain started off and suddenly got a signal reporting that the *Tirpitz* had suffered minor damage.
>
> N2133: Minor damage! When we sailed up there, we carried two hundred shipyard … on board. There was a repair ship already there.[34]

The *Tirpitz* was eventually sunk by the RAF on 12 November 1944. Naval intelligence via MI19's prisoners continued to flow. Sub-Lieutenant Striezel of U-1003 spoke to a junior Sub-Lieutenant (codenamed 42Z) about the new kind of U-boats being developed:

STRIEZEL: The new boats (Type XXI) were supposed to have been ready by Christmas. But it didn't come off. To start with, the Allies smashed half of them at Hamburg and at Bremen. There was a heavy air-raid just on the factories of Blohm & Voss and Deschimag and they smashed half of them then. Some are out – a certain number of the new boats are in use already. I had the nineteenth ... There are also racks (Greifer) up here: three, six, nine, twelve, and below there are two more, fourteen, sixteen, and another six by the tubes.

42Z: My God, twenty-two (torpedoes)!

STRIEZEL: It's a room on its own, i.e. two sections ... You don't need to worry any more about periscope depth and being spotted or the 'snorter' head being located etc. Nothing like that anymore. They are now working on it so that they can fire the torpedoes from 80 metres.[35]

In MI19 files, a sketch of the German Type XXI U-boat was reproduced as an appendix to the above report.[36] On a rare occasion, a prisoner was security conscious, as in the case of a telephonist from the *Scharnhorst* (N1552), who chatted to his cellmate (N2243), an able seaman from U-264 (sunk in the north Atlantic on 19 February 1944):

N.1552: What do they say in the security lectures?

N.2243: So far it has been correct: 'You will come to a camp where you will be interrogated from all quarters, by English and American officers and when you are in your rooms, you mustn't speak about your U-boat or about any service matters. There is apparatus installed through which they hear everything, even the slightest sounds.'[37]

With preparations under way for the D-Day landings, the intelligence gathering was gaining pace. Across the three CSDIC sites, interrogations produced new intelligence on the location of displaced German war industries, electrical sub-stations, and a large synthetic oil plant at Auschwitz.[38] Of particular value was information from prisoners on underground sites, particularly underground factories in Germany and Czechoslovakia that could not be identified from aerial reconnaissance missions.[39] An example of such a discovery was the Mittelwerk Niedersachsenwerfen, near Nordhausen, which manufactured V-2 rockets, Junkers aero engines and jet propulsion units.[40]

REPATRIATION OF CRAMER

During the week of 20 February 1944, Cramer and his batman Edelhäuser were set to be repatriated to Germany.[41] The day before their departure, Trent Park commandant, Major Denis Topham, went to see Cramer. The intelligence report gave an account: 'Cramer made a very nice speech to the commandant in which he thanked him for the excellent treatment he had had here. He stated that now that he was going he could reveal to the commandant that he had 25% English blood. He went on to say that every time he looked out of his window and saw the very smart guards, he was proud of his English blood.'[42]

Cramer attributed the high standards to Major Topham and would not fail to mention it to influential friends in Germany.[43] He told Topham that the German struggle was now hopeless and would lead to Germany's ruin.

After Topham had left the room, Cramer made another speech, this time to the British army officer. He reminded the officer that he had been Commander of the Afrika Korps and therefore wished to present a memento to him: 'Not only in his own name but in [the] name of all the officers of the Afrika Korps, as a token of their gratitude for the British "gentlemanly [behaviour]".' He gave the British officer his Afrika Korps armband from his uniform, with the remark, 'Even von Arnim isn't entitled to wear it'.[44]

General von Arnim stepped forward and gave Cramer two bars of soap because of the shortage of soap in Germany. The intelligence report said the bars of soap were: 'One for his wife and the other for his mistress.'[45] This appears to have set a trend, because when the other officers bade Cramer goodbye, they too were concerned about the lack of soap in their country and offered to give him more.

On the morning of departure, Cramer was escorted to Paddington Station by an unnamed British army officer. Driving through Regent's Park past many aircrew cadets, Cramer kept muttering: 'What a pity! What a pity! It is a scandal that these fine young men should be killed for the mistakes of the mad Führer.' The journey is recorded in the intelligence report for that week:

> All he [Cramer] hoped was that the war would be over without any necessity for us to invade. An invasion would cost rivers of blood to both sides, but the Allies were still bound to win as Germany could not hope to defeat the whole world. He intended to have a long talk on all this with his great friends Korten (of the GAF) and Dönitz. Cramer was not looking forward to his inevitable interview with Hitler.[46]

At Paddington Station, the British officer explained to a policeman that they would have to drive in because he had a German prisoner in the car. Out of vanity, Cramer took exception to that and told the British officer that he could at least have said there was a German general in the car.[47] The German batman who was with them got into the compartment of the train but Cramer objected to sharing a compartment with either his batman or a British private with a rifle. He was politely reminded that he was still a prisoner of war.

Given Cramer's anti-Nazi views, was it safe for him to be repatriated to the Third Reich? Rumours suggest he might have gone back on a secret mission, but no evidence has ever emerged. Cramer arrived back in Germany and was duly arrested by the Gestapo for his involvement in the July assassination attempt on Hitler.[48] He was held until 5 August 1944 at Prinz-Albrecht-Strasse prison, Berlin. From there, he was taken to Ravensbrück concentration camp. Due to an act of mercy, he was released to a hospital in Berlin, then placed under house arrest. After Allied forces crossed into Germany, he was taken up by the British army as Commander-in-Chief of all German POWs in Holstein.

After Cramer's departure from Trent Park, Crüwell decided to try to make himself ill enough to qualify for repatriation. He took cold baths every morning, which apparently 'made him very nervous', and he scratched the eczema on his legs in a hope that it would extend all over his body.[49] But there would be no repatriation for this pro-Nazi general before the end of hostilities.

That same week, Major Topham was posted to another camp, and a new commandant arrived. Before Topham left, he bade farewell to the generals in the common room. It was noted that von Arnim behaved very well during the meeting:

He thanked the commandant for his very reasonable treatment and efforts to lighten their lot. He then presented him with a picture as a token of their esteem. This had been painted in oils by von Liebenstein and framed by Bassenge. The whole business has led to one of the periodical uproars in the camp. The Nazis, led on by Crüwell, think it was below their dignity to assemble en masse for any British Major. They also object to the picture as they say that it makes it look as if they were currying favours.[50]

Von Arnim and Crüwell said that assembling to meet a commandant could not happen again and they summoned a British army officer and told him so. He took the wind out of their sails by stating that the new (unnamed) commandant wished to say a few words to them in the common room. Von Arnim replied that the commandant should visit each of the generals in their rooms instead. Von Thoma was furious at von Arnim's attitude and told the British officer that the commandant would be quite within his right to issue an order and the generals must obey. Bassenge told the British officer 'to tell the commandant that he must, on no account, give in to von Arnim's stupidity'. The intelligence report for the day concluded: 'Needless to say, the anti-Nazis consider that both Crüwell and von Arnim are ripe for the madhouse.'[51]

Within days, the generals had other matters to worry about. The Russian advance through Europe was considered a danger to everyone, and one that had been caused by the Allies supplying Russia with war material.[52] They discussed how Britain must now restore the balance of power in Europe. Von Thoma even expressed the belief that Britain might accept Germany as an ally against Russia before the war was over.

It was clearly von Arnim's intention, so the other generals believed, to try to gain a victory over the new camp commandant by bringing up all the old complaints about life in the camp.[53] The result was a memorandum, drawn up and signed by all the generals, except Crüwell, complaining about von Arnim's attitude towards the British.

THE FÜHRER'S BIRTHDAY

Within the camp, bitterness was never far from the surface and even spilled into arguments about how the generals would celebrate the Führer's birthday on 20 April 1944 – all recorded by the secret listeners. Crüwell suggested that he could make a short speech at dinner, after which they would toast the Führer's health. 'Pity it has to be English beer,' he remarked, 'but that can't be helped.'[54] He fretted about the possibility that von Thoma might refuse to participate in the toast and Bassenge might not make proper arrangements.

Crüwell decided that if Bassenge's preparations for the Führer's birthday were inadequate and von Thoma refused to toast, they would be expelled from the Officers' Corps and prohibited from eating in the Officers' Mess at Trent Park. This suggests that the generals believed that they were running the camp, with their 'puppet British minders' in the background. When the day arrived, the intelligence report gave a summary:

It was obvious on the morning of 20 April that this was not an ordinary day. The German batmen were dressed in their Sunday best – the officers were not! At 12.30 hrs, General von Arnim, supported by Captain Meixner, visited the batmen's dining room and a toast was drunk to Hitler, and von Arnim made a speech. Von Arnim also made a short speech during the officer POW's lunch, when a toast was drunk.[55]

The generals discussed not only Hitler and the Nazi leaders, but others too, both military and political. Von Thoma and Sponeck even showed admiration for British Prime Minister Churchill and contrasted him with their leader:

THOMA: Imagine, a 70-year-old man like Churchill travelling in a destroyer! He's a real soldier at heart.

SPONECK: Yes.

THOMA: He is personally appreciated everywhere. Hitler just sticks inside his fox-hole.

SPONECK: Actually, it would be the natural action of any decent thinking man to pay an immediate visit to a bombed town, as the King does over here.

THOMA: Whenever any ... the Queen arrives and enquires after the pets etc. What could be more touching!

SPONECK: If Hitler were at least to visit a divisional HQ up at the front, in order to see for himself the way the battle is being conducted. As it is, he speaks about the whole affair merely from the perspective of a runner in the Great War. One can't be a supreme commander and yet have no idea how things are going.[56]

The generals listened to a British broadcast of past speeches made by Hitler, Goering and Goebbels. Sponeck remarked to the other officers that it would be fine propaganda for Churchill if his speeches of a year ago were broadcast to Germany. Sponeck remarked that British statesmen had never made 'boastful promises or talked such rubbish as their German counterparts'.[57] The political analyses proved useful to British intelligence as a gauge to understand the regime and its weaknesses.

There was always the danger that information passed from MI19's intelligence sites to the army, Admiralty or air force might be disregarded. That sometimes happened with information gained from POWs on new German technology which could be deemed so advanced as not to be scientifically possible. But ignoring any kind of intelligence could naturally have consequences. One such example was given by US interrogator Heimwarth Jestin, who was working at Wilton Park. Ahead of D-Day, through careful interrogation, he established the location of a particular German fighting unit outside the tiny rural Normandy town of Carentan, not far from Cherbourg. He forwarded the intelligence to the War Office to pass to the relevant British forces who would be landing in that area after D-Day. Unfortunately, the information was dismissed as unreliable. Jestin commented: 'After D-Day, when the Allies reached Carentan area, they were attacked by Germany's 6th Paratroop Division (airborne unit) and we sustained very high losses.'[58] It is an example where the stakes in analysing whether intelligence was reliable or not, or failing to act on it, could cost lives.

The division was commanded by Major von der Heydte who would eventually be captured and brought to the 'special quarters' at Trent Park.

GENERAL KREIPE

Life at Trent Park was rarely dull. Soon to arrive was Major General Heinrich Kreipe, kidnapped from Crete in a daring mission by SOE on 26 April 1944.[59] His story has become the subject of several books and a film, *Ill Met by Moonlight*. Kreipe's personal MI19 file gives scant details of the kidnap: 'He was held up at night at a cross-roads by two traffic control sentries wearing German uniform. These were British officers who had carefully planned the whole operation. They kept him in hiding in Crete for 18 days before taking him to Cairo.'[60] MI19 considered him to be 'a rather unimportant and unimaginative anti-Nazi; rather weak character and ignorant'.[61]

Kreipe, born in Niederspier, Thüringen in 1895, had served as a regular soldier in the First World War. In 1941, as commander of 209 Regiment, 58 Division, he had served on the Russian northern front and been awarded the Ritterkreuz for sealing off Leningrad by thrusting forward to Oranienbaum.[62] He remained in Russia until April 1942, and by 1 September the following year was Commander of 79 Division. At the end of February 1944, he was transferred to Crete.

On arrival at Wilton Park on 22 May 1944, Kreipe was interrogated. A summary of his interrogation and several conversations with British army officers have survived.[63] British intelligence had prepared a number of specific questions for him. For example, did he command the 113 Infantry Division in Russia?[64] Was he in France between the time of leaving Russia and going to Crete? If so, did he command a division, and which division? Who commanded the flanking divisions? Was his sector regarded as a likely area for Allied landings? Are landings expected on the west coast or the Mediterranean? Did he come into contact with any preparations for reprisals against England by means of secret weapons?

On 25 May, Kreipe was transferred to Trent Park. The generals and senior officers immediately gathered in the common room to hear details of his kidnap.[65] Later, in conversation with Lord Aberfeldy, he discussed the event and the details were summarised in an intelligence report:

> He said the English major who had taken part in his capture had spent two years on the island [of Crete], with intervals of leave in Cairo, and that there were quite a lot of Britons in Crete, mainly officers and NCO instructors, organising and training the partisan bands. (This he knows only from observation after capture.)[66]

During his time at Trent Park, Kreipe discussed the secret weapon with the senior German officers, and reiterated his belief that its existence was not a bluff and that Hitler intended to bring the English to their knees with it.[67]

Kreipe was one of the few generals whom Kendrick entertained personally at his home 'Woodton' in Oxshott, Surrey. His wife Norah played the perfectly discreet hostess on the general's arrival. Grandson, Ken Walsh, remembered Kreipe coming to the house:

> I have vivid memories of Kreipe being entertained at my grand-father's house in Oxshott where I lived with my mother and sister for

over a year and where we also spent our school holidays. General Kreipe took a liking to me and made a little crane complete with a cab, a jib and a bucket. One of the cranes had an operator's revolving cabin on a strip used to seal fish paste jars. Kreipe was not the only General at my grandfather's house. The others were very relaxed and friendly. I suppose the idea was to bring them to a place with a family atmosphere and make them feel at home so they would open up.[68]

Kreipe enjoyed his visits to Kendrick's private home and came to respect him. It was said that they struck up a good rapport, even an amicable relationship.[69] Little did Kreipe know that 'Colonel Wallace', as Kendrick was known, was the spy who had been expelled from the Third Reich in 1938.

Discussions about an Allied invasion of the continent often featured in the generals' conversations.[70] Bassenge was of the opinion that the German air force was stronger than the Allies had reckoned, and they were all waiting for the signal to transfer to the Western Front to repel an Allied invasion attempt. Kreipe replied: 'I doubt whether the Allies really intend to invade.'[71] Lower-rank prisoners, too, discussed the likelihood or otherwise of the Allies making a landing and clearly believed it could not be successful. Prisoner A4188 (a bomber observer, captured 24 February 1944), commented to his cellmate (a bomber gunner):

They will never beat us from a military standpoint. We still occupy half of Russia, the whole of France, the Baltic countries, Holland, Belgium and everywhere. What have the English got? They have their island; and when they come they will come with their whole military power, and if we throw them out, then we've won the war.[72]

CHAPTER 11

Saga of the Generals

*We are not suffering an undeserved fate. We are being punished for letting a
national resurrection which promised so well, go to the devil.*

General Bruhn at Trent Park

On 6 June 1944, the Allies mounted the largest ever invasion of
Europe, landing over 150,000 troops on the Normandy beaches in
a single day.[1] D-Day became one of the greatest military triumphs of
the Second World War. Prisoners were captured after the landings
as Allied forces moved through France. The MI9 War Diary records
that, in June 1944, 13,742 POWs from Operation Overlord (the
invasion of Normandy) arrived via MI19's interrogation cage at
Kempton Park.[2] This number was exclusive of wounded POWs in
hospital. Each prisoner had to be interrogated and debriefed for intelligence, especially to establish the locations of Hitler's crack Panzer divisions and troops. Those thought to have strategic engineering or scientific
information were transferred for detailed interrogation and accommodation at one of CSDIC's UK listening sites. Joining CSDIC's team of
interrogators two days after D-Day was Hugh John Colman, a banking
and export merchant who had lived in West Africa in the pre-war years.
He was fluent in German, having been born in Germany in 1915.[3] In
July 1943, he transferred from the Royal Artillery to the Intelligence
Corps.[4] On 8 June 1944, he was formally attached to CSDIC as an
interrogator.

In July 1944, 18,082 POWs arrived at Kempton Park, and in August there was a new intake of an additional 24,731. During September, the new arrivals amounted to 48,444. In October 1944, the intake was a staggering 69,493 prisoners, now shared across the cages at Kempton Park and Devizes[5] where they were assessed and, if thought to have special intelligence, transferred to the CSDIC sites.

The Naval Intelligence section at Latimer House, under Lieutenant Commander Cope, continued to soften up its most valuable naval prisoners by taking them out to the Ritz Hotel. It caused a scandal and Cope received a letter from the Admiralty, complaining about the amount of money that was spent on the prisoners at the Ritz:

> Although this expenditure was sanctioned by the DNI [Director of Naval Intelligence], it is to be emphasised that care must be exercised as to how these funds can be used to the best advantage ... There are several items which are objectionable, viz: entertaining at the Ritz and purchase of considerable quantities of gin. If these facts became generally known, there might be good cause for scandal. Furthermore, I and many others are quite unable to enjoy these luxuries and it is out of all proportion that our enemies should.[6]

Successful campaigns in Normandy in the weeks and months after D-Day brought more generals and high-ranking commanders into captivity. In June alone, 490 German prisoners came through Kendrick's sites; the following month 587, and a new intake of 558 in August.[7] From D-Day to 31 August 1944, just over 1,600 POWs had come through Wilton Park and Latimer House – 523 of them were officers. Dealing with the intelligence side was a massive undertaking.

In total, 98 senior German officers would soon be held at Trent Park, 59 of them generals.[8] They were a diverse and colourful bunch who required careful handling. Their incarceration afforded British intelligence a detailed insight into the mind-set and strategy of the enemy. Amongst them were Admiral Walter Hennecke, the commander of all German sea defences in Normandy; General Lieutenant Karl von

Schlieben, the commander at Cherbourg; his second in command, Colonel Walter Köhn; General Lieutenant Ferdinand Heim, the commander of Boulogne; Colonel Andreas von Aulock, the commandant of the fortress of St Malo; and Eberhard Wildermuth, commandant of Le Havre. August 1944 saw the arrival at Trent Park of General Dietrich von Choltitz – the commander of Paris.[9]

ADMIRAL HENNECKE

As commandant of German sea defences in Normandy, Admiral Hennecke was a very valuable captive for the Allies. He was so important that the then Director of Naval Intelligence, Rear Admiral Rushbrooke, came out to Trent Park to see him on 21 July.[10] As the interview with Rushbrooke progressed, Hennecke became increasingly depressed about the threat of Russia and Communism. Rushbrooke noted: 'He is obsessed with the idea that there are hundreds of thousands of potential communists in Germany who are waiting to fall into the lap of the Russians.'[11]

Hennecke confided in Rushbrooke that, when he saw the vast resources the Allies had at their disposal during the invasion, he was convinced that Germany had lost the war. He and German forces in the region had been bitterly disappointed by the overwhelming Allied air superiority. He told Rushbrooke that he had not expected the invasion to begin before August and had expected to be able to repel it once their gun sites and defences had been completed along the Normandy coast. He revealed that he had been ill supplied with intelligence.

Rushbrooke asked him about the secret weapon programme and rocket sites along the Cherbourg peninsula. Hennecke had no information regarding these developments because only a few scientists were privy to that knowledge.

In the safety of Trent Park, the generals and senior German officers privately discussed how the war could not carry on:

HENNECKE: It can't go on like this. Just imagine it, in three days there have been three thousand bombers over Munich and so on, just imagine the damage that is being done and how it is increasing the chaos that will come later.

KRUG: That's what I say too. What did the Führer say? 'And if they smash up the whole of Germany, then we shall live underground!'

ROHRBACH: I heard that too!

HENNECKE: It's madness!

ROHRBACH: It certainly is![12]

Hennecke spoke about how he had been forced to retreat permanently to his concrete bunker at Cherbourg once the attack began.[13] British and American intelligence began to piece together German military strategy and order of battle from the bugged conversations, as well as vital information on U-boats and E-boats. Hennecke gave away that St Malo had become the new base for German E-boats instead of Cherbourg.[14] Von Schlieben talked about his friendship with Schmettow, the commander of the Channel Islands, and how the British could easily take them because Schmettow only had one battalion stationed there.

ANXIETY OF THE GENERALS

The D-Day landings and aftermath gave the generals plenty to discuss, especially with those who had been captured in 1943 and isolated at Trent Park for over a year. They were eager for news from the newly-arrived officers and to analyse amongst themselves the military disasters on the battlefields of France. Crüwell was anxious that the Allies were being allowed (by German forces) to land too much material at the bridgehead.[15] Neuffer replied that, comparing it with Germany's plans to invade England in 1940 in Operation Sealion, it would take at least three weeks for them to land sufficient material for an advance to continue.[16] Von Arnim declared that the German handling of the situation had been very clumsy, and it would have been wiser for them to have given up a few kilometres of ground during the initial (invasion) landings to enable more mobility for a German counter-offensive.

In a different conversation, von Liebenstein said that, in typical style, Field Marshal Rommel was 'throwing in the Panzer divisions piecemeal'.[17] Sponeck agreed that it was El Alamein all over again and that troops should have been held ready in a body further to the rear. The generals debated that this month (June 1944) would decide whether Germany continued to fight. Glasow believed the British and Americans might still be persuaded to come to peace terms rather than fight for every kilometre of Berlin. He told von Arnim, in true anti-Semitic Nazi style, that the Jews were at the helm of Russia and America and if they had their way, they would stamp out Nazi ideas.[18] He doubted they would achieve it, however.

Meanwhile, Neuffer and Bassenge concentrated their discussions on speculations about where the Allies would next land, which they believed would be around Le Havre or as far north as Holland.[19] They agreed that the war was as good as lost and would be over by the end of the year.[20]

General Bassenge had just returned from a mission with Lord Aberfeldy to negotiate the surrender of the Channel Islands.[21] The result is not discussed in CSDIC files. However, after the war, A.R. Rawlinson (head of MI19) wrote a three-part play for the BBC based on the intelligence operation at Trent Park, entitled *Lord Glenaldy* (to disguise the original use of Lord Aberfeldy).[22] Lord Glenaldy is cast as a fake aristocrat, working at a bugging site that holds German generals in a stately house.[23] In one scene in the play, Glenaldy and the German general (given the name von Hussen) do not succeed in achieving the surrender of the Channel Islands. They decide to stop off in Paris for the weekend without telling British intelligence.[24] By Sunday, they still had not returned to Trent Park. There was panic within British military circles until Kendrick (known as 'Tommy' in the play) received a phone call from Paris to say that Lord Glenaldy was partying in the capital with the general in tow.[25] The irony was that the general trusted him so completely that he did not attempt an escape.

At the time of its broadcast, the play was described in the press as 'factional'[26] as some of the scenes are remarkably close to the facts and antics that actually surrounded the real wartime intelligence operation and behaviour of the generals in captivity.

Over the summer of 1944, some generals were due to be transferred from Trent Park to camps in America. General Crüwell expressed considerable surprise and displeasure that his name was on the list.[27] He met with the new commandant and Lord Aberfeldy and insisted that he was a prisoner of war of the British.[28] His protestations led nowhere. His frustration was still running high when he conversed with Egersdorf later that day and told him that he was being shipped to America to make room for what he termed 'the Free German Movement' in the camp under von Thoma's leadership.[29] For the duration of his time at Trent Park, Crüwell had been the pillar and leader of the pro-Nazis.[30] He expressed disappointment to Egersdorf that all his efforts to feign illness had been in vain.

Von Arnim and Bassenge joined the conversation. 'It is contrary to the Geneva Convention to send me to America,' Crüwell complained to them. 'I'm not an American prisoner.'[31] Von Arnim did not seem bothered by Crüwell's imminent transfer and said to him: 'Well, I have no objection to the arrangement. It will be a change for you. The English have no say in the matter. They have to dance to the American tune.'

Bassenge added his contribution, saying, 'There's no point in protesting. Prisoners of war taken by Germany's allies are handed over to the Germans.' It was certainly rich of Crüwell to invoke the Geneva Convention when the Nazi regime, including its military commanders and generals, had committed so many atrocities and genocide.

With the departure of Crüwell, his worst fears were confirmed when anti-Nazi von Thoma was announced as the new camp leader. Von Thoma seemed quite amused by the turn of events and told the other generals that he did not plan to change anything. He told Bassenge, 'I'm rather surprised still to be here. But then, it must be a matter of prestige.'[32]

OPERATION VALKYRIE

At 1800 hours on 20 July 1944, a British army officer sent for Sponeck and gave him the news that an attempt had been made on Hitler's life, but he had survived with minor injuries. The assassination attempt 'caused a stir at No.11 Camp,' the intelligence report said.[33] MI19 prepared a special report on the generals' reactions to the news.[34] The failed putsch came as a shock to Sponeck who told the British officer that it was a put-up job by the Nazis as an excuse for a purge of the anti-Nazi generals.[35]

The bungled plot, led by German army officer Claus von Stauffenberg, an aristocrat, became widely known as Operation Valkyrie. He had smuggled a small bomb in a briefcase into a meeting room with the Führer at his Wolf's Lair field headquarters in East Prussia. Von Stauffenberg placed the briefcase between Hitler's legs, then made an excuse to leave.[36] Alfred Jodl, Chief of the Operations Staff of the German army, had called out 'Stay here!', but von Stauffenberg simply made an excuse that he had an urgent phone call to make and hadn't had breakfast. Outside the room, von Stauffenberg waited about 300 metres away and on hearing the bomb blast decided that no one could have survived. He boarded an aircraft to Berlin where he declared the attempt had been successful, without checking if, indeed, it had been, for at the crucial moment, Hitler had moved away from the briefcase and was only slightly wounded when the device went off.

Staff at MI9/MI19 were amongst the first to hear about the attempted assassination before it became public knowledge.[37] Commenting on those events, Catherine Townshend said: 'A camp bed was made up next to the scrambler telephone that had to be manned around the clock; a clerk and despatch rider were on hand in case of need. Most dramatic of all the news that arrived by scrambler telephone was the attempted assassination of Hitler ... We knew that retribution would be swift and merciless.'[38]

Hitler ordered von Stauffenberg's execution by firing squad the following day. His death caused consternation among the generals at Trent Park.[39] Weeks later, the failed assassination of Hitler was still a frequent topic amongst the prisoners, especially those who had been captured on the battlefields of France. The frustration of Bassenge was recorded in a transcript from the M Room: 'For God's sake, where is all this leading us?'[40]

Admiral Hennecke declared: 'This is the beginning of the end. There will be a blood-bath in Germany.'[41]

Von Broich quietly admitted to Sponeck that he had known von Stauffenberg because he had been on his staff at one time. He was 'a first-class man' and could not understand why he only used a small bomb. He deplored the fact that von Stauffenberg had failed in his attempt and now envisaged that a concentration camp would be set up for generals.[42] Reimann believed there would be another attempt on Hitler's life soon.[43]

The generals also questioned the levels of security around Hitler.[44] How was it possible to get the bomb into his headquarters so easily? The problem was that those closest to Hitler had been trusted completely. Von Choltitz told von Thoma and Sponeck that he was never searched when going into the headquarters: 'I could easily have had a pistol or a small egg-hand-grenade hidden away,' he said.[45]

Sponeck commented that 'nobody was really wounded. That seems suspicious to me. I mean, if it had been a real attempt on Hitler's life, none of them would still be alive.' In a separate conversation, Sponeck told Broich, 'I can only say I think it a great pity that Stauffenberg didn't succeed.'[46]

The generals deplored the fact that some of the perpetrators of the plot had been hanged as traitors and not shot according to the honour due to military men.[47] Eberbach told Schramm:

These people were not traitors. They first started to hang people in concentration camps. But those were mostly hardened criminals. Certainly officers who indulge in swindling might perhaps be put on the same level. But those officers – that should not have been done. And the worst of all is that the whole families of those officers have also been slaughtered.[48]

Schramm expressed disbelief that the families of the officers involved in the plot had been murdered. Eberbach added: 'They have disappeared. Whether they've been executed or gassed or what I don't know. Graf von

Stauffenberg's family, consisting of his wife and four children and a fifth expected is no more. I know about them because he lived in Bamberg where I live.'

The failed assassination was discussed between General Eberbach and his son, a naval officer, both being held at Trent Park:

SON: You've no idea how adversely this Stauffenberg business affected the Officer Corps. The fact that the individual soldier at the front was being killed, and that the officers at home were breaking their oath, infuriated the people. The fact that Lindemann, for example, through his own swinishness, let about 100,000 soldiers on the Eastern Front go to the devil – he let his whole front go to hell and went over to the other side with half his staff.

EBERBACH: It hasn't yet been established that Lindemann went over to the other side. Nothing is known about him.[49]

MI19 files noted the lengthy conversations on the von Stauffenberg affair: 'The possibility of a military coup d'état in Germany has been discussed among the senior officer POW for some time.'[50] How did the secret listeners react to the news of the attempt on Hitler's life? Fritz Lustig recalled:

We heard on the radio that same evening and that the plot had failed. By all accounts, Hitler was still alive and well. It may seem a strange reaction, but I was pleased that the plot had not succeeded because most of the names of the conspirators indicated that they belonged to the Prussian aristocracy and were high-ranking army officers. I figured that not much would change for the better in Germany if that particular class were to make peace with the Allies and then rule the country. No doubt millions of lives would have been saved if the war had ended in July 1944 rather than in May 1945, but how would the political situation in Germany have developed, and would it have led to democracy?[51]

POST D-DAY

After D-Day, as the Allies advanced through France, Germany's senior military commanders continued to be brought to Trent Park for the same softening-up treatment as those generals who had been captured in 1942 and 1943. General Dietrich von Choltitz, the commander of Paris who was captured on 25 August 1944, soon figures prominently in the bugged conversations at Trent Park. John Sinclair, then director of Military Intelligence, wrote to colleagues on 7 September 1944:

> You may care to glance through the latest CSDIC report on captured generals' conversations. The recent arrival of von Choltitz has unloosed their tongues, and gave this general an opportunity to put them wise about the latest situation in Germany . . . it shows the incredible state of mind of Hitler. The impression expressed by the generals is that Germany is now a mad house.[52]

During 1943, von Choltitz had commanded five German divisions in the Crimea. In July 1944, he was transferred to France and then posted as commandant of Paris. This monocled general, described by British intelligence as 'overweight, coarse, with an inflated sense of his own self-importance',[53] was captured when American forces entered Paris. Negotiations for an armistice had broken down and von Choltitz was arrested.

On 27 August, he was brought to Latimer House, then two days later transferred to Trent Park. His egotistic character played right into the hands of MI19 because he was boastful and spoke too freely in the presence of the other generals. They were only too eager to hear the latest news from the battlefields and about events in Germany from von Choltitz.[54] This updated information about Germany was extremely helpful for the secret listeners to record for British intelligence. Von Choltitz tried to ingratiate himself with his minders to appear in the best possible light. It was noted that he 'adopted the attitude that he had foreseen the outcome of the war because of his insight into historical necessities'.[55] He spoke about how Hitler had ordered him to defend Paris at all costs and to round up members of the underground resistance and execute them.[56] In a meeting with Hitler, von Choltitz had told him that he had inadequate supplies for a successful defence of Paris but the Führer did not listen.

Von Choltitz discussed secret weapons with comrades, with speculation from Neuffer about why these were not being used against the Allied invasion front.[57] Von Liebenstein supposed it was because the weapon was not yet ready and von Broich agreed, saying to von Choltitz and Elfeldt that the launch sites had been delayed because of bombing by the Allies.[58]

Other 'guests' at the hospitality of British intelligence included Colonel Andreas von Aulock, who surrendered at St Malo on 17 August 1944. Known as the 'mad Colonel of St Malo' by MI19, he was deemed to be 'an untrustworthy type who trims his sails to the wind and only thinks of himself and his well-being'.[59] The officer who escorted him to Trent Park described him as 'another typical, monocled, aristocratic German officer found to be pro-British and violently anti-Russian … with a high opinion of himself and his attraction to women'.[60] General von Thoma told Aulock that he had been very sensible to surrender the fortress. To which, Aulock replied, 'Well, there was nothing else to be done'.[61]

Heinrich Eberbach, general of a Panzer Division, 7th Army, had been forced to surrender on 31 August 1944 after failing to withdraw in time from Amiens where his division encountered Allied tanks. Three years earlier, he had seen action in the German advance on Russia and the capture of Roslavl (Smolensk Oblast, western Russia). That winter of 1941, he had contracted an illness related to the bladder and been forced to return to Germany. In November 1942, he was ordered to Stalingrad, wounded and returned to Germany again. In the autumn of 1943, he took over command of the XL Panzer Korps in Nicopol (Russia). By May 1944, he was back in Germany as an inspector of Panzer troops until being appointed commander of Panzer Gruppe West (France) on 10 July.

The day after his capture at the end of July, Eberbach was brought first to Wilton Park, then five days later to Trent Park. Eberbach proved to be another strong character with clear-cut views. He decided to join the 'generals' revolt' as an anti-Nazi. Although he had supported the Nazis for a number of years, he had never been a Party member. He came to recognise the Nazi regime as a criminal body to whom he no longer felt bound by his oath of allegiance.[62] His son, naval Lieutenant Colonel Eberbach, was captured and also taken prisoner. MI19 allowed him to visit his father at Trent Park and noted the son to have 'a fanatical trust in Hitler, although he admitted that he was not a 100% Nazi'.[63]

Fifty-two-year-old General Lieutenant Kurt Badinsky was captured in France on 20 August 1944. A professional soldier and anti-Nazi, he was careful not to display his open objection to the regime. He confessed a loathing of Himmler, called Hitler an ape and condemned Hitler's policy as disastrous.[64] He criticised the senior army command and expected Germany's complete defeat and total collapse. He was held at Trent Park until 23 September 1944.

General von Choltitz captivated the other generals with his tale of the famous Bayeux Tapestry which was being stored in the cellars of the Louvre in Paris. He told them how it was not to leave Europe but, on Hitler's orders, was to be secured for Germany.[65] Von Choltitz painted himself as a hero for saving it from being carried off. He had told his military colleagues, 'The tapestry won't leave Paris as long as I'm there! I'm not going to be party to that under any circumstances.'[66] Even when an SS delegation turned up to take the tapestry, he hid the keys to the cellars and successfully prevented its removal from the capital. Paris was liberated a short time after this incident.

Captured too were 48-year-old Colonel Hans Jay, commander of the Paris defence forces, and 53-year-old Colonel von Unger, Chief of Staff at von Choltitz's headquarters. Von Unger was, according to MI19, 'inclined to throw security to the winds'.[67] Jay was described as 'a very keen horseman who appears to have spent most of his time in Paris in contacting French racehorse owners'; he was relieved to be in Allied hands and had aided the arrests of prominent SS during the liberation of the city.[68]

THE FAKE MEDAL

On 19 September 1944, General Hermann Ramcke was captured in his bunker at Brest and found to be in possession of a large quantity of French brandy and liqueurs, a French mistress, an Irish setter, at least twenty uniforms, and a whole dinner service. Major General Hans von der Mosel was captured with him. They were taken to an airfield near the coast and separated. Ramcke was taken to barracks, surrounded by half a dozen guards and held in isolation. He recalled later: 'An officer with a pistol lying within reach kept watch over me in a room where the walls were covered with pictures of German aircraft. I was kept there for two days completely isolated.'[69]

Ramcke was brought to Wilton Park just two days after capture and housed in a cottage on site, along with Lieutenant Generals Heyking and Heim, and Vice Admiral Weber.[70] He wrote about this period in his memoirs:

> The following morning, I found myself in a small summerhouse in the upper rooms of which I discovered three generals, von Heyking, Heim and Weber. The house was bordered on two sides by high walls, topped by [barbed] wire and very well guarded. Next to the small yard was a tennis court, in some disrepair, upon which we were permitted to stroll. Two office buildings surrounded this area. In the ground floor of the gardener's house were two British soldiers who prepared our meals, which we took together in a small neighbouring room.[71]

Ramcke was a regular soldier who had risen up through the ranks; in MI19 files he is described as being 'inordinately vain and has a most extensive knowledge of distorted history'.[72] Ambitious, ruthless yet naive, he was an opportunist who began to change his views with the decline of the Nazi Party. It was noted that he could have led an underground movement if he felt it benefited him personally. He believed that Germany would go to war again within thirty years, and would fight 'for every stick and stone to the last man, woman and child'.[73] MI19 noted his view that 'it was better to be annihilated honourably, than to be defeated'.[74]

In his assessment of Ramcke, Lieutenant Colonel Corner concluded: 'If there is to be such a thing as a list of specially dangerous men to be kept under surveillance, General Ramcke ought to qualify as one of the first candidates.'[75] Ramcke's rudeness to his batman was recorded by the M Room. Ramcke asked his batman, 'Why are you always doubled up like that?'

> BATMAN: I've had two ribs removed, sir.
> RAMCKE: That's no reason. A lad of eighteen should be able to stand upright even without ribs.[76]

During his career, Ramcke made no secret of the fact that he was determined to win the highest decorations from the Führer, and had striven to do so by recommending his subordinates for high decorations – knowing that he would then have to be awarded higher decorations than them.[77] He did not initially open up in conversation with the other generals.

US interrogator 'Lt Col. Jenkins' (aka Heimwarth Jestin), an expert on German paratroops, was sent to interrogate him. He found Ramcke in the cottage with General von Heyking; the latter had been captured when he wandered too close to the frontline. Ramcke was dismissive of Jestin and boasted that he knew Jestin was an intelligence officer who had been sent to interrogate him. Years later in his memoirs, Ramcke wrote that Lt Col. Jenkins was 'a young American Lt Colonel of a Swedish type and elegantly clothed'.[78] Ramcke recalled his interrogation:

> I listened to some of his questions, without answering before saying, 'Colonel, I am aware that the Commander of the Corregidor fortress near Manila in the Philippines is a prisoner of the Japanese. Do you,

as an American officer, believe it is right if General Wainwright gave details of the organisation and strengths of the US forces?'

He stopped, visibly affected. 'Please don't expect anything different from me as you would expect from your own generals and officers, as I find it insulting'. He changed the subject to generally uninteresting subjects and then let me go.[79]

After the interrogation, Jestin wrote on Ramcke's personal MI19 file that he was 'an egotistical conceited Nazi. He is a firm believer in Hitler'.[80] Jestin found him cold and uncooperative. He needed to find a way for Ramcke to relax and talk. It was Ramcke's love of awards and decorations that played right into the hands of MI19, as Jestin recalled:

Captain Hamilton and myself drafted an artificial press release supposedly from a German newspaper. It announced an award to General Ramcke from Hitler himself, not merely the coveted Order of the Iron Cross, but the very highest level of the Order, the Knight's Cross with diamonds. The citation, which we invented, mentioned the general's bravery in defense of Brest. With this false release in hand and several of his own bottles of cognac, I visited General Ramcke that evening in the cottage. Saluting smartly, I informed Ramcke of the honor Hitler had bestowed upon him and suggested we celebrate the award. I produced the cognac which he did not recognise as his own. Despite obvious pleasure, he declined for a moment or two, but pride in his new distinction overcame his reticence and we proceeded to celebrate in great style.[81]

As more cognac was drunk throughout the evening, the more Ramcke, Heyking and Jestin talked about the superiority of Ramcke as a commander and the reasons why he had received the award.[82] Unfortunately, the generals could hold their drink better than the young American interrogator – for they were used to drinking cognac. By 11 p.m., Jestin found himself rather inebriated and had to call a guard to help him stand up. As Ramcke was spilling the beans, the secret listeners stood up in the M Room and cheered: he had inadvertently given away all the military strategy, details of glider installations, and troop information that Jestin had tried to gain in interrogation.[83] There was a postscript to the story, as Jestin explained:

A few days later, when General Ramcke learned that I was engaged to be married, he generously announced that from his possessions routinely confiscated from prisoners of war, I was to have his Luger and field glasses as a wedding present as well as his case of champagne for the reception. His statement was recorded by the M Room operators and could not be questioned by my commanding officer. The champagne, a rare luxury in war time London, was much enjoyed by the bride (MI19's Catherine Townshend) and groom and their guests.[84]

Ramcke's own version of his wartime decoration for bravery appeared in his memoirs years later:

That evening, he [Lt Col. Jenkins] came to me and General von Heyking. He asked for permission to join us for a little while. He unfolded a newspaper, which contained the news that Hitler had elevated me to the Iron Cross with Diamonds. He congratulated me on the award of this high honour and suggested that it should be celebrated. With the knowledge that our Fatherland was on the brink of collapse, I was in no mood to celebrate anything. The award, which had pleased me above all else, had also the bitter taste of the words, 'In vain, all in vain', which I had heard on the capitulation in 1918. However, with his friendly words, the Lt Colonel took out of his pocket two bottles of cognac which we knocked back with some excitement.[85]

Ramcke died in 1968, and never found out that his medal from the Führer had been fake.

ARNHEM TO ARDENNES

During August and September 1944, interrogation work became intense because of the relentless influx of POWs and senior German officers coming through CSDIC sites. One key priority was for interrogators to urgently locate 9th and 10th SS Panzer Divisions that seemed to have disappeared. They could not be plotted in the map room. Senior German officers captured in this period were interrogated for any knowledge of their whereabouts.

Lieutenant General Otto Elfeldt was captured south of Trun on 20 August 1944, during fighting in the Falaise Pocket. An affable, happy-go-lucky warrior type, with a fairly well-developed sense of humour and an easy manner, he was the first of the German generals to give a Nazi salute on arrival at Trent Park.[86] During interrogation, he was able to confirm the number of German troops that he knew had escaped the Falaise Pocket to fight another day. It included large elements of the Panzer and motorised divisions, but most of the infantry had suffered a dreadful fate there.[87] He stated to British interrogators his willingness to cooperate with Western Allies if Germany was defeated.[88]

Lieutenant General Paul Seyffardt, captured on 7 September 1944, was brought to Trent Park on 21 September, having been held at Wilton Park for ten days.[89] Since February 1944, Seyffardt had been in command of 348 Infantry Division stationed on the coast at Calais. In their character analysis, MI19 established that he took no active part in politics, but believed that one of the big mistakes made by the German Officer Corps was to have allowed themselves to become politically subservient to the Nazi Party.

On the same day as Seyffardt's capture, SS Oberführer Meyer was taken near Liège. The 34-year-old son of a factory worker had worked his way up the ranks of the SS and seen active service in Romania, Greece, Holland, Belgium and France. During late 1941, he was transferred to the Eastern Front until, suffering from jaundice, he was forced to take some sick leave. By 1944, he was back in action and commanded the 12th Panzer Division until wounded and captured by the Americans. During his captivity at Trent Park, details of terrible atrocities committed by him would come to light.

On 8 September, Major General Bock von Wuelfingen decided to surrender to the Allies at Liège rather than have his men wiped out. On arrival at Trent Park, he was assessed as being rather egocentric and not very bright.[90] His main interest appeared to be the survival of the German nobility. He told British army officers that Nazi ideology was firstly against the Jews, secondly against the nobility, and thirdly against professional officers.

Eberhard Wildermuth, the commandant of Le Havre, was wounded before finally being captured on 12 September 1944. He had defended the port and region to the last, resisting all requests by the Allies to surrender. The 54-year-old colonel was, according to MI19, fundamentally a liberal and 'a staunch German patriot, a brave officer, and violently opposed to the present regime'.[91] He showed an eagerness to re-educate the young Nazis and, in his own words, 'lead them back to the truth'.[92] He had been sounded out before the assassination attempt on Hitler and had expressed his willingness to cooperate.

Just days before Operation Market Garden, the Allied airborne assault on Arnhem, progress was made at Wilton Park on the location of the 9th and 10th SS Panzer Divisions from the interrogation of a dispatch rider captured in Belgium. Heimwarth Jestin recalled:

Having noted the exact positions of the SS Panzer Divisions, I immediately sent an urgent message to higher authorities. Nevertheless, a few days later, on 17 September, the British Airborne Division, together with some Polish forces, dropped by parachute and descended by gliders at Arnhem. Immediately they were surrounded and almost totally annihilated by the German panzers hidden in nearby woods ... The Allied losses at Arnhem and Nijmegen and the damage done to the British Armored Division on the road from Neerpeldt are recognised as a major – and unnecessary – disaster.[93]

Jestin never understood why this vital strategic intelligence coming out of Wilton Park just days before Arnhem was ignored. His future wife, Catherine Townshend, also recalled the despair felt in the office at Camp 20 at Wilton Park 'that the airborne operation had not been cancelled or postponed'.[94]

November 1944 saw the capture of Major General Bruhn who had been surrounded by American forces and seized west of Saverne whilst on reconnaissance. During his captivity at Trent Park, he used his time to write an autobiography, from which MI19 was able to extract his full detailed military career. He was seen as 'the most intelligent of the generals, combining personal charm with an air of integrity'.[95] During captivity, he had time to reflect on the brutality of the Nazi regime. He came to see that Germany would lose the war as a result of this brutality and now believed that Nazism had to be rooted out to allow 'good' Germans to put their house in order. He switched allegiance to the anti-Nazis at Trent Park and saw himself as one of the 'good' Germans who must rebuild Germany. Like other senior officers there, he was ardently anti-Communist.

Lieutenant Colonel von der Heydte was unexpectedly captured at Monschau (West Germany) on 23 December 1944, during the German winter offensive that became known as the Battle of the Ardennes. He was brought to Wilton Park four days after capture, and interrogated by Heimwarth Jestin. A Catholic, with a splendid castle, Schloss Egglkofen in Upper Bavaria, the 37-year-old von der Heydte was a professional soldier who had proven his skills as a paratroop commander in France, Italy and Crete. Originally an enthusiastic Nazi, he became disillusioned by 1943/44, turned anti-Nazi and genuinely wished to cooperate with the British in bringing about the end of the war.

Jestin initially found him tough in interrogation: 'A fine officer and gentleman, he was a difficult prisoner of war for me to "break" and I found it was only possible to do so politically.'[96] Von der Heydte felt he had been let down by his troops, and this was the weak point on which Jestin could play. MI19 files say that von der Heydte eventually gave interrogators a significant amount of information on German paratroops in the Ardennes counter-attack, and sketched a plan for an Allied airborne landing in north-west Germany.[97]

Lieutenant General Heinrich Kittel (captured on 22 November 1944, whilst defending Metz) was characterised by MI19 as 'a professional soldier of exceptional intelligence who, in the course of the war, had been connected with most of the major political happenings in Nazi Germany'.[98] He detested the SS and a Nazi state within a state; however while in custody, he was not prepared to go against his oath to Hitler or say anything which might damage the war effort and the Reich. He had 'a strong sense of humour and takes a philosophical outlook on life'.

In April 1942, Kittel had received promotion to the rank of major general and became commandant of Stalino (Ukraine). In August 1942, he was transferred to Rostov as commandant during a period of mass murder of Jews – something which he discussed in some detail with the other generals at Trent Park. Kittel was on the Russian list of war criminals and was held responsible for the poisoning of 18,000 Russians. These were not the only war crimes levelled against him. During his time stationed north of Dvinsk (Latvia), the SS and SD carried out mass executions of Jews in the region. Kittel denied all responsibility for the slaughters.

After capture, many of these military men tried to distance themselves from their past by claiming they were only obeying orders – a defence which would re-emerge during the Nuremberg Trials.[99] Others were not so quick to renounce their Nazi loyalties. Major General Hans von der Mosel, captured at Brest, gave the impression that he was '100% behind the Nazi regime and underlined this fact by a clicking of heels and a Hitler salute'.[100]

A summary intelligence report was eventually written up by CSDIC on the Ardennes Campaign, outlining and analysing the intelligence gained from those commanders with direct experience of it, including Field Marshal von Rundstedt (also being held by CSDIC).[101] He told Kendrick's officers that the campaign was bound to fail because, although the Battle Order had been planned by Hitler and the Wehrmacht High Command (OKW), all counter-proposals were rejected. Under these circumstances, the campaign was bound to fail, commented von Rundstedt.[102]

As the Allies made successful advances through France, secret listener Fritz Lustig received a telephone call from Lieutenant Colonel Cassels, the officer in charge of the M Room. He told Lustig that he was improperly dressed. Lustig did not reveal it, but he knew the phrase to be a jocular way of informing someone of their promotion.

'How is that, sir?' Lustig replied. 'Well, Lustig, I understand that you still have a crown on your sleeve, although now you are a RSM.' Lustig had been promoted to Regimental Sergeant Major or Warrant Officer First Class, the badge of which was a coat-of-arms. He was extremely proud. He had come to England as a refugee from Nazism, and had now reached the most senior non-commissioned rank. Like any officer rank, and ironically like the German generals, he was now entitled to a batman to polish his boots, make his bed and wake him in the morning.

CHAPTER 12

War Crimes and the Holocaust

On 17 December 1942, concern about the fate of Jews in Poland and other Nazi-occupied countries received the full attention of the British parliament when Anthony Eden read the Allied Declaration to the House of Commons. The declaration included words of condemnation from other nations, including the United States, Soviet Union and various governments-in-exile: Belgium, Czechoslovakia, Greece, the Netherlands, Norway, Poland and Yugoslavia. All were united in condemnation, 'in the strongest possible terms of this bestial policy of cold-blooded extermination ... None of those taken away are ever heard of again. The infirm are left to die of exposure and starvation or are deliberately massacred in mass executions.' In reference to the deportation of Jews, MPs were shocked to hear from foreign secretary, Mr Eden: 'I regret to inform the House that reliable reports have recently reached His Majesty's government regarding the barbarous and inhuman treatment to which Jews are being subjected in German-occupied Europe.'

The House rose to its feet for a two-minute silence for the victims of Nazism. At London's Wigmore Hall, the Women's International Zionist Organization was being addressed by Prime Minister Churchill's wife. She referred to Hitler's 'satanic design to exterminate the Jewish people in Europe'. Affirming complete solidarity, she told the female audience: 'I wish to associate with you in all your grief, and I pray your meeting may help to keep the attention of the British people focussed upon the terrible events which have occurred and are impending in Nazi Europe.'

At MI9/MI19's secret bugging sites, details of war crimes were overheard from lower-rank prisoners at Latimer House and Wilton Park, and the generals at Trent Park.[1] In his summary intelligence report for the first six months of 1942, Kendrick wrote that most prisoners spoke about the severity of German measures in Poland.[2] General von Thoma was well aware of the horrors and spoke about it to his fellow generals in bugged conversations in 1942.[3] He argued that the name of Germany had been disgraced by the mass extermination programme and Germany would have to pay. The intelligence report noted:

He [von Thoma] describes the Warsaw ghetto, where every presentable Jewish woman was pregnant, and talks of the brutalisation of German youth. Atrocities by the SS against the population of Kiev, Minsk, and in the Crimea were mentioned today (shooting of women and children). Von Thoma saw one man himself who said: 'Today I've killed 400 people. I can't go on, I've had enough.'[4]

The bulk of detailed information on war crimes came in bugged conversations from 1943. MI19 amassed substantial evidence that covered most of what is known today about the Holocaust and concentration camps.[5]

Horst Minnieur, a 21-year-old seaman gave an eye-witness account of executions in Lithuania to his cellmate (a U-boat crewman): 'They had to strip to their shirts and the women to their vests and knickers and then they were shot by the Gestapo. All the Jews there were executed ... Believe me, if you had seen it, it would have made you shudder.'[6]

Kendrick's summary reports noted that a German prisoner spoke about 300,000 civilians shot; another that boys and girls had been killed.[7] There was talk of 'armed conflict between the SS and members of the other armed forces because the latter would not commit atrocities, and mention too of the suffering of Jews in the Lodz ghetto'.[8] One prisoner, whose sister had worked in a hospital in Lodz, spoke about 'the poverty and disease amongst the people, their complete disillusionment and the rigid control exercised by the SS who supervised the hospital'.[9]

A German parachutist (A1373) told his cellmate that 80,000 Jews were shot at Lublin in Poland: 50,000 were shot first, followed by 30,000 more Jews who had been brought in from Germany.[10] Pilot Dette (a blockade runner, captured 29 December 1943) relayed the story that he was

… driving back in his car from visiting some staff near Lvov and at the side of the road they heard shots. They approached and found about two hundred Jews, the men in just their pants and the women in knickers and brassieres … Some of the women had children in their arms. They were all shot in the back of the head, two rounds with a tommy-gun. We shall have to pay for that.[11]

EVIDENCE FROM PRISONER HAUPTMANN

German parachutist rank of Hauptmann (Captain), captured in Italy on 18 October 1943, provided the most information from a single prisoner about the extent of the Nazi genocide. Many transcripts survive of his conversations with a British army officer who was a fluent German speaker. He was given the codename M350 by MI19.[12] All that was noted about him was his claim to have been a fugitive after shooting a Nazi official in Hamburg. MI19 was not sure what to make of some of his statements in interrogation and, unusually, added to his transcripts: 'He has given a certain amount of information, some of which appears to be accurate and some highly improbable. His statements should therefore be treated with reserve.'

With the benefit of hindsight, it can now be shown that M350 was remarkably accurate. He spoke to a British army officer about Sachsenhausen and Dachau concentration camps, and told him that Sachsenhausen had seven to eight thousand people there and considerably more in Dachau.[13] The British officer asked him if there were only three concentration camps, to which M350 replied, 'Oh, there are a lot.'

In a separate conversation that day, possibly with the same British officer, M350 talked about Hitler's use of 'stud farms' to breed a pure Aryan German race.[14] This was part of the regime's *Lebensborn* programme to create a perfect master race. Such breeding camps or 'farms' existed across Nazi-occupied Europe. M350 explained that good German girls agreed to conceive a child with an SS officer. A few days before the girl went into labour, she was taken to one of the special 'stud farms' where the baby was born. The baby was immediately surrendered to the Nazi regime and the mother never saw her child again. Hauptmann commented that '[the baby] is looked upon as a child of the Führer'.[15]

The British army officer (below, BAO) probed further: 'Are these SS men specially selected?'

> M350: It's a thoroughbred stud farm. They are the military stallions. I know a BdM leader [League of German Girls] who has already presented the Führer with two children.
> BAO: Are only SS men employed as 'stallions'?
> M350: Yes.
> BAO: Is there no 'stud fee'?
> M350: No.
> BAO: Can the SS man select the girl?
> M350: Hmm. That's of no importance.

M350 confirmed that the girls were examined beforehand to see if they were suitable breeding stock. The British army officer asked, 'Was there a parade of "stallions" beforehand or afterwards, in order to entice the girls?'

M350 laughed. 'Unfortunately not. They are men from the Führer's bodyguard. They do that as a single line. While other men go to brothels, they go to this stud farm. There's a better selection.'

The above transcripts lay in classified government files at the National Archives until the late 1990s. In the 1980s, the first details of these breeding farms became public knowledge from a different source, when some of the children who had been fathered by SS officers and had lived a life of shame and trauma, decided to reveal their shocking past. What the MI19 files demonstrate is that British intelligence knew of the existence of 'stud farms' long before the survivors came forward. The transcripts also independently corroborate the testimonies of the women who had succumbed to the Nazi breeding programme.

The significance of these conversations is that British intelligence knew of this shocking 'breeding programme' at the time it was happening – something that would not be known by the public for some forty years. It serves to underline, too, that the information in the bugged conversations was remarkably accurate and not fabricated by the prisoners. MI19's bugging operation proved to be reliable not just for military and technical information, but also regarding the lives of Germans.

PRISONER M320

On 31 October 1943, an SS officer was brought to Latimer House after capture in Italy. He was no ordinary SS officer, but from one of Hitler's infamously brutal and merciless death squads – Einsatz-Kommando 3, Sicherheits-Polizei (Security Police). Holding a rank equivalent to sergeant major, this SS Hauptscharführer came from one of the highest positions in Hitler's Secret Police. Special reports generated from the M Room merely give him the codename M320. In an unguarded conversation with another POW (named M322) he spoke about Auschwitz. His cellmate appears not to have heard of it, but certainly knew about other concentration camps.

> M320: I know the Auschwitz concentration camp in Poland by hearsay. Actually you can see it from the train. It is a hutted camp for Jews. I heard say that there's a crematorium there, and that no one who enters the camp comes out alive.
>
> M322: I heard a lot in Vienna about Mauthausen.
>
> M320: I personally haven't seen any concentration camp, apart from Auschwitz, which I saw from the train. It's not far from Cracow.
>
> M322: Oh, down there.
>
> M320: Yes. When you go through by train you can see it.
>
> M322: Were mainly Jews sent there?
>
> M320: Yes. I should be interested to know what they have done with all the Jews in the Reich, and then the ones from Austria, since

they started to get rid of the Jews. I wonder whether they've slaughtered them?[16]

In a different conversation, this time with a British army officer (below, BAO), M320 spoke at length about mass executions by firing squads in the village of Ananyev in the province of Kherson, and referred to the shooting of as many as 5,000 Jews there in a single day.[17]

BAO: How many people were shot at a time?

M320: They were always shot in groups of ten.

BAO: With tommy-guns?

M320: With rifles. One man to each. Ten men with rifles to ten –

BAO: Did they simply fall down into trenches or what?

M320: Yes. They had to get down into a trench – it was a kind of anti-tank trench. It was about two and a half to three metres deep and wide as this room, we'll say. You had to shoot down at them from above.

BAO: Were they all killed instantaneously?

M320: Yes. There were men with tommy-guns who finished them off. The cars drove away one after the other and they could see the others being taken up and shot, and they knew that it might be their turn next. You'd see a woman holding a little child on each of her arms, and she might be pregnant as well – and there were whole families.[18]

M320 was one of the longest-held lower-rank prisoners at Latimer House, possibly because of his position in the SS death squad. He was still being questioned by British intelligence into 1944.

MOBILE GAS TRUCKS

Bugged conversations revealed that the Nazi regime used mobile gas trucks to kill Jews before the gas chambers were constructed in the concentration camps.[19] In 1942, Luftwaffe officer Heimer told his cellmate:

They [Jews] were taken right through to Poland, and just before they reached their destination they pumped in some sort of stuff, some sort of gas, cool gas or nitrogen gas – anyway some odourless gas. That put them all to sleep. It was nice and warm. Then they were pulled out and buried. That's what they did with thousands of Jews! (*laughs*)[20]

On 12 October 1943, a conversation was recorded between a naval lieutenant and transport officer (of a Panzer Regiment) which provided one of the earliest references to mobile gas trucks amongst lower-rank prisoners. The transport officer had visited a concentration camp and witnessed the mass deportation of Jews from Berlin in 1940. He said:

In Poland, they are called reprisal measures for atrocities … Killed off indiscriminately, some shot in the neck and with some they did it more simply, they pretended to drive them to work in closed lorries and on the way they all died of the exhaust gases which filled the lorry … The Polish intelligentsia also, and the great landowners and so on, were decimated in revenge.[21]

On Christmas Day 1943, British forces captured a lieutenant of Nebeltruppe, 56 Regiment, in Italy. By March 1944, he had been brought to one of Kendrick's centres and a British army officer primed to converse with him about war crimes. The prisoner was designated M363 in reports and spoke about a special SS Kommando unit at Simferopol. He revealed that the SS unit ordered Jews to hand over their belongings and were told that they were being transferred by truck to another location.[22] In reality, he explained, they were going to be ushered into the mobile gas lorries. This corroborated information already given by other prisoners and was held to be reliable.

Prisoner M320 told the British army officer that he had seen the use of mobile gas trucks to kill Jews at Theodosia and Sudak:

BAO: How many do you think were killed there?

M320: There was talk of about fifteen hundred at Theodosia.

BAO: A great many were said to have been killed at Simferopol, weren't they?

M320: They even spoke of sixteen thousand there.[23]

On 23 February 1944, another important conversation about the gas trucks was recorded. This time, M320 spoke in detail of exactly how the early Nazi killing machine worked. He had first noticed it when he was stationed at Sudak and travelled to Theodosia to collect stores. He told a British army officer:

M320: I saw the gas lorry there for the first time and how the people were shoved in, and then I was interested to find out what kind of a lorry it was. It was explained to me that it was a gas lorry – that exhaust gases were used in it. There had been some talk earlier of the existence of such a lorry, but I hadn't seen it before. The people were told some tale about being taken to another place, so they climbed into the back of the truck.[24]

BAO: Were they men, women and children?

M320: Yes. Once they were inside they were shut in, the engine was turned on, and in a few minutes they are dead.

BAO: How long does the engine run?

M320: Ten minutes, and in four, or at most five minutes, they should be dead.

BAO: What happens then?

M320: They are then driven away, buried and –

BAO: Where were they buried, do you know?

M320: Generally in anti-tank ditches.

BAO: Where were the anti-tank ditches?

M320: They were in various places. One was between Starikrim and Saaly and then there were some more in the direction of Kerch ... I saw a large anti-tank ditch about 3 or 4 km away from Kherson. There was a hell of a lot of corpses there.

BAO: When was that?

M320: That was round about August/September, 1942. The Teilkommando was then disbanded and others from Einsatzgruppe C then took over the area and Einsatzgruppe D moved on further ...

This transcript provides a source of evidence about the mobile SS death squads 'Einsatzgruppe C' and 'Einsatzgruppe D' that carried out mass executions of Jews in Nazi-occupied areas.

At Trent Park, information about the mobile gas trucks was also picked up from the unguarded conversations of the generals. On one occasion Köhncke spoke about the trucks and said, 'Would you ever have thought it possible, sir, that the German people would fit up gas cars in order to kill people?'[25] Cramer replied: 'I didn't believe that at first either, but one must believe it now. It is true.'

In a different conversation, Generals Rothkirch and Ramcke said that 'all the gassing institutions' were near Lvov in Poland.[26] He admitted that the gassings were by no means the worst and that he had been interrogated about them by British officers at Trent Park. Rothkirch denied responsibility, but the conversations showed that he did nothing to prevent them either. He told Ramcke:

To start with the people dug their own graves ... Thousands of people were shot. Afterwards they gave that up and gassed them. Many of them weren't dead and a layer of earth was shovelled on in between. They had packers there who packed the bodies in, because they fell in too soon. The SS did that, they were the people who packed the corpses in.[27]

He explained to Ramcke how children were taken by the neck and shot with a revolver and said: 'in Lvov, just like people catching fish with a net, ten SS men would walk along the street and simply grab any Jews who happened to be walking along. If you happened to look Jewish, you were just added to their catch (*laughs*).'[28]

These particular conversations are historically significant because they demonstrate that British intelligence knew about the mobile gas trucks being used to kill Jews at least three to four years before their terrible use became public knowledge. Until the declassification of these files, the only knowledge of the mobile gas trucks came after the liberation of the camps in 1945.

SS MUTINY AGAINST THE REGIME

The involvement of the SS and death squads in the annihilation of Jews has been well documented; but the M Room material has revealed something previously unknown. In early July 1943, secret listeners at Latimer House recorded a conversation between a British army officer and a prisoner in the rank of lance corporal, codenamed M222, who had been captured in Tunisia. M222 described two separate mutinies amongst SS guards in an unnamed concentration camp prior to 1937. Nothing like this has ever come to light before and, if true, requires a re-evaluation of previous knowledge about the SS and resistance to the atrocities. The two attempted mutinies occurred in the period before Hitler's formulation of the Final Solution and before the concentration camps in Poland were constructed. Because of the importance of the conversation, it is quoted at length below. A British army officer asked M222:

BAO: What sort of people were these SS men? Had they been criminals or – ?

M222: No. They were people from outside, who happened to be in the SS; they had all volunteered as guards. I have sometimes spoken to some of them. They said they didn't all get work immediately. Several were there for three or four days or a week and then went off again. Others felt really happy there … In 1936, at Easter, or I believe it was 1937, some of the guards even fired on each other.

BAO: Why was that?

M 222: We were told that this is what happened. There were three guard platoons with 100 men in each, making 300 in all. It was the turn of one platoon to be on guard every third day, the second had to go out with the working party, and the third was off duty. It was, so to speak, standing-by. It was resting. Round about midday shooting suddenly started: one platoon was trying to disarm the guards and let us out, but that wouldn't have succeeded in any case.[29]

The exact identity of M222 is not given in the files. He appears to have been a guard or SS officer in the camp. There was a similar incident a couple of years prior to that. There are gaps in the conversation where the listeners were unable to distinguish some of the words.

M222: Shortly before Christmas 1935, we had sixty men killed. It happened like this. It was pretty cold and had snowed a little too, and, as sometimes happens, for we only had on our thin blue uniforms . . . When a sentry saw that, he said: 'Come here, if you're cold!' Then he had some sort of things erected on the grass and they had to get on them with their caps off and stand at attention with their faces to the wall. In the course of time, there may have been about twelve figures standing there. I don't know how it happened, but at any rate one man said: 'That's too much of a good thing in this cold.' Then one of the sentries said. 'They are mutinying!' and as soon as he shouted: 'They are mutinying!' they fired into them with their machine guns. Then the camp commandant came out. A whole number of us had been killed. You can well imagine that when you are all working bunched together one beside the other and they fire into you with machine guns, there are bound to be some killed. The camp commandant had a look at things and then he said: 'The remainder will be shot.' The remainder, there may have been about a hundred of them or a little more, I can't remember exactly, were to be shot too. He said it was mutiny.[30]

M222 said that in another camp: 'Many of them [SS] were killed; you have no idea how many SS men were shot there [in the camps].'[31]

The conversation highlights that British intelligence was interested in information about SS involvement in war crimes, but also in at least two previously unknown SS mutinies against the regime. The concentration camp is not named, but enquiries by the author to the archivists at Dachau and Sachsenhausen confirmed no trace of a mutiny there. It could possibly have happened at Bergen Belsen which was built as a large military complex from 1935. The workers were housed in camps near Fallingbostel. It became a prisoner-of-war camp, before being extended to be a concentration camp.

The transcript leaves unanswered questions: what provoked the first mutiny? Was there any sense amongst these SS guards that the killing of Jews and political opponents was wrong? Did the mutiny occur for other reasons? What does emerge is that for a short time, some men of an SS battalion in a concentration camp 'broke out' emotionally against the situation in which they found themselves. Where the two mutinies took place still remains an open question.

Interrogators were primed to ask about the Nazi killing machine and the concentration camps.[32] An example of one such detailed interrogation took place in September 1944 when a Czech POW, who had been conscripted into the German army from Dachau concentration camp, was captured by the Allies at Brettenville in France on 13 August 1944. During interrogation, he gave comprehensive information about conditions in Dachau and, in particular, the experiments that he was subjected to by a German air force experimental station in the camp. It makes for particularly difficult reading.[33]

British intelligence intended to hold the Nazi regime accountable and ensure justice would be carried out at the end of the war.[34] The focus was not limited to gathering military, political and operational intelligence.

Perhaps most surprising amongst MI19 files are the detailed sketches of the layout of concentration camps, drawn by prisoners who had first-hand experience of them. Sketched plans of Dachau and Auschwitz date from September 1944 – at least four to six months before the liberation of the concentration camps.[35] It is not known what British intelligence intended to do with these ground plans, but they are comprehensive and show the barracks, prisoners' huts, the crematoria, SS barracks and brothel, railway lines into the camps and the perimeter fences. The liberation of the concentration camps in 1945 showed these maps to have been remarkably accurate.

WAR CRIMES IN POLAND AND RUSSIA

The flip side of the farcical life and political power-struggles of the generals had a deeply dark and disturbing aspect. The bugged conversations provided further evidence of the systematic extermination of Europe's Jews and killing of Russians and Poles. The unguarded conversations of the generals revealed to the intelligence services that Germany's military commanders not only knew about the war crimes committed, but some were complicit in it. The transcripts are significant because they dispel the long-held view that the Wehrmacht (German army) played no part in the Holocaust.[36] For decades, the German army's reputation had remained intact. Shockingly, Hitler's generals did not only boast about the number of people killed, but often spoke in chilling and graphic detail.[37]

The generals realised that as the Allies advanced through Nazi-occupied territories, it was only a matter of time before they would reach the areas where mass atrocities had been committed. In April 1943, a conversation was recorded between General von Thoma and Crüwell. Von Thoma said: 'The Poles have been making enquiries about the murdering of the 8,000 officers in Russia. That business will cause a lot more unpleasantness, but that is of no consequence in this war. I expect the Russians will open up the graves of the Jews in Sebastopol and Odessa some time!'[38]

On 10 July 1943, Neuffer was overheard saying to Bassenge:

What will they say when they find our graves in Poland? The OGPU [Russian Intelligence] can't have done anything worse than that.

I myself have seen a convoy at Ludowice, near Minsk. I must say it was frightful, a horrible sight. There were lorries full of men, women and children – quite small children. It is ghastly, this picture. The women, the little children who were, of course, absolutely unsuspecting – frightful! Of course, I didn't watch while they were being murdered …
The German Jews were also sent to the Minsk district and were gradually killed off …[39]

After hearing the BBC Midnight news in German on 19 December 1943, the same two generals were recorded, speculating on the number of Jews killed so far:

> BASSENGE: They dished up the mass executions of Jews in Poland. They estimate here that altogether five million Jews – Polish, Bulgarian, Dutch, Danish and Norwegian – have been massacred.
> NEUFFER: Really? Not counting the German ones?
> BASSENGE: Including the German Jews, during the whole time. They furnished evidence that an enormous number from camp so-and-so between such-and-such a date, fifteen thousand here, eighteen thousand there, twelve thousand there, six thousand and so on – I must say that if 10 per cent of it is correct, then one ought to –
> NEUFFER: I should have thought about three million.
> BASSENGE: You know, it really is a disgrace.[40]

Cavendish Bentinck at the Foreign Office received a copy of the above transcript. In response, he wrote to Norman Crockatt (the head of MI9) with a specific request:

> I notice that Generals Neuffer and Bassenge are disquieted at the prospect of the Russians reaching places where the Germans carried out large scale liquidation of Jews, Poles and Russians. We [at Foreign Office] should be grateful if you would try to find out from your guests by the various means at your disposal exactly where these places are.

We can then give the Russians some spots to carry out exhumations, and shall perhaps hear less about Katyn, which has begun to pall.[41]

In a different conversation, General Felbert asked Kittel whether he knew of places where Jews had been taken to be executed. Kittel answered: 'Yes.'[42]

Felbert asked whether it was carried out systematically. Kittel again replied: 'Yes.' Felbert said: 'Women and children?' Kittel replied: 'Everyone.' The conversation continued:

FELBERT: Were they loaded into trains?

KITTEL: If only they had been loaded into trains! The things I've experienced! For instance in Latvia, near Dvinsk, there were mass executions of Jews carried out by the SS or Security Service. There were about fifteen Security Service men and perhaps sixty Latvians who are known to be the most brutal people in the world … Three hundred men had been driven out of Dvinsk; they dug a trench – men and women dug a communal grave and then marched home. The next day along they came again – men, women and children – they were counted off and stripped naked; the executioners first laid all the clothes in one pile. Then twenty women had to take up their position, naked, on the edge of the trench. They were shot and fell down into it.

FELBERT: How was it done?

KITTEL: They faced the trench and then twenty Latvians came up behind and simply fired once through the back of their heads … I went away and said: 'I'm going to do something about this.' I got into my car and went to this Security Service man and said: 'Once and for all, I forbid these executions outside, where people can look on. If you shoot people in the wood or somewhere where no one can see, that's your own affair. But I absolutely forbid another day's shooting there. We draw our drinking water from deep springs; we're getting nothing but corpse water there.'

FELBERT: What did they do to the children?

KITTEL (*very excited*): They seized three-year-old children by their hair, held them up and shot them with a pistol and then threw them in. I saw that for myself.[43]

Kittel explained that although the orders were given by Germans, the slaughter was executed by the Latvians. He continued: 'The Jews were brought in and then robbed. There was a terrific bitterness against the Jews at Dvinsk, and the [local] people simply gave vent to their rage.'[44]

In the common room, after a German radio broadcast about Nazi barbarism in Russia, General Broich admitted to von Choltitz and Rothkirch: 'We shot women as if they had been cattle.'[45] Broich explained how he had seen a large quarry where ten thousand men, women and children were shot the previous day. He commented: 'We drove out on purpose to see it. The most bestial thing I ever saw.' Von Choltitz said: 'One day after Sebastopol had fallen – whilst I was on my way back to Berlin – I flew back with the Chief of Staff, the CO of the airfield was coming up to me, when we heard shots. I asked whether a firing practice was on. He answered, "Good Lord, I'm not supposed to tell, but they've been shooting Jews here for days now."'[46] Von Choltitz told the other generals, 'The Führer gave orders, shouting at me furiously, that a report be sent him every day in which at least a thousand Jews were shot.'

Rothkirch asked, 'Only in Germany, or where?'

Von Choltitz replied, 'No – everywhere. I presumed he meant Poland. 36,000 Jews from Sebastopol were shot.'[47]

General von Thoma spoke about atrocities perpetrated by the SS and mass executions at Minsk. He confessed to Crüwell that he would not have believed it if he had not seen the executions himself, and added, 'No one can accuse me of having been in any way responsible for it … Orders were actually given that all Jews were [to be cleared out of] the occupied territories – that is the great idea, but, of course, there are so many in the east that you don't know where to start.'[48]

Reimann talked about being present when the Russians were being transported from Korosten, outside Lvov:

> They were driven like cattle from the trucks to the drinking troughs and bludgeoned to keep their ranks. There were troughs at the stations; they rushed to them and drank like beasts; after that they were given just a bit of something to eat. Then they were again driven into the wagons. There were sixty or seventy men in one cattle truck! … [At the stations] children came up and brought them pumpkins to eat. They threw the pumpkins in, and then all you heard was a terrific din like the roaring of wild animals in the trucks. They were probably killing each other. That finished me.[49]

Elfeldt and Meyer spoke about the shooting of whole innocent Russian families. Elfeldt called it 'an outrageous business!'[50]

ADMISSION OF GUILT

In an astonishing turn of events, the generals divulged their own guilt to each other. In a conversation recorded on 29 August 1944, von Choltitz confessed to von Thoma: 'The worst job I ever carried out – which, however, I carried out with great consistency – was the liquidation of the Jews. I carried out this order down to the very last detail.'[51]

Von Thoma's reply laid the blame on Hitler for issuing the orders, as he sniggered: 'Ha! Ha! Ha! It's a good thing that you can now produce such unimpeachable proofs.' Even von Thoma's laughter was written on the transcript of the conversation.

Two months later, the secret listeners picked up another frank admission from von Choltitz: 'We are also to blame. We have cooperated and have almost taken the Nazis seriously . . . I've persuaded my men to believe in this nonsense … I feel thoroughly ashamed of myself. May be we are far more to blame than those uneducated cattle [the Nazis].'[52] Von Choltitz appeared only to express remorse after he knew he could face charges of war crimes and the death penalty.

General Liebenstein told von Thoma, 'We once shot forty thousand Poles in a concentration camp.'[53] Von Thoma replied, 'Out at Dachau in 1940 were a great part of the Polish intelligentsia, university professors, doctors, lawyers – that's the pathological part of it, this mania.' In a separate conversation, von Thoma said the killings were committed on Hitler's orders.[54]

Neuffer and Bassenge discussed crimes committed by the German army.[55] Bassenge told Neuffer that the Goering Regiment was a wild lot.

'I know officially,' Bassenge said, 'because part of the paratroops were formed from the Goering Regiment.'

'Did they commit murders?' asked Neuffer.

'Yes,' replied Bassenge. 'They secretly condemned and murdered people in the barracks and the officers took part.'

In September 1944, General Eberbach and his son discussed the killing of Jews in these terms:

EBERBACH (senior): In my opinion, one can even go so far as to say that the killing of those million Jews or however many it was, was necessary in the interests of our people. But to kill women and children wasn't necessary. That is going too far.

EBERBACH (junior): Well, if you are going to kill off the Jews, then kill the women and children too, or the children at least. There is no need to do it publicly, but what good does it do me to kill off the old people?

EBERBACH (senior): Well, simply that it is contrary to humanity, in the end it hits back at you, simply because it instils a certain brutality into the people.[56]

Other senior officers spoke about the struggle to liquidate the Warsaw Ghetto. Seyffardt commented to Heyking and Admiral Tresckow: 'For three whole weeks, they [a Panzer division] fought behind the front, with tanks and everything, against the Jews. The Jews had 8.8 anti-tank guns and everything … A whole division. In order to suppress the Jews in the ghetto!'[57]

How much did the generals know about the concentration camps and how early? Their discussion in May 1945 reveals the true extent of their knowledge:

> DITTMAR [*re. concentration camps*]: What did we know about them?
>
> SCHLIEBEN: Everybody knew that dreadful things happened in them – not exactly what, but just that dreadful things happened – every one of us knew that as far back as '35.
>
> ELFELDT: We knew [what happened] in Poland to the hundreds and thousands of Jews who, as time went by, disappeared, were sent away from Germany and who after '39 were said to be accommodated in ghettos and settlements in Poland.
>
> SCHLIEBEN: They all disappeared.
>
> ELFELDT: Whoever got to know that millions of these people – as the Russians now assert – perished or were burnt in Auschwitz and whatever these small places are called?
>
> BROICH: Certainly none of us.
>
> ELFELDT: We heard about Auschwitz when we were in Poland.
>
> BROICH: I visited Dachau personally in '37.[58]

Lieutenant General Feuchtinger, who was captured in Hamburg on 3 May 1945, had not previously believed it possible for mass shootings in the thousands to have been carried out until he himself visited Pinsk (now in Belarus) where he was told that:

> The previous year there had still been 25,000 Jews living there and within three days, these 25,000 Jews were fetched out, formed up on the edge of a wood or in a meadow – they had been made to dig their own graves beforehand – and then every single one of them from the oldest grey-beard down to the new-born infant was shot by a police squad.[59]

Apparently that was the first time Feuchtinger had heard about mass executions. Likewise, Bodenschatz said that he knew about the expulsion of Jews from Germany in the 1930s but not of the concentration camps and killings.[60] He spoke about the looted works of art and where they were being taken and how.[61]

It became apparent that ordinary Germans knew much more about what was going on than they were prepared to admit to the Allies after the war:

> HEYDTE: There's another camp which is even worse than Lublin. It's in Czechoslovakia. Half-a-million people have been put to death there for *certain*. I know that *all* the Jews from Bavaria were taken there. Yet the camp never became over-crowded.
> WILDERMUTH: Yes, I've heard of that too.
> HEYDTE: But I don't only know that all the Jews from Bavaria were taken there. I know that all the Jews from Austria were taken there, and still the camp wasn't over-crowded.
> WILDERMUTH: From all over Germany. It appears that most of the Jews from Germany were either sent to Lublin or to that place.[62]

The generals unwittingly revealed how far Hitler was prepared to go to create his vision of a pure Aryan race. Those who did not fit the Nazi ideal of racial perfection were singled out for annihilation. Wildermuth, Broich, Elfeldt and Wahle had an intense discussion on the subject. Wildermuth said he had evidence at his disposal that led him to estimate that '70,000 to 80,000 mental defectives had been put to death'.[63]

Seyffardt said he 'knew about the liquidation of the insane'.[64] Secret listeners overheard him telling other generals:

> There was a provincial lunatic asylum near Baden-Baden where there were harmless lunatics who worked in the vineyards, but who were no use for anything else. Then one day, they all suddenly died. Then, after they had turned it into a hospital for people who had limbs

amputated, they put up a huge notice board: *From lunatic asylum to a home for cripples – Adolf Hitler.*[65]

Even today, decades later, it is alarming to read the transcripts of eyewitnesses describing in such detail how the Final Solution was carried out. The evidence from prisoners' conversations raises pertinent questions today. With such a knowledge of the Final Solution and genocide, why did the Allies not bomb the railway lines to the camps? It is a legitimate question that requires further scholarship. The M Room intelligence establishes firmly on record precisely what information was being picked up by British intelligence, and how early – namely, as early as 1940.[66] Gathering intelligence had moved beyond the realm of political judgment and military secrets to cataloguing Hitler's annihilation programme for the Jews of Europe in readiness for the Nuremberg Trials at the end of hostilities. There was every expectation that the perpetrators would face justice for their war crimes.

CHAPTER 13

Breaking the German Will to Resist

On New Year's Day 1945, the German air force mounted Operation Bodenplatte – an attack by 700 German fighter aircraft, aimed at crippling the Allied air forces stationed in liberated Belgium, Holland and France. The German objective was to regain air supremacy that had been lost earlier in the war. It failed and was to be the last major air offensive by Germany. At the time, Allied forces were making preparations for the final push towards the invasion of Germany. At CSDIC headquarters at Latimer House, there was a frenzy of activity as a German Group Commodore captured during Operation Bodenplatte was imminently expected on site.[1]

'There have never been so many guests. All the cells are full,' wrote interrogator Matthew Sullivan. 'Fifty German names have been chalked on the blackboard in the main office with their units, interrogators and report editors.'[2] Felkin and the interrogators uncovered details of another unnamed operation by German night fighters. 'Carmichael', the blonde ATS driver, was dispatched to Bomber Command with urgent papers. Felkin called a meeting to summarise Operation Bodenplatte and said it had been 'a brave show, well-planned, but poorly executed because of the inexperience of the German pilots'.

The Group Commodore finally arrived in a closed, unmarked van. An Austrian and a defiant Nazi, he was escorted straight to his cell. Felkin left him to stew for a while, before sending interrogator Sullivan (aka 'Forrest') to make polite conversation with him.[3] When Sullivan raised an issue of politics, the Group Commodore exploded and started to shout at him, saying: 'I'd rather fight to the last drop of my blood and die in the snow, than live again those days of poverty and unemployment.'[4] The Nazi kept up his aggressive front, accusing the American forces of opening fire on German pilots who bailed out. The whole conversation was picked up by the secret listeners from the M Room.

Interrogator 'Forrest' left the cell. His two American co-interrogators were briefed on the prisoner's views. They stormed into the cell and, according to Sullivan, 'blow so much air about him that he [the prisoner] apologises for his general behaviour.'[5] The prisoner continued to hold out against all attempts to undermine him, but was relieved when, late that evening, Felkin invited him into his sitting room for a whisky. Slowly, the breaking-down of the prisoner began to work. A trip into London further undermined the prisoner's confidence that Germany had bombed England into submission; meanwhile Felkin appeared to be the only friend in the camp who could protect the prisoner from the 'unfriendly Americans' who wanted to have him court-martialled. Around midnight on 21 January, the prisoner finally caved in – three weeks after capture.

LIFE AT TRENT PARK

The generals continued to try to improve their conditions. Bassenge made a request to Lord Aberfeldy for cinema tickets to attend performances in central London, there was a petition for extra cigarettes for the batmen, and a request was made for new uniforms to be brought over from Germany for the batmen.[6]

Von Thoma declared that he was enjoying his life as a POW. The intelligence report for the week of 11 January 1945 noted: 'Von Thoma denounces Gestapo rule in Germany; embarks on the story of the beginnings of the Party, but is interrupted by the tea gong.'[7] He began to criticise the slow progress of the Allies through the Netherlands and towards the invasion of Germany.

On 23 February 1945, General von der Heydte arrived at Trent Park from Wilton Park. The other generals were interested in his military experiences, and asked him to deliver a lecture on the history and operations of the German airborne forces, which he duly gave in Sir Philip Sassoon's former dining room.[8]

The following month, Lord Aberfeldy wrote from 'Trent Park Camp, Barnet' to Captain Evans (MI19) that General von Thoma had had a slight heart attack late the previous evening and a stimulant had been administered.[9] The medical officer had advised that the attacks were likely to recur and he might even have a stroke. Lord Aberfeldy wrote: 'He must not excite himself but, of course, all these innumerable internal rows in this camp, do not tend to keep him calm – and the mere mention of the word Hitler sets him off ... We never have a dull moment here, do we?'[10]

NEGOTIATING PEACE

With the impending defeat of Nazi Germany, MI19 and Chiefs of Staff had already mulled over plans to use the anti-Nazi clique of German generals at Trent Park.[11] Could the generals be persuaded to broadcast to Germany and bring an end to the war?

Lord Aberfeldy submitted a list to Lieutenant Colonel Rawlinson (head of MI19), with the names of senior German officers whom he felt would cooperate.[12] In such an undertaking, only a high-ranking British commander would appeal to their egos. It was decided to dispatch General Sir Andrew Thorne (General Officer, Commander-in-Chief, Scottish Command) to Trent Park. He arrived on 3 April and met with Eberbach, Bassenge and Wildermuth.

General Thorne began by reassuring the generals that the discussion between them would remain secret. He explained that he was acting on the instructions of General Eisenhower to 'enlist their cooperation in putting an end to the senseless slaughter and annihilation that was taking place at a time when there could be no other possible outcome of the war but the defeat of Germany.'[13] The radio networks of the British Empire and America would be at their disposal to make a historic broadcast asking their nation to surrender.

In response, the generals made several points: first, they recognised the inevitable defeat of their country and they would do all in their power to avert unnecessary bloodshed. However, their hands were tied because of reprisals that would be taken against their own families, and so they could not agree to their names being used publicly.[14]

Second, they argued that the military men with the real power (Field Marshals von Rundstedt, Kluge and Kesselring) had not been captured.

Third, they feared that, with the end of the war, German soldiers could be held as prisoners for years, with some even being deported to Russia. Seeing how brutally the Russians treated POWs, they argued that German soldiers would rather die in battle than face the prospect of being a POW in Russian hands.

The following evening at dinner, von Thoma made an announcement to the other generals about the meeting. His speech was recorded via the bugging devices hidden in the dining room. A hushed room turned its attention to von Thoma's speech, which was recorded word for word in the M Room:

> The Camp Commandant approached me requesting that General Eberbach, General Bassenge, Colonel Wildermuth and myself attend a conference on post-war questions with an English general, an emissary from General Eisenhower … The conference took place yesterday afternoon. They were asked to say whether they would be prepared to draw up and sign a proclamation to the Wehrmacht to lay down its arms. The proclamation would be broadcast by means of the radio and leaflets. They turned it down with one accord. I am in complete agreement with their point of view…[15]

The subsequent reactions over the dinner table were recorded by the secret listeners. Eberbach told Elfeldt that the focus should be on trying to persuade the Allies to stop using the term 'unconditional surrender' which was bad propaganda for soldiers who had been defending the Reich for six years.

A final written decision from the generals was given to Lord Aberfeldy within days of General Thorne's meeting, and a copy circulated at a meeting of the Joint Intelligence Committee in London on 11 April 1945. It said:

An appeal from German generals in captivity for the cessation of resistance even with the sole object of preventing further senseless destruction of the basis of German existence would – even in the present war situation – constitute an action which would not be understood by the troops in the field or by the German people.[16]

The generals did not believe that their retreating troops on the Western Front would have time to listen to wireless broadcasts, and leaflets rarely reached the frontline. On a political note, they said that the Nazi Party had already begun to blame them for the defeat of Germany; their betrayal was deemed to be the cause of Germany's downfall. In their eyes, the only way forward was the elimination of the men currently in power in Germany; namely, the eradication of the Nazi Party. In a separate statement to Lord Aberfeldy, Bassenge told him that the generals had essentially the same aim as the Allies – to bring a rapid end to the war.

TOWARDS TOTAL DEFEAT

Just weeks before Germany's unconditional surrender, Kendrick's three sites were brimming with senior German officers. His staff were now processing the top echelons of the surrendering German forces, tasked with their interrogation and debriefing for intelligence data. The MI19 official diary provides an impressive list of fifty senior officers captured in April 1945 alone.[17] Amongst some of the vivid descriptions of the 'new guests' was MI19's assessment of 50-year-old Major General Paul Goerbig, captured in Germany on 10 April 1945. He was described as 'a thoroughly despicable figure' and 'determined to treat his captors courteously in the hope of obtaining personal advantage … He states his hobbies to be old furniture and young women.'[18]

The conversations of senior German officers turned to Russian atrocities in areas along the Elbe. Holste spoke with von Thoma about how he had crossed the Elbe on 3 May and: 'I saw a sight near Kuhnhausen (?) – perhaps 1000 or 2000 young German women on the banks of the Elbe. At that moment, Russian tanks and Cossacks appeared, who immediately fired into this crowd of women and lashed out with whips. They then picked up many women and carried them off, and hundreds of German women jumped into the river and drowned.'[19]

Von Thoma asked: 'Didn't the women get away from the Russians?' He received the reply, 'Well, they raped them immediately. It was bestial. You've no idea.'[20]

Bodenschatz discussed Nazi looted art with Bassenge, telling him that he knew Goering was buying paintings, but not the range and quantity of them.[21] He confirmed that hundreds of paintings from the German State galleries were hidden in the zoo in Berlin, until Hitler suggested that they be moved to a tunnel near Berchtesgaden. 'The paintings bought in Paris and Amsterdam,' said Bodenschatz, 'were mainly paid from money which they obtained from the sale at very high prices of degenerate paintings to Switzerland and other countries. The Führer received hundreds of millions for these paintings and used the money to buy better ones.'[22]

Their conversation turned to concentration camps and the scenes which Bodenschatz believed must be 'rejected and condemned'. He argued that these scenes were nothing in comparison to the Allied air attacks on residential areas: 'If you could see Dresden. I was there; 51,000 women and children were killed in one night.'[23]

Johann Kogler, a 33-year-old Austrian commander of a fighter unit, had ninety wartime flights to his name and four victories to his credit:

His native charm as an Austrian gave place to the studied boorishness of a would-be Prussian. When it suits him, he can still be as personally charming as he is politically reprehensible. His morale and security were both initially exceptional but his Prussian personality, artificially conditioned in resentment and inherently 'phoney', was fertile ground for doubts springing up with realism of the true facts. The bluster is gone and the conceited and very 'German' German has become a comparatively reasonable Austrian with nascent enthusiasm for Austrian nationalism.[24]

British minders didn't fail to notice that, on first arriving in the dining room at Trent Park, Kogler gave a Nazi salute, which Major General Ullersperger returned with enthusiasm.[25]

Lieutenant Colonel Josef Ross was captured at Wesel on 24 March, brought to Wilton Park on 4 April, then four days later taken to Trent Park.[26] Interrogators learned how his bunker had been attacked by Allied infantry regiments after the Rhine crossings, and Ross had surrendered with his surviving men. In interrogation, Ross refused to give any information about his activities as commander of Wesel and only told the interrogator that he was a senior German officer, located in a certain area, and tasked with defending it.[27] However, once back with the other generals, Ross gave a full account to Bassenge of the fall of Wesel.[28] The personal intelligence summary concluded: 'He [Ross] would gladly work with the Allies for the building up of a new Germany after the war is over.'[29]

HITLER'S SUICIDE

By April 1945, Hitler had retreated to his bunker in Berlin for the final battle. Albert Speer had already written to him that the war was militarily and economically lost, and beseeched him not to take Germany to total destruction.[30] On 20 April, on what turned out to be Hitler's last birthday, Goebbels's broadcast to the German nation to 'blindly follow their Führer and the stars'. Some of the senior German officers at Trent Park listened to his birthday speech for the Führer in the common room. One of the officers (unnamed in reports) turned off the wireless half way through the German National Anthem. Kittel was outraged and complained that one officer had walked out during the anthem and the others had remained seated, calling them scoundrels and cowards.[31] He told whoever was listening to him that he preferred death at Metz (where he was captured) than life at Camp 11. Major General Wahle complained to Heim that Goebbels's speech was nothing but hot air, while Major General Bruhn told Felbert that 'the speech was tripe'.

Three days later, Hitler ordered the following announcement to be made across Germany: 'The Führer is in Berlin. The Führer will not leave Berlin. The Führer will defend Berlin to the last.'[32]

On 30 April, rather than surrender in the besieged city, Hitler and his new wife Eva Braun committed suicide in the bunker. Whether the generals ever foresaw that Hitler would take his own life was not clear. They displayed no emotion at the news of his suicide and did not mourn his death. Instead, they began to focus on the suitability or otherwise of Admiral Doenitz to be his successor.[33] Schlieben referred to Doenitz as 'a damned fool'.[34]

News of Hitler's death came to the secret listeners via radio broadcasts and newspaper reports. Although there were no celebrations amongst the secret listeners at any of Kendrick's centres, this was what Fritz Lustig and the other émigré listeners had waited for. Hitler was dead. The man who had singled out the Jewish people and themselves for annihilation was himself dead. Lustig commented: 'We felt instinctively that Hitler would not allow himself to be captured by the Allies. In that sense his suicide came as no great shock. For days prior, everything had been pointing at Soviet forces overwhelming Berlin's defences. We were realistic about the end game. At last Hitler got his come-uppance.'

Kendrick must have felt a sense of satisfaction that Hitler was finally dead, after thirteen years of autocratic and brutal rule, tracked since the 1930s by Kendrick himself for SIS. The end was now swift and, within a week, on 7 May 1945, Germany signed an unconditional surrender.

DEFEAT OF THE THIRD REICH

War was finally over and a new era dawned on a Europe devastated by thirteen years of the Nazi regime and six years of war. On a personal level for Kendrick and the secret listeners, it had been a long road to victory. On the day that Germany capitulated, secret listener Fritz Lustig and his fiancée Susan Cohn went into central London for the evening to witness the victory celebrations.

> Piccadilly Circus was crammed full of people, some sitting on the roof of buses, others hanging out of windows or climbing lamp posts. It was a unique experience. We made our way through the crowds to Parliament Square, where we listened to a speech by the King, which was broadcast through loudspeakers in the street – nobody spoke a word. We then proceeded to Buckingham Palace where the Royal Family appeared on the balcony. It was now getting dark. We went back to Whitehall, where we heard Winston Churchill make a short speech from the balcony of the Home Office, lit up by searchlights.[35]

At Trent Park, the German generals celebrated VE Day by drinking wine – much to the disgust of their batmen who believed this was not in the German spirit and quite a scandal.[36] One of the batmen was overheard saying that the generals were celebrating 'their own funeral'.

European hostilities may have ended, but MI19's work with German POWs was far from over. The task of deciding the future of the thousands of POWs and their re-education would take up much of its time, as well as the ongoing incarceration of Hitler's generals. That month of Germany's capitulation, Kendrick's three sites received an influx of 106 senior German officers, amongst them Field Marshal Erhard Milch and SS Obergruppenführer General der Waffen SS Maximilian von Herff.[37]

Maximilian Herff, a high-ranking SS commander, was captured at Flensburg on 9 May and brought to Latimer House on 16 May, then moved to Trent Park on 14 July. MI19 noted that the circumstances surrounding his capture were unknown, but found him cooperative. He was, however, described by his fellow officers as 'a shady character and an opportunist'.[38] Although he protested his innocence they failed to believe him, saying that a man in his influential position could only have got there through compulsion and ambition. Herff died of a stroke on 6 September 1945 whilst a POW in British custody and is buried at the German Military Cemetery, Cannock Chase.

Arriving at Trent Park at the end of May 1945 was Lieutenant General Edgar Feuchtinger. He had been condemned to death in Germany in March 1945 for allegedly being engaged in misappropriation and looting, and released on the personal intervention of Hitler.[39] While in British custody, he tried to portray himself as an anti-Nazi, but MI19 saw through his façade and commented that he was 'in reality a whole-hearted supporter of the Nazi regime'.[40] His quick promotion in the German army supported the view that he was an ardent Nazi. As part-owner of a publishing house in Leipzig he tried to ingratiate himself with British Army officers with a view to a role in post-war Germany.

There was concern that some high-ranking officers might commit suicide to avoid justice. There was particular concern for Rear Admiral Scheer who had been transferred to No.1 POW camp at Grizedale Hall in the Lake District. A memo was sent on behalf of Kendrick to Camp 20 at Wilton Park, raising concerns about Rear Admiral Scheer:

> We have reason to suspect that the above [Scheer] has a phial of poison hidden on his person or in his belongings. Although a search has been carried out we have failed to locate it. As this POW has now been dumped to Grizedale, you will no doubt wish to inform the Camp Commandant without revealing the source of our informa-tion. Care will also have to be taken, of course, to ensure that POW does not know that we suspect him.[41]

The Allies had every reason to be vigilant: Heinrich Himmler committed suicide with a cyanide pill on 23 May whilst in British custody in Germany and escaped justice. It was a scenario that British intelligence wished to avoid for Hitler's other commanders.

FIELD MARSHAL VON RUNDSTEDT

The most senior German officer to be held at Trent Park was 69-year-old Field Marshal Gerd von Rundstedt, Hitler's Commander in Chief in the West. He and his son Lieutenant Hans von Rundstedt were captured together at Bad Tölz on 1 May 1945.[42] The previous year the Field Marshal had presided over the Court of Honour that had tried officers involved in the failed 20 July attempt on Hitler's life. At that time, he was the most senior officer in the German army, until replaced by Field Marshals Model and Kesselring in 1945.

St Clare Grondona received a phone call to expect the arrival of Field Marshal von Rundstedt. On 5 July 1945, father and son arrived at Wilton Park where they were held for a month. The Field Marshal was found to be 'the product of courtliness itself and willing to give information'.[43] His name had often been canvassed by senior German officers as a possible leader of an anti-Nazi movement to bring an end to the war in the West, but they had concluded he was too old and lacking in purpose. In turn, he told them that he could never contemplate such a move, which he considered 'high treason'.

A large party of German generals was now being housed in the White House at Wilton Park. With von Rundstedt and his son were General Busch (second in command to Goering in the Luftwaffe) and General Dittmar. St Clare Grondona noted:

In anticipation of their arrival, all windows were made secure, the flood-lighting system was installed and all other security measures were laid on. About an acre of ground in a field near the White House was enclosed in a thick, high barbed-wire fence overlooking which were two raised Bren gun posts ... The feelings of those Germans as – red-tabbed, gold-braided and erect – they walked inside their barbed wire enclosed exercise ground for an hour each morning and afternoon, must have been indeed bitter; but I never sensed that their bitterness was against their captors.[44]

The two field marshals were already both very sick men when they arrived at Wilton Park. Even so, no parole was offered to them; as St Clare Grondona noted: 'We had recently been appalled by the details of the discoveries at Buchenwald and Dachau, and feelings were running very high that humanity had been thus outraged.'[45]

Joining them for a short time from Trent Park was another sick commander, General von Thoma, who spent two periods in hospital. Once back at Wilton Park, he and Kurt Dittmar decided to turn an acre of land beyond the tennis courts into allotments:

Dittmar was as enthusiastic a gardener as he was a great talker and, stripped to the waist, he and his helpers toiled exceedingly, so that in a few months, they were producing salads and other vegetables, baskets of which were sometimes sent with their compliments to our officers' mess.[46]

Bassenge was transferred back to Wilton Park for a short time. He was busy protecting the cherry orchard from being besieged by the local birds. For days, he was totally occupied with:

… pieces of wire, a soldering iron, a variety of tins – ranging from tobacco containers to petrol cans – on which he got to work with snips, hammer and homemade rivets. He constructed an impressive range of windmills from tin cans which rotated and rattled to prevent the birds from eating the fruit in the orchard. He acquired some turkey feathers which he made into the shape of an aeroplane, added buttons from trousers for eyes and finished with a product that looked scarier than a hawk.[47]

Bassenge's room was full of tools for making all kinds of gadgets. He generously carved a walking stick for the frail von Rundstedt, which von Rundstedt gave to St Clare Grondona when the former left Wilton Park.[48]

DEATH OF A GENERAL

Field Marshal Ernst Busch, Commander of all German forces in north-west Europe, was never transferred to Trent Park. He remained at Wilton Park because of ill health. On 17 July 1945, he died of a heart attack in his room at Wilton Park before his batman could summon any help. Given his status as a Field Marshal, it is perhaps surprising to find no personal MI19 file for him or any official report of his death. His funeral and burial went ahead without the customary issuing of a death certificate. One was finally issued on 14 September 1945, signed by Registrar W. Stokes, nearly two months after the date of death, and Nottingham hospital was given as the place of death, not Wilton Park.[49] Why the death was kept secret for two months is not clear, but probably to protect the existence of Wilton Park as a special POW camp from the public eye. The informant of death was Major Commandant St Clare Grondona of No.7 P.W. Camp (Annex) Beaconsfield and the cause was given as chronic myocarditis (heart attack), diagnosed by Dr J.S. Smith.

Immediately after the death, St Clare Grondona awaited instructions from the War Office about the funeral. An urgent reply came through that Busch's body was to be removed from the White House at Wilton Park by motor hearse to Aldershot the following day. The body could be accompanied by 'reasonably appropriate military honours'.[50] Regular British troops practised the funeral drill for two hours ahead of the ceremony and staged an impressive ceremonial parade:

> Next morning, two lines of troops with heads bowed over their reversed arms were drawn up between the steps of the White House and the hearse on the wide carriageway; and another party stood ready to slow-march ahead of the short column as it moved 400 yards to the South gate of the inner perimeter. Von Rundstedt and about 20 generals walked to the rear of the hearse, with British officers behind them. Then, as the gate was approached, there was a brief halt while the advance party formed two lines on either side of the hearse, and, as it moved on, they presented arms. Von Rundstedt raised his Marshal's baton and we all came to the salute till the hearse had passed through the gate – when it accelerated in setting out on its journey.[51]

The other generals immediately discussed amongst themselves the kind of funeral that they would arrange for the Field Marshal and submitted their requests to Captain Lang, the Intelligence Liaison Officer in charge of prisoners at Wilton Park. Later that day, St Clare Grondona received instructions from the War Office that eight German generals and Field Marshal von Rundstedt would be granted permission to attend the funeral. The following day, St Clare Grondona, Captain Lang and four armed guards escorted the delegation from Wilton Park to the Aldershot military cemetery for the funeral. They were driven in an army coach, the blinds drawn down over the windows. St Clare Grondona recalled:

> As we entered Eton, I thought it would be as well to let these Generals see that life hereabouts was going on as usual, so I had the blinds raised sufficiently to enable them to see, without being seen, until we had passed Windsor Castle. But, as we drew clear of Windsor Great Park, the blinds were drawn down again. The Germans had been very interested to see the Eton boys and were quite excited when we passed the Castle.[52]

During the journey, von Rundstedt asked St Clare Grondona whether there would be a firing squad from the Brigade of Guards at the ceremony. St Clare Grondona was non-committal in his response and said, 'I have no idea what arrangements have been made by the War Office'. He later reflected:

> I marvelled at the outlook of this man who had seen all our newspaper's gruesomely illustrated accounts of the terrible discoveries made at the concentration camps, and who even yet imagined that a party of the King's Household Brigade would now be detailed as a guard of honour at a German General's funeral. He was soon disillusioned. The burial was conducted with a minimum of ceremony.[53]

On return to Wilton Park, St Clare Grondona received a message that von Rundstedt wished to see him in his room. When St Clare Grondona entered, von Rundstedt asked him to be seated. They were alone. He said to St Clare Grondona: 'Herr Kommandant, you will receive a letter from me expressing our appreciation of the ceremony which marked the departure of our late colleague's body from this place. But, can you tell me why he was buried today with none of the honours due to a soldier and with no respect whatever for his rank?' Von Rundstedt was clearly quite emotional, as he finished by saying: 'None of us who were present at Aldershot today will ever forget what was a very bitter experience.' St Clare Grondona's response was careful: 'You must understand the state of public opinion. There is no small amount of outrage at the concentration camps.' Not until 1963 were Busch's remains exhumed from the Aldershot Military Cemetery and re-interred in the German Military Cemetery, Cannock Chase in Staffordshire.

CHAPTER 14

British Intelligence, POWs and War Crimes Trials

Fritz Lustig was working in the M Room at Latimer House when he read in the newspaper about the liberation of Belsen on 15 April 1945. Photographs and film footage, recorded by the Allies sent shockwaves throughout the world. Earlier that month, American forces had liberated Buchenwald concentration camp and similar horrific scenes had confronted US soldiers. Nothing had prepared the liberating forces for this. Lustig commented:

> When I saw film footage of Belsen for the first time I was deeply shocked at the emaciated survivors and heaps of naked dead bodies lying around. Although coming from Nazi Germany I had known about concentration camps, I was not prepared for this. Seeing the extent of the Nazi disregard for human life raised questions about how such unspeakable acts could have been committed in the civilized country of my birth.[1]

Overhearing details about concentration camps was particularly painful for the secret listeners. Many had left families behind in Nazi Germany and spent the war years worrying about their fate. When they eavesdropped on the conversations about mass shootings of Jews into shallow-dug pits in Russia, Poland or Latvia, they could have been overhearing descriptions of the murder of their own parents, sisters, brothers and friends. For them, this must have been one of the most difficult parts of their work. Secret listener Peter Hart recalled overhearing from prisoners about Buchenwald concentration camp:

> We came across many a horror story. One of the worst that I can remember was when we heard from a prisoner that the wife of the Commandant in an extermination camp, had her lampshades made from human skins taken from the inmates, selected before they were put to death, because of their attractive tattoos. We had this confirmed more than once … We also heard gruesome stories from prisoners who had been employed in extermination camps … Some of the worst reports from the extermination camps which shocked us most, were those which described the callous use made of victims' bodies after they were gassed.[2]

When asked about it too, Fritz Lustig replied:

> We all tried to be professional in our approach to hearing prisoners discussing war crimes, which meant that irrespective of the personal circumstances of our own families, we tried not to become emotionally involved in what we were hearing. We knew the terrible truth which the world would see in all its horror after the camps were liberated at the end of the war. Because we were told by Colonel Kendrick to keep the acetate records of conversations of war crimes, there was the expectation that justice would eventually be done.[3]

Clearly the secret listeners who had left family in Germany in the 1930s must have suffered when they overheard the harsh details of the holocaust. Peter Ganz learned after the war that his grandfather had been murdered in Auschwitz in 1944. Fritz Lustig was fortunate in that he lost no family members at all. Rudi Oppenheimer learned that his 4-year-old niece, Eve, had survived Belsen, together with her brothers Paul and Rudi. The brothers came to England a short time later, but Eve was too young at age four to travel. In the chaos of post-war Europe, many family survivors of camps became separated. In the autumn of

1945, Kendrick granted compassionate leave to Rudi Oppenheimer to travel to Holland, where Eve then was and bring her to England. The Oppenheimer family learned that Eve's parents perished in Belsen just months before its liberation by British forces. It was to be an all too familiar story for so many of the émigré men and women.

DISGRACED FOR ALL TIME

MI19 decided that the generals at Trent Park should be shown film footage and photographs of the concentration camps.[4] Their reaction to what they saw was secretly recorded in the M Room, and the 'cut' records to be kept. Copies of black-and-white photographs of Belsen, Buchenwald and Dachau were circulated, alongside copies of the forth-coming White Paper on Buchenwald.[5] This provoked some broad comments by the generals that the photographs had been faked.[6]

General Felbert admitted to von Schlieben, 'We are disgraced for all time and not a thousand years will wipe out what we've done.'[7]

Amongst other generals, there was disbelief. Broich commented to Wildermuth that the camp stories, whether true or not, were the best possible propaganda for the Allies. Von der Heydte told a British army officer that it was useless for the senior German officers to deny knowledge of the camps because 'practically every German suspected that that sort of thing went on'.[8] He commented that Goebbels's propaganda, which made inmates in the concentration camps look sub-human, had been so successful that the German people did not care what happened to Jews; he even feared that photographs of the liberation of the camps would not be sufficient to convince the German people of the true horror of the situation. He appeared to be the only general at Trent Park to suggest some kind of personal recompense for the crimes committed by Germany.

It has long been debated how much ordinary Germans knew about the concentration camps.[9] The generals speculated on this issue.[10] General Bassenge, who was an eye-witness to the camps (especially in Poland), told a British army officer that not even one half of one per cent of Germans knew about Buchenwald, or generally what went on inside concentration camps.[11] He added that people living in the neighbourhood might know, but anyone who spoke about them would immediately find themselves inside one. He claimed to have told fellow generals stories about the camps, but these were discounted as propaganda.[12]

Major General König spoke to Franz Lustig about a proposed permanent memorial at Belsen: 'This projected memorial to perpetuate [commemorate] the Belsen concentration camp will make every German itch to blow it up, for it is only a few beasts of the SS who are to blame for the atrocities. It's still too early for that sort of thing. The first thing is the reconstruction of our homeland.'[13]

The generals looked to their own future and how they could do their utmost 'to show they were not guilty of atrocities'.[14] But MI19 had 'abundant evidence' of their guilt in occupied countries.[15]

REACTIONS TO FILM FOOTAGE

By now, Trent Park was holding fifty-nine German generals and almost forty senior German officers.[16] Kendrick decided that it was compulsory for them to view film footage of the liberation of the camps. The footage is believed to have been screened in the Sassoon sports hall where the generals had regularly exercised, and the only place large enough to hold ninety-eight senior German officers. Their reactions were recorded by the listeners from another M Room under a nearby single-storey building.[17]

After the film screening, Dittmar and Holste agreed that the scenes were revolting, but could not be compared to what had happened to Germans in Russian camps. They could not understand why the SS had not destroyed all the damning evidence before the Allies reached the camps. Siewert said: 'It's a very effective film; it's a fine sort of recommendation from us! It really was like that, I saw it. The worst thing was that anyone could have anyone else put in such a camp without a sentence.'[18]

Later, Bruhn philosophically commented to Schlieben: 'I believe that when the policy of extermination overtakes us, which we have actually merited by our shedding of blood, the blood of our children will have to be shed too or perhaps that of our relations.'[19]

For the generals and senior officers, images of Belsen were soon over-shadowed by the news that Hitler had committed suicide in his bunker, and the suitability or otherwise of Admiral Doenitz to take over the reins of government.[20] Then their concerns swiftly turned to whether they would stand trial for the crimes of the regime. Now they tried to distance themselves from the past, agreeing amongst themselves that they would say that they were 'only obeying orders'. This line of defence continued amongst those generals still at Trent Park in the autumn of 1945.

MI19's intelligence report noted: 'Various of the senior officer POWs are expecting to be called as witnesses at the Nuremberg War Crimes trials.'[21] Eberbach was one of them. In conversation with von Thoma and Wildermuth, he said:

Either they want me about the shooting of the Canadian POW – I have already once proved to them that it happened before I went there. Or they want to interrogate me about the transfer of the police into the armed forces in connection with preparations for the war. I joined two years before the law was enacted. Or Speer has named me as a witness; I can tell only good of him.[22]

Wildermuth advised him to say as little as possible on the matter. Von der Heydte interrupted them: 'If I may butt in, I do not believe that it will be a staged trial.'[23] Eberbach, Heim, von der Heydte and Wildermuth spoke about the duties and obligations of a witness under oath. Wildermuth commented that it would not be appropriate for any of them to shake hands with the accused whom they knew, and advised Eberbach 'not to remember' if he was in doubt as to the implications of any given answer.

In a different discussion, Elfeldt expressed his belief to von der Heydte that all senior military officers would be tried by the Allies in due course. They both agreed that the British and Americans wanted to annihilate the German military and academic classes. They condemned Hitler's use of the gas chambers, but stated that, in their view, the Germans had already been sufficiently punished. Elfeldt told Heim that too much fuss was being made about the German maltreatment of Jews: 'After all, many more Germans died in this war than Jews died in gas chambers.'[24]

The generals were very preoccupied with the war crimes trials and reacted to news that Field Marshal von Rundstedt was to be put on trial as a war criminal, and that General Dostler was wanted by the French.[25] General Blumentritt engaged much of his time, with von der Heydte's assistance, marshalling evidence and arguments to be used in defence of his former chief, should the occasion arise.

Another alleged war criminal and captive at Trent Park, SS Kurt Meyer, requested of General von der Heydte that he undertake to defend him before a war crimes tribunal. Von der Heydte refused:

> He [Meyer] is charged with the fact that POWs were shot in front of his position. Two cases are particularly serious – in the first, nine were shot 200 metres from his battle HQ … Of course, as a regimental commander, I can well imagine that in the heat of battle, I might not know what was going on 200 metres in front of my battle HQ – I've other things to do and think about. But that there were many cases of shootings of POWs – that POWs were shot – is incontestable. It has been ascertained who shot them and the people involved are, of course, falling back on the excuse of orders received from [SS Kurt] Meyer.[26]

Kittel suspected that he might be named as a war criminal. His explanation: '18,000 Jews were killed at Rostov. Of course I had nothing to do with the whole affair! But it is down on my account because I was the only known general there.'[27]

Eberbach asked him: 'Who is really responsible for the affair? There's no doubt at all that the Führer knew all about this massacre of the Jews.'

In typical fashion, Kittel blamed the Jews and replied: 'Well, those Jews were the pest of the east! They should have been driven into one area and employed on some useful occupation.' He added that he was going to hold his tongue about the things he knew until he was called to give evidence:

After the fall of Rostov, the Russians accused me, in a great official solemn declaration on the radio, of having poisoned 18,000 Russians. As regards that I can only say: until then I knew nothing whatsoever about the whole affair in which so many people were killed ... Wildermuth also told me in the strictest secrecy that he has signed about forty sentences of death in his official capacity as Field Commander. Yes, I have some anxiety on that score![28]

Discussions about culpability intensified further after SS Meyer had been notified that he was to appear before a War Crimes Court of Enquiry.[29] On 26 March 1945, General Bassenge – in his capacity as new camp leader – notified Meyer that he would be transferred to London at midday, in readiness for a court appearance at 8.30 a.m. the following morning. Meyer told Eberbach: 'He [Bassenge] didn't know what it was all about. It's quite possible that it is in connection with that question I raised some time ago.'[30]

On return from the Court of Inquiry, Meyer was full of it and recounted the experience to Elfeldt, Kittel and Kogler:

'They wanted me to answer 'yes' or 'no' to their questions.'

'Did they tell you who accused you?' Elfeldt asked.

'Yes, they never stopped doing that,' replied Meyer.

'Did they first tell you the charges under which you were accused?' Kittel asked.

'No,' Meyer replied.[31]

The conversation continued, then with some frustration Kittel said:

I gave the order for the shooting of Russians, allegedly. I gave the order myself – allegedly ... They can wipe out the whole of the officer corps, it won't matter to them. Then that will be the end of us.

He decided that, if it came to it, he would dispute the legality of the Court of Inquiry and plead to be heard only in a German court.

He finished by saying, 'The Allied courts can do what they like with me, but I am under no obligation to say anything more than appears in my pay book.'

Later, in another conversation, Kittel told his fellow officers: 'You are under an obligation of silence.' Effectively he was arguing with them that they were not obliged to say anything if called to a Court of Inquiry.

As the reality of defeat finally sank in, the generals became quite philosophical about the atrocities. Bruhn commented:

Have we deserved victory or not? No, not after what we've done. After the amount of human blood we've shed knowingly and as a result of our delusions and also partly instigated by the lust of blood and other qualities, I now realise we have deserved defeat. We've deserved our fate.[32]

M ROOM FILES AND NUREMBERG

When the mountain of evidence for war crimes was finally presented at the Nuremberg Trials, there was one vital part missing – the transcripts from bugged conversations of German prisoners of war. Enquiries to various government departments on whether these acetate discs have survived today have been unsuccessful; although it is still possible that they lie forgotten in a basement.

Throughout the war, Kendrick had instructed his secret listeners to keep all recordings of atrocities, indefinitely, and mark the acetate discs with a big red 'A' (for atrocity). He genuinely believed that the conversations would be drawn upon at the various trials.[33] The volume of information provided enough evidence to bring to justice the Nazi war criminals and POWs who had passed through one of MI9/MI19's sites. However, declassified MI9 files now reveal that a fierce debate broke out in intelligence circles over whether the bugged conversations could be released to the war crimes trials. Secret listeners, like Fritz Lustig and Eric Mark, would not find out until decades later why the evidence they had gathered was never released.

By mid-May 1945, pressure was mounting within MI9/MI19 to release files for the war crimes trials. The matter was raised by Cavendish-Bentinck of the Foreign Office, as part of the agenda of the Joint Intelligence Committee which met on 15 May 1945 and again on 5 June.[34] He reported that the leaders of the German armed forces were likely to do their utmost to show that they were not guilty of atrocities, a tactic which, of course, was already known from M Room transcripts. Senior German officers at Trent Park had already denied any complicity in war crimes to British army officers. MI14's representative on the committee said:

> I regard it as of the utmost importance that everything possible should be done to discredit the German General Staff and Officer class in such a way that they may never regain their former influence … There is abundant evidence of atrocities committed under the authority of German Armed Forces' leaders in the occupied countries. It should therefore be possible to conduct an effective propaganda campaign both inside and outside Germany.[35]

The meeting of the Joint Intelligence Committee on 5 June 1945 deliberated whether recordings discussing the atrocities could be played in court as evidence for war crimes. One main objection was the impossibility of proving 'that the voice of any individual is, in fact, the voice alleged to be reproduced on the record'.[36] It was further stated:

> Even if this could be established, the basic security, from the point of view of the future, of CSDIC [MI19] methods as developed in this war must be considered. A large measure of success has been achieved by the methods we have employed, and it is the measure of success which has been attained which is of even greater security importance than the methods themselves which have actually been used. From this angle, the greater effect of playing back these records in open court, the more deeply will the future use of CSDIC's be compromised.[37]

However, some concessions were made. 'If the records and reports were made available on a TOP SECRET basis for the purpose of briefing the cross-examiners at the trials (in order that the accused may be induced to confess or be so shaken that he is discredited), then it would appear that Security would be preserved and the main object of discrediting the accused achieved.'[38]

It was the new head of MI9, Lieutenant Colonel Sam Derry, who made the final decision.[39] The original source on war crimes and the death camps via bugged conversations could not be released because it would blow current methods of eavesdropping that were still in practice at the end of the war.[40] The files would have become public property and neither MI6 nor MI9 were prepared to allow this to happen.

Europe had also entered the Cold War with new dangers from an old adversary – the Soviet Union. Like other top-secret sites of the Second World War, any possibility of leaking the original source of intelligence potentially put at risk other ongoing operations. Information could only be used at the trials if it could be corroborated from another source known to the enemy. Having intelligence and being able to act on it are two different matters. The Allies could not risk the source of their information being leaked into the public domain, especially to hostile or enemy states (like the Soviet Union) because then the method of obtaining that intelligence could no longer be used. It explains why British intelligence did not declassify the M Room files until the late 1990s, after the Berlin Wall had come down and the Cold War was effectively over.

Not everyone in intelligence circles agreed with the decision to withhold M Room files from the war crimes trials in 1945.[41] Three surviving letters in a slim file provide an insight into the frank exchange and feelings of those within British intelligence at the time. The first, dated 31 October 1945, is from the time when the twenty-one surviving leaders of the former Nazi government were being held at Nuremberg Prison, ahead of their trial (which would finally open on 20 November). The letter was written by the Military Deputy of the Military Department at Judge Advocate General in Whitehall, in which he expressed no objection to evidence from MI9/MI19 files being used in the war crimes trials, as long as the methods of obtaining that information were kept secret:

> I understand the DMI [director of military intelligence] may take objection to members of CSDIC staff giving evidence of what they heard a prisoner of war say, in the circumstances. In my opinion it may, in some cases, be essential to call an officer of CSDIC [MI19] staff as a witness. He could say that he overheard a conversation between the POWs and give the context of the conversation without saying how he came to overhear it. On the other hand, it appears to me now obvious that the Germans were fully aware of the procedure adopted by CSDIC, and it is clear from investigation in the Dulag Luft case that the Germans employed exactly the same methods. The matter, therefore, does not appear to be so secret as it was during the war.[42]

On 16 November, Derry replied in firm language that anything that drew attention to the wartime work of CSDIC and MI19 could not be disclosed under any circumstances, even though the Germans may be aware of it after the war.

> In spite of warnings, memories are short and POWs continue to talk indiscreetly, but anything which will tend to increase security-mindedness on the part of an enemy should at all costs be avoided … It does not require much imagination to visualise the sensational Press articles to which such disclosure might well give rise. In short, what up to now has been known to comparatively few (and those mostly persons who are directly interested and are under oath of secrecy) would become common knowledge.

Derry highlighted that any use of bugged conversations would lead to the disclosure at the trial of the names of POWs – some of whom had been persuaded to work for the Allies, often as stool pigeons. He finished by saying: 'Nor would we view with equanimity the calling as a witness of an officer who had been employed in the particular branch concerned who would have to submit to cross-examination which might easily result in the disclosure of information which was then and still is Top Secret.'[43]

The third surviving letter is dated 28 November 1945, from a brigadier whose signature is illegible:

> I must return to the attack. It is unfortunate that war criminals should avoid the consequences of their misdeeds because evidence cannot be given of what they said quite voluntarily while a prisoner of war to another prisoner of war. If the MI [Military Intelligence] are of an opinion that it is undesirable that evidence should be given in open court, orders can be given that an application should be made to hear the evidence in camera or the names of witnesses suppressed … A point raised by MI9/MI19 that cross-examination might result in the disclosure of information which is Top Secret can be got over by the witness claiming the privilege under the Official Secrets Act. Will you please take this matter up again with DMI.[44]

None of the generals ever faced trial for the war crimes which they admitted during their unguarded conversations at Trent Park. SS General Kurt Meyer, commander of the 12th Panzer Division, captured by the Americans near Liège in Belgium, was not brought to justice based on anything he said there. As one of Hitler's most decorated warlords, Meyer had served in the major campaigns of the German offensive.[45] During 1945, he was finally extradited to Germany to stand trial for the shooting of Allied soldiers earlier in the war. For this atrocity, he received the death sentence, later commuted to life imprisonment. But he had admitted in conversations at Trent Park to massacring the population of a Russian village near Kharkov, for which he never stood trial. This was because much of MI19's evidence of war crimes could only be used to steer post-war investigations, by advising legal teams and prosecutors at Nuremberg that a particular prisoner was believed to be guilty, and that a confession should be sought.[46] If the prisoner confessed, then he could be sent for trial. If not, then he was repatriated. It under-lines how the M Room material had limitations, in the end, with regard to the war crimes trials. It also highlights the moral dilemmas facing intelligence chiefs in which intelligence gathered in wartime sometimes has to be discarded or set to one side to avoid compromising other ongoing operations and in the interests of national security.

CHURCHILL AND THE M ROOM

Prime Minister Winston Churchill's views on the whole bugging operation became clear in a Personal Minute dated 16 February 1944, issued to Sir Percy Grigg (Secretary of State for War) and General Hastings Ismay (for the Combined Chiefs of Staff). Churchill wrote that the records of conversations between enemy prisoners of war at CSDIC 'afford an excellent insight into the German character and the results of the Nazi regime.'[47]

Churchill wanted a book written, using a summary of conversations.[48] He received a favourable response from the Joint Intelligence Committee, but it would have to wait until after the war. In the end, it was a parallel scenario to the evidence gathered on war crimes by the secret listeners. British intelligence refused to release any of the files or knowledge of their contents into the public domain. Neither were the unit's existence and clandestine operations during wartime acknowledged. Consequently, around 75,000 transcripts from the M Room remained closed until at least 1996 and some were not released until the period between 2004 and 2006.

CHAPTER 15

Always Listening

The Axis powers may have been defeated, but the Allies faced a huge task in the denazification of Germany, the hunt for Nazi war criminals and the reconstruction of post-war Europe.[1] There was also a new, more dangerous threat from Europe's old enemy, the Soviet Union. Winston Churchill had raised international awareness to the Soviet threat in his speech on 5 March 1945 in Missouri, USA where he famously coined the phrase 'Iron Curtain': 'From Stettin in the Baltic to Trieste in the Adriatic, an iron curtain has descended across the continent.' It would characterise much of the Cold War where the battlefield shifted from direct physical combat to the arms race and superiority in the technological spying game. The challenges facing British intelligence would prove as difficult as during the hostilities of 1939–1945. British and American forces raced to snatch German scientists and technologists before they fell into the hands of the Russians.

Kendrick's secret listeners were not demobilised immediately. A small number were posted to the former London Cage in Kensington Palace Gardens, when it became the War Crimes Investigation Unit until 1948.[2] Some were posted to new listening posts in Germany and others to Farm Hall near Cambridge. There was still vital work for them to do.

OPERATION EPSILON

British and American special teams such as 'T Force', Counterintelligence, Fleming's 30 Assault Unit, and Field Security units successfully hunted down the key German atomic bomb scientists and brought them to England, before their eventual transfer to the United States. From May until December 1945, they were held at Farm Hall, a comfortable Georgian country house in Godmanchester near Cambridge, and code-named Operation Epsilon.[3] Ten chief German atomic scientists were held there, with no explanation for their detention. Amongst them were two Nobel Prize winners: Max von Laue and Otto Hahn (the latter heard about his award of a Nobel Prize whilst at Farm Hall).[4]

The files of their bugged conversations survive in the National Archives; amongst them are copies of their reactions to the dropping of the atomic bombs on Hiroshima and Nagasaki in August 1945.[5] As with the German generals during the war, the scientists did not suspect that their conversations were bugged from the M Room. The listeners ironically overheard them saying: 'The British are too stupid to bug our conversations.'

This highly top-secret site came under the daily running of Major Rittner, one of Kendrick's wartime intelligence officers. A number of secret listeners were posted to the site, as noted by Major Rittner in a report dated 17 June 1945:

Lieutenant Commander [Eric] Welsh and I went to Farm Hall where arrangements had already been made to install microphones. I had asked for such an installation from the day I took charge of the professors. We arranged with Colonel Kendrick to transfer the necessary staff from CSDIC (UK) to man the installation. We were fortunate also in obtaining the services of Captain Brodie from CSDIC (UK) to act as Administrative Officer.[6]

The secret listeners there were known to include George Pulay, Herbert Lehmann, Heilbronn and Peter Ganz.

Farm Hall represented a prime example why intelligence files could not be made public after the war and released to the war crimes trials. Nothing could be allowed to jeopardise Operation Epsilon, from which the British and Americans expected to obtain the most important scientific secrets in the new era. The Cold War, that would last forty years, was a period now deemed as more dangerous than the Second World War because for the first time in history, the world faced the real threat of its own total destruction by nuclear war. There could be no admission that the intelligence services were bugging the conversations of personnel being held at special sites. That would jeopardise the vital new intelligence gathering and hence, the security of Europe.

NO.74 CSDIC, BAD NENNDORF

As Allied armies had swept through Western Europe after D-Day, the intelligence services were already preparing for the occupation of Germany and that included plans to set up a bugging operation in Germany.[7] The site opened as No.74 CSDIC in July 1945 at Bad Nenndorf, 25 kilometres west of Hanover. It was commanded by Colonel Robin 'Tin-eye' Stephens, who had run MI5's interrogation centre at Latchmere House, Ham (as Camp 020) during the war. Stephens was tough and had dealt with the captured German spies who had landed on Britain's shores, a number of whom he successfully turned as double agents as part of the Double Cross System.[8] In a different uniform, the monocled colonel could have passed as a Nazi – and he was ideal for instilling fear into captured German spies. Questions were later raised about Stephens's handling of prisoners amidst allegations of brutality, and even torture.[9] Although he was acquitted at a court martial, rumours of a cover-up still circulate decades later.[10]

The task of No.74 CSDIC was to interrogate and listen into the conversations of German internees, often civilians and political dissidents, and suspected Nazi war criminals. There was concern by the Allies that die-hard Nazi resistance movements which had gone underground would rise up again. The secret listeners at Bad Nenndorf were taken from the pool of wartime listeners.[11]

The administrative work and some of the interrogations were carried out by women from the wartime CSDIC sites and a small number who had transferred from Bletchley Park.[12] It was not all about interrogation and listening; former secret listener Frank Falk was given piles of documents to translate that had been seized by the Allies from the Reichs-Chancellery and German Foreign Office,[13] many of which bore Hitler's signature. One particular document stood out for him – a letter from Hitler to Admiral Horthy (the Hungarian Regent), instructing him to deport Hungary's Jews from the country to the death camps.[14]

TRENT PARK

Trent Park continued to hold high-ranking German officers until December 1945.[15] Among them was Lieutenant General Walter Dornberger, who had overseen the general supervision of Germany's rocket development programme since 1937 and been responsible for developing the site at Peenemünde. He had been promoted to the position of Chief Advisor to the Department for Development and Testing of Weapons.[16] It was noted that he persuaded the German Army Ordnance Branch 'to take up liquid-fuel rocket propulsion, as a result of which Peenemünde experimental site came into being.'[17] Captured on 2 May 1945 at Garmisch-Partenkirchen, a Bavarian ski resort, he was brought to Latimer House on 5 August, then moved to Trent Park the following day.[18]

Dornberger spoke quite freely with Bassenge. He revealed to him that the Russians had attempted to make a secret deal with him and double whatever offer the Americans had made for him to work for them. He also said that the Russians had attempted to kidnap the German engineer Wernher von Braun: 'They [Russians] appeared at night time in English uniform; they didn't realise it was the American zone. They came to us and wanted to come in. They had a proper pass, but the Americans were quick to realise it and wouldn't let them in. Real kidnapping; they don't stick to the boundaries at all.'[19]

There was clearly concern over the fate of Germany's scientists because, during his time at Trent Park, Dornberger talked with General Fink (German air force) about Hitler's plans for them. The intelligence summary of their conversation stated: 'Himmler had been ordered by the Führer not to let Braun, Dornberger and the 450 scientists and technicians at Peenemünde fall into Anglo-American hands but to liquidate them all beforehand.'[20] Dornberger also provided confirmation that as many as 720 people had been killed in the first raid on Peenemünde in August 1943.

On 8 August 1945, Field Marshal von Rundstedt and his son were transferred together to Trent Park. On VJ Day, 2 September 1945, the Field Marshal sought out the British army officers to offer his 'congratulations on a great victory'.[21]

Arriving at Trent Park at the same time as von Rundstedt and his son were Generals Halder, Student, von Manteuffel, von Falkenhausen, Blumentritt, Careis, Kruse and Müller-Hillebrand (Chief of Staff to the 3rd Panzer Army).[22] General Günther Blumentritt had been captured at Hohenaspe on 2 May, just days before Germany's unconditional surrender. His personal file contains little comment, except that he was 'a regular, friendly Bavarian infantry officer' and cooperated with Allied forces after capitulation.[23] He arrived at Wilton Park on 1 June 1945 and then transferred to Trent Park on 8 August. Before promotion to the rank of general, he had served as Chief of Staff to Field Marshal von Rundstedt and then General von Kluge. During the Nuremberg Trials, Blumentritt was held as a key witness at the same time as von Rundstedt.

Franz Halder, chief of the German General Staff in 1938–42 and later a witness at the Nuremberg Trials, was also captured just days before the German surrender in May 1945 and eventually escorted to England. At Trent Park, his fellow officers described the 61-year-old general as 'the most capable General Staff Officer produced by the post-1919 German Army.'[24] Halder gave the impression of 'a mild, inoffensive and exact civil servant ... an exceptionally lucid brain and great hidden reserves of strength.'[25]

Fifty-four-year-old General Karl Bodenschatz, formerly head of the Personal Ministry of the Supreme Command of the Luftwaffe and Chief of Staff to Hermann Goering, had acted as liaison officer between Goering and Hitler's headquarters.[26] With a reputation for being a convinced Nazi, his high-level contact with Nazi leaders made him unpopular amongst officers in the German air force.[27] Bodenschatz had sustained serious injuries during the assassination attempt on Hitler's life in July 1944.

Another particularly important 'guest' was Infantry General Alexander von Falkenhausen, who finally arrived at Trent Park in August, after a month at Wilton Park. Von Falkenhausen had been military governor of Belgium and Northern France, captured on 5 May at Pragser Wildsee (South Tyrol). He was respected by the other senior officers at Trent Park for 'his sense of fairness, uprightness and moderation'.[28] He was even seen as a possible negotiator in post-war Germany or even an acceptable Prime Minister for the new Germany.[29] It is not possible to provide a complete list of all senior German officers at Trent Park in this period, and their colourful conversations and daily lives – all captured by the secret listeners in the M Room. That would take another book. What is clear is that British intelligence believed they still had vital military and strategic information to offer the Allies.

The generals were fooled until the very end. In September 1945 they presented a gift (unknown item) and certificate to the camp interpreter Captain Hamley on his leaving the camp and in appreciation of his kindness towards them. From Trent Park, Field Marshal von Rundstedt wrote a personal letter on behalf of the senior German officers and told him:

> We all regret your departure very much! You have never seen in us the 'victims' of a mis-directed policy, the 'enemy', but always the 'human beings' ... [you] lighten the heavy burden of captivity for every one of us . . . our sincerest wishes for your further welfare and assure you that we shall always preserve a true and grateful memory of you.[30]

The last of the German generals and senior officers were transferred to Camp 11 at Bridgend in Wales, and a few sent to Grizedale Hall in the Lake District.[31] Others had gradually been transferred to America where they underwent a programme of re-education.[32]

In December 1945, Trent Park finally closed as 'special quarters' and there ended a chapter of its secret history that would remain unknown until the declassification of its files sixty-five years later. By 1948, the generals were all repatriated to Germany. General von Arnim, for example, found that his home was now behind the Iron Curtain and confiscated by the Russians. He made a new life, quietly, in West Germany and died on 1 September 1962 at Bad Wildingen. The generals were keen to keep their heads down and fade into the background, lest they should be noticed and cases of war crimes suddenly brought against them. However, none of them ever faced justice for their crimes.

Ian Thomson Munro – Trent Park's fake aristocrat – was promoted to the rank of major in 1945. After the war, he worked for MI6, as confirmed on his army record, and was 'specially employed not remunerated from army funds, MI6'. In 1950, his name appeared on a passenger list for the Far East where he was on his way to a posting in Japan. He was tragically lost at sea on that voyage. Probate listed his occupation as diplomat, with no relatives.

Between January 1946 and the summer of that year, a team of engineers quietly dismantled any trace of the wartime bugging operation at Trent Park. If the files had not been declassified in the late 1990s, its wartime role would have remained a closely guarded secret. From autumn 1946, Trent Park became an emergency teacher training college, under a new requisition order by the Ministry of Education. By 1952, it became the subject of a compulsory purchase order for use as Barnet Teacher Training College, that also included the use of nearby Ludgrove Hall. It then became Middlesex Polytechnic, and Middlesex University before the site was vacated in 2013 and sold to a Malaysian education company whose operations and offices, however, did not materialise. The estate was purchased in 2015 by Berkeley Homes to create residential homes on site while preserving spaces and historic rooms across the ground floor and basement of the mansion as a museum to the secret listeners.[33]

LATIMER HOUSE

After May 1945, senior German officers continued to be brought via Latimer House before their transfer to Trent Park. The Naval Intelligence section now had vital work in post-war Germany. Commander Cope, as

Staff Officer (Intelligence), was dispatched to Germany with Naval Party 1735 that left from HMS Cockfosters.[34] In the early part of the war, HMS Cockfosters was a land naval base located at Trent Park for the interrogation of prisoners and initially located in an Italian-style villa called the White House, once part of the wider Trent Park estate.[35] In 1944–45, HMS Cockfosters was located in 'Parkfield' and 'Corbar', two houses in Beech Hill, Hadley Wood (an area adjacent to Cockfosters).[36] This was one of a number of Naval Party units dispatched from HMS Cockfosters to impound German naval equipment and documents throughout Germany, work which was similar to Ian Fleming's 30 Assault Unit.[37]

Colin McFadyean, who was working out of the Admiralty (NID 1/ PW), was present at the arrest of Admiral Doenitz (Hitler's successor) on 23 May 1945 at Flensburg on the Danish–German border.[38] Ralph Izzard, Charles Wheeler and George Blake became part of the Naval Intelligence's special Forward Interrogation Unit (FIU).[39] FIU was tasked with capturing vital technologists, interrogating U-boat crews and seizing documents and German naval equipment and new technology.[40] In 1946, Blake took over from Wheeler in Hamburg as head of the Naval Intelligence team there;[41] subsequently he was attached to SIS in the Netherlands. It later transpired that he was passing secrets to the Soviets and he was eventually prosecuted and imprisoned for betraying British agents to their deaths.[42] He escaped from prison, defected to Russia and became one of the infamous traitors of the Cold War, alongside Guy Burgess, Kim Philby and Donald Maclean.[43]

In terms of prisoners, the operation at Latimer House as a joint services interrogation centre was winding down.[44] Since March 1945, a special aircraft had flown into Britain twice a week, sometimes more frequently, for the sole purpose of bringing special prisoners to ADI(K) headquarters at Latimer – the Air Intelligence section under Denys Felkin.[45] Impounded documents were being brought to ADI(K) from Germany by the crateful – in sacks, crates and boxes – such that Felkin's team could not cope with the sheer volume. It all needed to be translated and sifted for intelligence. Felkin's section had to take on an extra thirty-six German-speaking ex-refugees to help with the workload. The material was microfilmed and distributed to the relevant authorities for their intelligence.

The office space at Latimer was totally inadequate for the volume of work, and in April 1945, new accommodation was taken up in the Air Ministry building in Monck Street,[46] yet the crates of documents continued to arrive. The following month, the volume was too much again, and a new combined Anglo-American centre was set up in a block of flats at 55 Weymouth Street, London. Staff increased to between four hundred and five hundred, thirty of whom came from ADI(K). It became known as the Air Documents Research Centre (ADRC). In November 1945, it moved out of Weymouth Street to 12a Stanhope Gate, London.[47]

After the German surrender in May 1945, most members of the German air force high command had gone into hiding. They were rounded up by the British and Americans and taken to a camp near Berchtesgaden for interrogation, until their fate was decided.[48] In August 1945, it was agreed that they should be brought over to England and held temporarily at Latimer House.[49] The highest Luftwaffe officers, such as Field Marshal Hugo Sperrle, Karl Koller (Chief of the General Staff) and General Adolf Galland, were captured and brought there, together with many of the civilian technicians holding the most interesting information.[50] It was rumoured that Hermann Goering was briefly brought to Latimer and interrogated by Felkin, although this has not been officially verified.[51] Latimer became No.2 Personnel Holding Unit: a centre capable of holding up to 300 German air force personnel.[52] For the next three months, this air force section came under the command of Squadron Leader A. Macleod, aided by Flight Lieutenant A.A.D. Maconochie as station administration officer.[53]

The unit received its first quota of German air force officers on 1 September, flown into nearby RAF Bovingdon. It consisted of 150 officers, 86 NCOs and 33 female staff.[54] That same day, an intelligence element of ADI(K) arrived under F/Lt L. Taylor.

The following day saw the arrival of seventy more German air force officers, thirteen other ranks and eleven German women. German air force personnel continued to arrive on a daily basis throughout September 1945. The majority remained on site until December 1945, when they were taken under American military escort to the port of Dover for return to Germany.

Denys Felkin was awarded an OBE and an MBE for his services during the war, as well as the Belgian Order of Chevalier with Swords (1945) and American Legion of Merit. His work did not cease with the closure of Latimer House. He headed ADI(K) which undertook the interrogation of German air force prisoners, civilian scientists and technicians being held at a clandestine site known as 'Inkpot' in Wimbledon, South London.[55]

The CSDIC side of Latimer House under Kendrick formally closed on 7 November 1945. One of his last tasks was to collate copies of the personal files of all the German generals and senior officers held by MI19. The thick file of profiles of 98 officers was sent by his colleague Norman Crockatt to the head of MI6, with a covering letter:

Dear C,

The enclosed notes on Senior German Officer prisoners of war who passed through our hands at Cockfosters were compiled for DMI [Director of Military Intelligence]. The latter has now gone on leave pending handing over and has returned his folder to me. It occurs to me, however, that either you or he (in his future appointment) might find some use for these jottings, and I am, therefore, sending them to you.[56]

Lord Chesham never occupied his home again: it was the subject of a compulsory purchase order. From 1947, Latimer House became a site for the Joint Services Staff College, with new buildings constructed within the estate, and later became the National Defence College. Today, it is a luxury hotel and conference centre.

Wilton Park became No.300 POW Camp, where thousands of German POWs underwent a vital re-education and denazification programme in readiness for their repatriation to Germany. Afterwards, it continued to have military links and by the 1980s had become an army languages centre. It has since been sold to a developer for hundreds of houses to be built on site. All traces of its wartime heritage have disappeared.

THE SECRET LISTENERS

What happened to the secret listeners? They finally witnessed the end of the regime which had destroyed their lives in Germany, and persecuted and murdered members of their family and friends. It was the end of a regime which had systematically annihilated six million European Jews, and five million others. For the secret listeners there could be no going back to Germany to reclaim what was lost or rebuild their lives there permanently. Britain was now their home. After being demobilised around 1947–48, they received British nationality and the majority made their homes in Britain.

In post-war civilian life, they settled down, perhaps to marriage and a family, and went on to make a valuable contribution to business, education and academic life, politics, economics and the arts. Peter Ganz, for example, had a distinguished career in academia as a Germanist and medievalist.[57]

Fritz Lustig lost contact with George Pulay after the war but, in 2012, in a twist of fate, he met up with George's daughter Jessica Pulay, and George's nephew, the late Roger Lloyd-Pack, an actor. Roger had no idea of his uncle's wartime work until a chance discovery during the research for this book. The late Peter Hart, who was immensely proud of his role as a secret listener, reflected in his memoirs: 'It is the duty of the older generation to leave an authentic record of their experiences during the Second World War for the benefit of posterity. Without it, history would simply be hearsay.'[58]

COLONEL THOMAS JOSEPH KENDRICK, OBE

After Latimer House closed, Kendrick was assigned to 'special duties' with MI6, although the precise nature of the work was not revealed. His personal army file noted: 'To be specially employed (and not remunerated from army funds), MI6.' For his services to American intelligence, Kendrick was honoured with the Legion of Merit. His citation, signed personally by Harry S. Truman, read:

Colonel Thomas Joseph Kendrick, British Army,
rendered exceptionally valuable services as commanding officer
of a special center for interrogation of enemy prisoners of war
for the British War Office from June 1942 to May 1945.
He willingly made available to the United States intelligence
units all facilities at his command, and contributed greatly
through his earnest cooperation to the effective training
of American intelligence personnel.

Kendrick worked for MI6 until his retirement in 1948. He died in 1972 at the age of 91. A Roman Catholic funeral service took place in Cobham, Surrey, and was followed by burial in the municipal cemetery in Weybridge. Grandson Ken Walsh recalled: 'I attended his funeral and stood next to my mother. I noticed some chaps in long raincoats. I asked my mother who they were. She replied: "Oh, they're from the Foreign Office and MI6." As we left the church they shook hands with us. They were just like spies out of a film.'[59]

Even in his twilight years, Kendrick never spoke about his work. Until recently, MI6 did not officially exist. Kendrick went to his grave carrying many secrets. The cloak of secrecy surrounding his life adds to the sense of mystery, enhanced by the shadowy figures at his funeral.

EPILOGUE

Secrets To The Grave

For decades, Lustig speculated whether their work had any impact on the outcome of the war. Although not privy to precisely how it changed the war, Lustig could take comfort from the words of Kendrick on his first day at Latimer House: 'What you are doing here is as important as fighting on the front line or firing a gun in action.'[1]

Did they contribute to the Allied victory in Europe and defeat of Nazism? It would take Lustig nearly seventy years to discover how their unit, alongside Bletchley Park, impacted the intelligence war. Lustig passed away in December 2017 at the age of 98 and was one of only a handful of intelligence personnel who lived to see the declassification of the official files and gain an appreciation of their enormous contribution to the war. Although the work of the secret listeners is now recognised as being 'of considerable national and international historical interest which bears comparison to the code-breaking work at Bletchley Park,'[2] it remains an area of Second World War history yet to be fully studied and evaluated by historians. Today, with the benefit of hindsight, it is easy to be complacent about what is now known about the war and to overlook the volume of intelligence and significance of material that the secret listeners amassed for British intelligence. They often picked up information that had not been gathered by any other British wartime unit.

The pages of this book have sought to provide a comprehensive history of the intelligence gathered, the mechanics of gaining that intelligence and the day-to-day lived experiences of the POWs, largely drawn from information contained in declassified Special Reports and General Reports. They preserve the rare but verbatim wartime conversations which in turn shed light on a moment in time and provide unique insight into life as a German general or enemy POW at the hands of British intelligence and its spies.

The sheer volume of material from the bugged conversations provided Britain and the United States with a comprehensive picture of the Nazi war machine and its threat. The M Room yielded a wealth of information about the new technology the Germans were developing for use in warfare, which could not have been secured in direct interrogation. It is highly doubtful that the Allies could have kept ahead of the 'tech war' without it. Operational intelligence from the M Room enabled the Allies to develop counter-measures to the new technology being developed before it was first used by the Germans. The M Room provided intelligence which ranged from the first discovery of X-Gerät (the new Y beam technology fitted to Luftwaffe planes) to Knickebein, radar, magnetically-fused torpedoes, mines, new technology on U-boats and Luftwaffe aircraft, Hitler's plans for a gas attack on Britain, German battle plans and positions of troops, U-boat bases and construction programmes, the Battle of the Atlantic, German secret weapon programmes (V-1, V-2 and V-3), and guided projectiles.[3] At the end of hostilities, it was reported that the unit proved to be 'one of the most valuable sources of intelligence on [German] rockets, flying bombs, jet propelled aircraft and submarines'.[4]

The bugged conversations shed a lot of light on German radar, including night fighter radar appliances and tactics, so that when a postwar investigation was made in Germany, it was estimated that the Air Intelligence section, ADI(K), had reports on the subject that covered '95% of the whole developed and developing field of German radar and anti-radar devices with accuracy little short of 100%'.[5] A special report recognised how this alone had made 'an enormous contribution' to minimising Allied losses in night attacks over Germany.[6]

The theatrical scenes and dramatic episodes that unfolded, particularly in the 'special quarters' at Trent Park, often seemed to belong more to fiction than history. No 'third degree methods' (rough treatment or torture) were ever used at the M Room sites.[7] Instead, the files provide a glimpse into the often unruly life of the German generals. This can make for surprising reading – as seemingly frivolous behaviour on the part of the intelligence services (such as treats and trips to London) is pitched against a bitter rivalry between Hitler's own top commanders. But it is pertinent to draw back and ask: how else could the Allies have successfully gained the vast array of operational intelligence? Despite the 'mad hatter's tea party' of daily life at Trent Park, it underlies a deeply serious intelligence operation. Success was accomplished with devastating efficiency and good old-fashioned British humour (which would not seem out of place in an episode of the TV series *Dad's Army*). The stakes were high. No wonder Kendrick slid a pistol across the desk when intelligence officer Charles Deveson first started at the unit – and said to him: 'If you ever betray anything about this work, here is the gun with which I expect you to do the decent thing. If you don't, I will.'[8] There was no room for traitors or accidentally spilling the beans – the secrecy of this operation had to be protected at all costs. Kendrick is to be credited with masterminding a cunning operation that enabled the Axis prisoners, and specifically Hitler's top commanders, to relax in comfort in captivity. Little did they suspect that the walls had ears...

Few people have ever heard of Thomas Joseph Kendrick. His clandestine wartime sites had provided pivotal information through a highly efficient 'human intelligence' organisation, and influenced the course of the war. One reason for his obscurity is that he and the majority of his staff had to take their secrets to the grave. They had all signed the Official Secrets Act. Towards the end of the war, Norman Crockatt (head of MI9) wrote to Kendrick:

> You have done a Herculean task, and I doubt if anyone else could have carried it through. It would be an impertinence were I to thank you for your contribution to the war effort up to-date: a grateful country ought to do that, but I don't suppose they will.[9]

The nation could not yet thank Kendrick, nor the men and women who had secured a free Europe and laid the foundations for contemporary espionage into the Cold War and beyond. Their secrets were consigned to the basement of the War Office; and it would be over sixty years before the files were quietly released into the National Archives and anything revealed about Trent Park, Latimer House and Wilton Park.

Even after the files were released between 1999 and 2004, it took another thirteen years for formal recognition of the unit's significance, which came only after a high-profile public campaign in which the author was involved, after developer Berkeley Homes purchased Trent Park in 2015 and planned to turn the historic rooms into luxury apartments. A weighty endorsement of the site's significance by Historic England was taken seriously enough by Berkeley Homes to save the key historic spaces within the mansion as a museum dedicated to the work of the secret listeners.[10]

Today, it is possible to argue that the M Room shortened the war and saved lives. However, analysis of the M Room's legacy is only in its infancy. Its files have rarely, if ever, been consulted for books on the Second World War. Further research is essential to assess its implications for operations on land, air and at sea and to understand the wider link between intelligence gained and campaigns launched.

With this story emerging from the shadows, the nation can finally pay tribute to its women and men and the commanding genius of its spy chief, Thomas Joseph Kendrick. As one of Britain's greatest spymasters, his legacy can take its place in the nation's history. The events described in this book, however outlandish, did unfold and significantly contributed to the M Room's mission to protect Britain's shores from the gravest of threats. The stakes during the Second World War had never been higher:

> Had it not been for the information obtained at these centres, it could have been London and not Hiroshima which was devastated by the first atomic bomb.[11]

Appendix of Intelligence Staff

ARMY INTELLIGENCE WHO SERVED WITH CSDIC

Overall Commandant: Colonel Thomas Joseph Kendrick, OBE.

Assistant Commandant (Intelligence): Lieutenant Colonel Charles Corner, MVO

Assistant Commandant (Administration): Lieutenant Colonel F. Huband, MBE, MC, DCM

Commandant at Wilton Park: Major Leo St Clare Grondona.

Captain H.G. Abrahams, Captain F.G. Adams, Captain George Ernest Austen, Captain S.F. Austin, Lieutenant A.J. Bauers, Lieutenant C.A.W. Beaumont, Lieutenant Blyth, Captain R. Boothroyd, Captain M.O. Brigstock, Lieutenant Patrick Brodie, Lieutenant A. Buesst, Lieutenant J.G. Bullock, Captain John Edgar Burgoyne, Captain C.E. Calderari, Major Frank Cassels, Lieutenant K.O. Chetwood-Aiken, Lieutenant W. Cochraine, Hugh John Colman (Hans Joachim Colman), Lieutenant G. Cooper, Captain G.P. Copping, Captain B. le Cren, Captain M.D. Davidson, Lieutenant H.W. Davis, Captain S.H. Davis, Captain Charles Deveson, Lieutenant Colonel Henry V. Dicks (camp psychologist), Lieutenant F.E. Edmunds, Colonel Richard Prior Edwards, Lieutenant E. Egger, Lieutenant H.R. Evans, Lieutenant W.G.G. Fairholme, Lieutenant R.D. Fermo, Lieutenant E.M. Fitzgerald, Captain W.E. Foss, Captain W.P. Gatliff, Lieutenant H.S. Gervers, Lieutenant Gross, Captain R. Hamilton, Lieutenant H.P. Hare, Major Harrison (CSDIC, Middle East), Captain W. Hartje, Captain C.C. Hay, Captain

D. Heaton-Armstrong, Lieutenant J.S. Heber, Captain M. Hilton, Lieutenant A.E. Hind, Lieutenant J. Hunter, Captain W.J. Ingham, Captain H.R. Jahn, Captain J.E. Johnson, Captain Charles Juulmann (Karl Ferdinand Juulmann), Captain E.E. King, Captain G.A. Kitchen, Captain Victor Lang, Major C.H. LeBosquet, Lieutenant F. Lonergan, Lieutenant Macintosh, Captain Macmillan (CSDIC, Middle East, technical), Captain E.W. Marin, Captain Norman S. Marsh, Captain E.A. Morton, Lieutenant L. Muirhead, Captain Ian Thomson Munro, Captain F.W. Murray, Captain A.B. Nash, Captain A.H. New, Lieutenant A. Oakey, Major Leslie E. Parkin, Captain J.E. Parnell, Captain C.D. Perring, Captain H. Phare, Captain L.L.M. Pokorny, Lieutenant E.A. Poupard, Lieutenant F.W. Read-Jahn, Captain C.H.B. Readman, Lieutenant H.W. Reynolds, Major Thomas Rittner, Captain A.C. Robertshaw, Captain H.B. Romberg, Lieutenant M. Rowe, Lieutenant M.E. Rubin, Lieutenant G.A.F. Sandor, Captain W.H. Serin, Lieutenant D. Simon, Captain A.G. Speirs, Lieutenant R.H.C. Steed, Lieutenant O.H. Strafford, Captain L.G. Struthers, Lieutenant G.A. Thompson, Captain B.S. Vickerman, Captain J. Walmsley, Lieutenant M. Walshe, Lieutenant John Weatherley, Lieutenant Jan August Weber, Lieutenant E.W. Zundel.

Female officers: Subaltern Lucy F. Addey, J/Commander P.M. Agar-Robartes, J/Commander M.R.K. Bennett, Subaltern E. Bernert, J/Commander M.B. Boak, Subaltern E.W. Bobby, J/Commander M. Braun, Subaltern S.J. Caldwell, 2/Subaltern M. Crutchleigh-Fitzpatrick, 2/Subaltern C.J. Davis, 2/Subaltern A.G.M. Doyle, 2/Subaltern P.G.R. Doyle, J/Commander K.M. Falwasser, J/Commander M.J. Frise, Subaltern M. Grugeon, Subaltern S.P. Hall, Subaltern J.P. Horrigan, Subaltern E. Iles, J/Commander G.H. Leigh, J/Commander H.M. Lishman, Subaltern J.E. Little, Subaltern B. Maile, J/Commander T. Masterson, J/Commander R. Morris, Subaltern G. Ouseley, J/Commander V.M. Robins, J/Commander Dawn Rockingham-Gill, Subaltern P.M. Rubin, J/Commander A.D. Skoyles, Subaltern M. Sworder, 2/Subaltern L.M. Thomas, J/Commander E.M. Thwaits, J/Commander Catherine Townshend (Jestin), J/Commander E.F. Van Bergen, Subaltern F.F. Watt, J/Commander J.D. Woodhead, 2/Subaltern H. Zillwood.

SECRET LISTENERS

The names below are as complete a list as currently possible of the German-speaking refugees who served as secret listeners. In some cases, only their anglicised name, or part of full name, is available:

Robert Aufhäuser, Peter Baer (Peter Baines), Hubert Bailey, Rudolph Bamberger (Bambi), Otto Lothar Barber (William Peter Barber), Fritz Berger (Freddie Benson), Walter Beevers, Erwin von Bendemann (H.I. Bertham), Peter Bendix, Bentham, Berchstecher, Fritz Bierer (Fred Bentley), Blake, Egon Brandt (Ernest Brent), Bratu, Garry Casey, Hans Friedrich Eisler (Sean Graham), Emanuel Ekler (Eric Ellis), Bruce Eldon, Max Ernst Erlanger (Ernest Max Langley), Kurt Ernst (Brian Henson), Erskine, Friedrich Falk (Frank Falk), Werner David Feist, Alfred Fleiss, Hans Francken (Hannen Geoffrey Francken), Ludwig Heinrich Franken (Lewis Franklin), Felix Konrad Fullenbaum (Felix Kenneth Fraser), Peter Ganz, Hans Göhler (John Gay), Lev Golodetz (?), Eberhard Gottstein, Innozenz Grafe, Sidney Graham, Ludwig Kurt Grunwald (Kenneth Grandville), Oscar Hamm, Heilbronn, Kurt Heinsheimer (Frank West), Walter Oscar Heller (Walter Hellier), Francis Hellman, Peter Klaus Herz (Peter Hart), Adolf Hirschfeld (Alan Henley), Hans Ernst Hoffmann (John Housman), Albert Hollander, Willie Hornstein (John Horton), Franz Huelsen, Erich Huppert, Harry Jakobs, Jellinek, Hans Kallmas (Herbert Kellett), Wolfgang Kals (William Kennedy), Fritz Katz (Frederick Geoffrey Katz), Karl Heinz Kaufmann, Leo Kaufmann, Leon Kendon, Siegfried Kissin (Stephen Kissin), Erich Konrad (Eric Arthur Conrad), Konrad Paul Korn (Paul Douglas), Ernest Korpner, Kraft, Herbert Kyval, Walter Leatham, Ernst Lederer, Herbert Lehmann, Lindsay, Charles Lipton, Alexander Lowy, Fritz Lustig, Otto Mandel, Mann, Bobby Manners, Robert Mannheimer (William Manners), Siegfried Männlein, Marefield, Erich Mark (Eric Mark), Claus Mayer, Hans Adolf Mayer (Herbert Anthony Marshall), Joseff Merfeld (Peter John Morton), Wolfgang Meyer (William Meyer), Arthur Morgenthau, Robert Neave, Herbert Neuhaus (Herbert Newhouse), Neumann, Rees Nichols, Heinrich Nickelsberg (Hilary Nichols), Rudi Oppenheimer,

Helmut Orgler, Erich Peritz (Eric Stephen Pearce), Oskar Henryk Prentki, George Pulay, Johnny Rapp, Sabersky, Heinz Jürgen Sahlmann (Henry Saunders), Edward Solomon Salti, Teddy Schächter (Teddy Chester), Eric Schaffer, Godfrey Scheele, Robert Schneider (Robert Lacey), Ernst Schönmann (Ernst Scott), Segell, Francis Seton, Father Shipton, Hubert Simon, Sirot, Spiller, Werner Stark, Hans Stern (David Stern), Richard Paul Adolf Stern, Frank Stevens, Hans Strauss (Hugh Strauss), Wolfgang Tietz (Leonard Deeds), Albert Tugendhat, Franz Türkheim (Peter Türkheim), Michael Ullman, Fritz Carl Ullstein, Vigart, Wilhelm Vollbracht, Max Wassermann (Martin Warner), Fritz Wechselmann (Arthur Fred Wellmann), Norbert Wegner (Norman Willert), Fritz Weis (Fred Wells), Peter Weisz, West, Wulwick.

THE K ALBUM

The main source is a booklet called 'The K Album' which list the names of members of ADI(K) – Air Intelligence.

Commanding Officer: Samuel Denys Felkin.

Squadron Leader W.L. Antrobus, Flight Lieutenant W.B. Atkinson, Squadron Leader L.P. Bamford, Section Officer C.R. Baring-Gould (Mrs Bottenheim) (female), Section Officer E.J. Bembaron (female), Flight Lieutenant R. Benson, Flight Lieutenant C.R. Bingham, Squadron Leader B.E. Bishop, Section Officer H.M. Black (female), Captain E.H. Boehm, Squadron Leader A.K. Boning, Captain M.P. Borchert, Squadron Leader G.W. Bragg, Flight Officer W.O. Brayton, Section Officer J.Y. Brooks (female), Captain L.A. Brunner, Flight Lieutenant E. Campbell, Flight Lieutenant V.I. Clark, Flight Lieutenant M.D.M. Cockraine, Flight Lieutenant R.J. Cole, Flight Lieutenant L.E. Collier, Flight Officer K.R. Costello (female), Squadron Leader G.L.D. Cox, Flight Lieutenant D. Culver, Captain C.C. Davis, Flight Officer J.E.M. Davis (female), Squadron Leader L.V. Davis, Wing Commander R.M.C. Day, Flight Lieutenant J.F.R. Druce, Lieutenant Colonel E. Englander, Section Officer F. Fairburn (female), Flight Lieutenant W. Forbes-Watkins, Section Officer E.A. Ford-Hutchinson (female), Wing Commander R.H. Francis,

Captain W.A. Frank, Flight Lieutenant R.H. Gould, Squadron Leader H.R. Gray, Flight Lieutenant B.B. Gregory, Squadron Leader H.O. Gregory, Major K.M. Grubb, Flight Officer V.L.A. Gundry-White (female), Wing Commander P. de Haan, Section Officer M.E. Harcourt, Squadron Leader L.F. Hartje, Flight Lieutenant D.F. Haslewood, Flight Lieutenant M.A. Hicks, Flight Lieutenant R. Hirsch, Lieutenant Colonel J.D. Holtzermann (US), Flight Lieutenant A.R.J. Humphrey, Squadron Leader John X. Hunt, Flight Lieutenant J.C. Hutchinson, Commandant G. Ittel (French Air Force), Squadron Leader L.A. Jackets, Squadron Leader T.E. James, Squadron Leader W. Jamieson, Wing Commander G.B. Jepson, Section Officer M. Jopp (female), Squadron Leader H.H. Keen, Captain W.M. Kloetzer, Section Officer C.M. Krause (female), Squadron Leader P.N. Labertouche, Flight Lieutenant S.A. Lane, Squadron Leader C.M. Lawler-Wilson, Flight Lieutenant N.E. Leigh, Flight Lieutenant P.K. Lickford, Flight Lieutenant J.R. Littlefair, Flight Lieutenant E.A. Littlefield, Captain S.R. Litton, Flight Lieutenant M.J. Longinotto-Landseer, Flight Lieutenant J. Lord, Squadron Leader Ludovici, Flight Lieutenant A.J.R. Lyon, Flight Lieutenant I. Macrae, Captain G.D. Mandelik, Flight Officer S.M. Manduell (Mrs Jackets), Wing Commander C.H. March, Flight Lieutenant H.G.R. March, Squadron Leader W.W. Marks, Flight Officer E.J. Masterman (female), Flight Lieutenant E.H. Mayer, Flight Officer E.M. Mayes (female), Flight Lieutenant E.E. Medland, Lieutenant J.H. Mehl, Squadron Leader N. Miller, Wing Commander W.L. Minter, Flight Lieutenant G.I.A. Moes, Flight Lieutenant J.E. Mullholland, Wing Commander J.B. Newton, Wing Commander Newton-John, Flight Lieutenant P.G.A. Norman-Wright, Flight Lieutenant E.C. Norris, Flight Lieutenant J.G. Nowell, Flight Lieutenant J. Odde, Section Officer O. Oppenheimer (female), Captain F.E. Overley, Squadron Leader J.E.H. Park, Flight Lieutenant A. Parkin, Flight Lieutenant Pelham-Toll, Flight Lieutenant E.C. Peters, Flight Lieutenant V.J.R.D. Prendergast, Captain Pyper (South African Air Force), Wing Commander R.M. Rickett, Flight Lieutenant G.M. Robbins, Flight Lieutenant J.S. Robinson, Flight Lieutenant B.P. Roche, Wing Commander H.N. Roffey, Captain

H. Rosenhaupt, Flight Lieutenant Ruse, Captain O.A. Saborsky, Squadron Leader E. Sankey, Captain C.D. Schneider, Squadron Leader R. Scrivener, Squadron Leader J.F.A. Segner, Squadron Leader R.H. Siddons, Flight Officer L.M. Sieveking (female), Flight Lieutenant A.J. Sington, Flight Lieutenant W.M. Skeffington, Wing Commander V.O. Slesser, Squadron Leader C.H. Smith, Squadron Leader D.A.G. Smith, Captain M.M. Sommer, Wing Commander Peter Soren, Squadron Leader G.W. Spenceley, Squadron Leader C.K. Squires, Squadron Leader H.M. Stokes, Captain M. Sulkes, Squadron Leader B.B. Sullivan, Flight Lieutenant A. Taylor, Flight Lieutenant J.L.S. Taylor, Flight Officer I.D. Thornhill (female), Captain Willis Thornton, Squadron Leader J.P.C. Tooth, Major Max van Rossum Daum, Flight Lieutenant S.Y. Vitalis, Captain R.E. Vollprecht, Flight Lieutenant C.H.R. Wade, Lieutenant Colonel E.M. Warburg, Flight Lieutenant H.J. Ware, Flight Lieutenant G.C. Waterston, Squadron Leader H. Webb, Captain H.E. Weingartner, Flight Officer H.M. Weir, Captain J.M. Whitten, Flight Lieutenant A.C. Wilberforce, Flight Lieutenant R.R. Witter, Squadron Leader T.S. Wyatt.

NAVAL INTELLIGENCE STAFF

Personnel who served in, or were attached to, the Naval Intelligence section of the bugging sites:

Lieutenant Leslie Atkinson, Lieutenant George Blake (RNVR), Lieutenant John Wilfred Carey, Sub-Lieutenant Brian Connell (RNVR), Lieutenant Commander Burton Cope, Lieutenant Commander Edward Croghan, Lieutenant Commander Charles Everett, Lieutenant J.G. Halstead, Lieutenant Commander Ralph Izzard (RNVR), Lieutenant Julius Lunzer, Lieutenant John McDonnell, Lieutenant Commander Colin McFadyean (RNVR), Lieutenant R.D. Macpherson, Lieutenant John Marriner, Lieutenant Richard Pennell, Commander Leonard Rideal, Lieutenant Wilfred Samuel, Lieutenant Harry Scholar (Czech), Lieutenant Colonel Bernard Trench, Lieutenant Richard (Dick) Weatherby (RNVR), Captain John Weatherby, Lieutenant Commander Donald Burkewood

Welbourn (RNVR), Captain Selwyn Charles Wheeler, Sub-Lieutenant David Williamson (RNVR).

Female interrogators and intelligence staff: Evelyn Barron, Miss M. Barton, Third Officer B. Collis, Miss E. Duckers, Jean Flower, Claudia Furneaux, Ruth Hales, Miss Hyde, Miss King, V. P. Lennard, Esme Mackenzie, Gwen Neal-Wall, Miss K. Pearce, Celia Thomas.

OFFICERS' MESS, TRENT PARK

Daily Camp Commandant: Major Topham
Medical Officer: Captain Young
Interpreter: Captain E.A. Hamley
Captain Drumgold, Lieutenant Simmons, Captain Coulson, Lieutenant Maule, Lieutenant Cheshire, Lieutenant Danks.
Others who worked for this unit: Cynthia Crew, Daphne Joan Houckham, Elizabeth Rees-Mogg, Joan Stansfield
Adjutant at Wilton Park: Captain Kenneth Morgan

notes

PROLOGUE: DECADES OF SILENCE

1. SRX 1635, 11 March 1943, WO 208/4162. Sketches of V-1 and V-2 launching equipment (ramps) contained in WO 208/4292.
2. Helen Fry, *Spymaster: The Secret Life of Kendrick*.
3. Kendrick's personal service record, copy from Barbara Lloyd.
4. Keith Jeffery, *MI6: The History of the Secret Intelligence Service, 1909–1949*, pp. 202 and 301.
5. Fry, *Spymaster*, pp. 39–58; Jeffery, *MI6*, p. 202; and letter from Consulate General to Sir Nevile Henderson (British ambassador, Berlin), 22 August 1938, copied and released to the author by the Foreign Office in 2013 under Freedom of Information Act.
6. Fry, Spymaster, pp. 57–8, 144–7.
7. Martin Gilbert, *Beyond the Call of Duty: British Diplomats and Other Britons Who Helped Jews Escape from Nazi Tyranny*. The crisis facing Kendrick and his staff in trying to get Jews out of Austria is reported in detail in FO 372/3284. See also Jeffery, *MI6*, p. 301.
8. George Weidenfeld, *Remembering My Good Friends*; Eric Sanders, *From Music to Morse*, privately published autobiography. Both men were interviewed by Helen Fry for *Spymaster*.
9. Fry, *Spymaster*, pp. 115–17.
10. Ibid., p. 116.
11. KV 3/116.
12. Fry, *Spymaster*, pp. 90–8, 155–9. See also KV 3/116.
13. British Consulate General to Sir Nevile Henderson, 18 August 1938, FO 371/21691.
14. Cypher to Sir Nevile Henderson, 23 August 1938, FO 371/21691.
15. Cypher to Sir Nevile Henderson, 19 August 1938. Copy released to the author by the Foreign Office under FOI in 2013. News reports of charges of espionage: *News Chronicle*, 19 August 1938; *Sunday Express*, 21 August 1938; *Daily Telegraph*, 20 August 1938.
16. Jeffery, *MI6*, pp. 295, 310–11.
17. Michael Smith, *The Secrets of Station X*; David Kenyon, *Bletchley Park and D-Day*.
18. Jeffery, *MI6*, p. 319.
19. 'The Story of MI19', pp. 1–2, WO 208/4970.
20. Memo 2 September 1939, signed by Major M. Perceval, WO 208/3458. In 1940, the unit became a part of MI9, and then MI19.
21. Summary report by Denys Felkin (history of the unit), 31 December 1945, AIR 40/2636. Also 'Prisoner of War Interrogation 1939–1945', ADM 223/475.
22. Interview with Barbara Lloyd.
23. On 29 March 1910, Kendrick married Norah Wecke, the daughter of Frederick Wecke (manager of a diamond mine near Lüderitzbucht in German-occupied South-West Africa

(now Luderitz in Namibia). Interviews with family members, Barbara Lloyd and Ken Walsh.

24. WO 94/105 is dedicated to the setting up of the bugging operation in the Tower of London. Various correspondence for January 1939.

1: THE TOWER OF LONDON

1. Minutes of the meeting, entitled 'Co-ordination Arrangements for the Interrogation of P/W', KV 4/302.
2. Letter from MI1 via the War Office to the Admiralty, 23 March 1939, ADM 1/10579.
3. Interviews with Evelyn Barron and Melanie McFadyean.
4. Memo, ref: C/1196/A, 21 August 1939, WO 94/105.
5. Memo issued by MI1(a), 2 September 1939, WO 208/3458.
6. Memo, ref: C/1196/A, 21 August 1939, WO 94/105.
7. Memo, 3 September 1939, WO 208/3458.
8. Nigel West, *Historical Dictionary of International Intelligence*, pp. 41–2.
9. See FO 371/22321, and Fry, *Spymaster*.
10. Felkin took over from Pollock on 20 December 1939. See 'Intelligence from Prisoners of War', report by Denys Felkin, 31 December 1945, p. 2, AIR 40/2636.
11. Anne Walton (Felkin's daughter). See also Fry, *Spymaster*.
12. Biographical information from Anne Walton.
13. Interview with Anne Walton.
14. Confirmed by their individual medal cards, the National Archives.
15. Memo from MI1(a), 3 September 1939, WO 208/3458.
16. Correspondence with the author.
17. After the war, he returned to work in Germany as general manager of Cable and Wireless Ltd.
18. Trench diary, 28 September 1939.
19. ADM 116/4572. He was mentioned in Dispatches in August 1942 for resolution and leadership as the senior officer of 1st S.G.B. Flotilla.
20. Pennell was decorated with a DSC on 15 September 1942, and mentioned twice in Dispatches (2 October 1942 and 9 October 1943).
21. Felkin's history of the unit entitled 'Intelligence from Prisoners of War', 31 December 1945, AIR 40/2636.
22. Peter Leighton-Langer, *The King's Own Loyal Enemy Aliens*; and Helen Fry, *Churchill's German Army*.
23. Interviews with the late Roger Lloyd-Pack, nephew of George Pulay.
24. Fritz Lustig, interviews with the author.
25. 'Intelligence from Prisoners of War', report by Denys Felkin, 31 December 1945, AIR 40/2636; 'The Story of MI19' in WO 208/4970.
26. Memo, ref: C/1196/A, 21 August 1939, WO 94/105.
27. Count Anthony de Salis died in 1952, France.
28. 'Admittance to Prisoners of War Enclosure: Instruction 5', issued 7 October 1939, WO 94/105.
29. 'Prisoner of War Collecting Centre – HM Tower of London', ref: C/1195/Q, 3 September 1939, WO 94/105.
30. Major Dunne to Governor of the Tower of London, 22 September 1939, WO 94/105.
31. Governor of the Tower of London to Major Dunne, 30 September 1939, WO 94/105.
32. 'Intelligence from Prisoners of War', report by Denys Felkin, 31 December 1945, section 52–63, AIR 40/2636.
33. Report, 3 October 1939, WO 208/4141.
34. 'Intelligence from Prisoners of War', report by Denys Felkin, 31 December 1945, section 68–76, AIR 40/2636.
35. AIR 40/2394 and WO 94/105.

36. *The Guy Liddell Diaries, Vol. 1*, ed. Nigel West, p. 20.
37. Trench diary entry for 17 September 1939. Full interrogation reports survive in AIR 40/2394.
38. German U-boats of WWII on uboat.net, 17 February 2010.
39. Nominal roll in WO 94/105.
40. Trench diary, 18 September 1939.
41. Ibid., 20 September 1939.
42. Trench diary, 22 September 1939.
43. Report entitled 'U-27: Interrogation of Crew, September 1939', AIR 40/2394.
44. 'Procedure on Arrival of Prisoners of War', 14 September 1939, WO 94/105.
45. Trench diary, 26 September 1939. See also Report entitled 'U-27: Interrogation of Crew, September 1939', AIR 40/2394.
46. Report entitled 'U-27: Interrogation of Crew, September 1939', AIR 40/2394.
47. Undated report on information from the wireless operator of U-27, AIR 40/2394.
48. Ibid.
49. Ibid.
50. Undated translation of Beckmann's coded letter, AIR 40/2394.
51. Sophie Jackson, *Churchill's Unexpected Guests*.
52. Trench diary, 27 September 1939.
53. Ibid., 28 September 1939.
54. Report, 3 October 1939, WO 208/4141.
55. Ibid.
56. Ibid.
57. Trench diary, 5 October 1939.
58. Trench diary, 15 October, 17 October and 29 October 1939.
59. Report, 27 October 1939, AIR 40/2394.
60. Document: 'Enemy Prisoners of War: Treatment on Capture', WO 32/10720.
61. Ibid.
62. Report by Pollock, 15 November 1939, AIR 40/2394.
63. Ibid.
64. SR 1, 2 November 1939, WO 208/4117.
65. The first members of AI1(K) with Felkin were F/O W.O. Brayton, F/O H.O. Gregory, F/O H.N. Roffy, and F/O C.H. Smith – see list in KV 4/302. This section became ADI(K).
66. Report from AI1(K) to AI.3, 3 November 1939, WO 208/2394.
67. SR 2, 2 November 1939, WO 208/4141.
68. Ibid.
69. Ibid.
70. Hochstuhl remained in the Tower until 18 November 1939.
71. SR 7, 22 November 1939, WO 208/4117.
72. Ibid.
73. SR 3, overheard on 26 October 1939 (report dated 9 November 1939), WO 208/4117.
74. Ibid.
75. Ibid.
76. Felkin's report of 31 October 1939, WO 208/5158. For later discussion on bacteriological warfare, see GRGG 210, 11–12 October 1944, p. 2, WO 208/5622.
77. A copy of the Oslo Report in AIR 40/2572. References also appear in Naval Intelligence files, see ADM 1/23905.
78. From the British Legation (Oslo) to Admiral Boyes, 6 November 1939, ADM 1/23905.
79. SRX 4, 22 December 1939, WO 208/4158.
80. SRX 7, 23 December 1939, WO 208/4158.
81. SRA 18, 26 January 1940, AIR 40/3070.
82. Directive from the War Office, 13 October 1940, WO 208/3540; 'Intelligence from Prisoners of War', report by Denys Felkin, 31 December 1945, AIR 40/2636.

83. MI9 War Diary, 21 December 1939, WO 165/39.
84. MI19 War Diary, WO 165/41. All entries were signed by Rawlinson.
85. 'The History of CSDIC', p. 3, WO 208/4970.
86. Damian Collins, *Charmed Life*.
87. The Hess files are contained in FO 1093/1-16. See Charles Fraser-Smith, *The Secret War of Charles Fraser Smith*, pp. 135–8. For other prisoners held in the Tower in WWII, see lists in WO 94/105.
88. Matthew Barry Sullivan, *Thresholds of Peace: German Prisoners and the People of Britain*, p. 51.
89. Hermann Ramcke, memoirs, pp. 79–80.
90. Trench diary, 30 November 1939 and 4 December 1939.
91. Trench diary, 4 December 1939.
92. Ibid., 4 December 1939.
93. Ibid., 9 December 1939.
94. KV 4/302; and references to Camp 11 in WO 208/3504.

2: M ROOM OPERATIONS

1. 'Inventory of Equipment Supplied and Installed at Cockfosters Camp', copy in WO 208/3457.
2. Letter from RCA to Kendrick, 14 February 1940, WO 208/3457.
3. It was shipped aboard the RMS *Lancastria* – the British Cunard liner that was later sunk on 17 June 1940 during the Dunkirk evacuations.
4. Cypher from Military Attaché (Washington) to DMI, 1 December 1939.
5. Kendrick to Rawlinson, 15 January 1940, WO 208/3458. See also 'The Story of MI19', p. 2, WO 208/4970.
6. Copies of their signed declarations, witnessed by Kendrick, survive in WO 208/3457.
7. Letter from RCA to Kendrick, 14 February 1940, WO 208/3457.
8. Ibid.
9. WO 208/3458, and a typed notice of 9 December 1939 in WO 94/105.
10. 'The History of CSDIC', WO 208/4970.
11. The army intelligence officers in this period were: Captain Charles Corner, Captain Leslie Parkin, Captain D. Heaton-Armstrong, Captain Frank Cassels, Captain Thomas Hardwick Rittner, Lieutenant M.E. Rubin, Lieutenant John Edgar Burgoyne, Lieutenant M.S. Marsh, Lieutenant R.H.C. Steed, Lieutenant G. Cooper, Lieutenant Charles Juulmann (Karl Ferdinand Juulmann), Lieutenant W. Hartje, Lieutenant S.H.S. Davis, Lieutenant J.E. Parnell, Lieutenant C.A.W. Beaumont, Lieutenant F.W.W. Murray, Lieutenant W.G.G. Fairholme, Lieutenant Victor Lang, Lieutenant H.P. Hare, Lieutenant Patrick Lennox Brodie, Lieutenant R.H. Boothroyd and Lieutenant J.M. Weatherley.
12. Biographical information courtesy of Paul Biddle. Juulmann (b.1885) served with the Royal Engineers, Signals Service in France in WWI, then 45th Battalion Royal Fusiliers in Russia as an interpreter.
13. Born 1893 in Ayr. At the outbreak of the First World War, Burgoyne was on a walking trip in Germany when he was arrested and interned in Ruhleben, then repatriated in 1917. In the inter-war years, he resumed his studies in French and German. By 1939, he was head of Modern Languages at the Royal High School and lecturer at Herriot-Watt College, Edinburgh.
14. Courtesy of Alasdair MacLeod.
15. 'Intelligence from Prisoners of War', report by Denys Felkin, 31 December 1945, section 68, AIR 40/2636.
16. The family always understood that Brin had been a stool pigeon and also spent time at Trent Park. Email correspondence with Steve Mallinson in April 2015.

17. Note dated 14 December 1940 about SPF/4, WO 208/4196.
18. Brin transferred to Bletchley Park in 1942.
19. Letter 9 December 1945 to Guy Liddell (MI5) from Rawlinson (MI9), KV 2/3767.
20. Letter to the Home Office, 25 March 1941, KV 2/3767.
21. 'The History of CSDIC', p. 6, WO 208/4970. Some special reports from stool pigeons survive in WO 208/4196.
22. They worked at Latimer House and Wilton Park, alongside Matthew Sullivan and US interrogator, Heimwarth Jestin. See Heimwarth Jestin, *A Memoir, 1918–1946*, p. 14.
23. 'Inventory of Equipment Supplied and Installed at Cockfosters Camp', WO 208/3457.
24. 'Installation and Use of Microphones at CSDIC (UK) P/W Camps 1939–1945', appendix G of 'The History of CSDIC', WO 208/4970.
25. Letter from RCA to Kendrick, 14 February 1940, p. 2, WO 208/3457.
26. Ibid., p. 3.
27. Overseeing the squads of listeners were Captains Brodie, Hartje, Davis and Serin, and Lieutenants Blyth, Rowe, Read-Jahn, Reynolds, Gross, Bauers and Weber.
28. Cassels had served in the First World War from 1914 and was wounded at Ypres in October 1918. In the inter-war years, he worked for the Foreign Office and as district controller, Inter-Allied Plebiscite in Upper Silesia until 1921. This was followed by a year in New Zealand, six years in Canada, as well as time in the Argentine Republic. He was fluent in German, Spanish and French.
29. Interview with the author. This account is borne out by the summary of M Room operational work in 'The History of CSDIC', appendix E, WO 208/4970.
30. Ibid.
31. Ibid., appendix F.
32. Ibid.
33. These files are to be found primarily in War Office series WO 208 and Air Intelligence section AIR 40 at the National Archives.
34. Felkin report, 28 November 1939 and 23 December 1939, WO 208/5158.
35. Departments that regularly received copies rose to include for example, MI10, 21 Army Group, Ministry of Information, Airborne Troops, Foreign Office, SAS, SHAEF, ETOUSA and MIS (Washington).
36. WO 165/39, 30 April 1940.
37. 'The History of CSDIC', p. 6 and appendix F (section 9), WO 208/4970.
38. Sullivan, *Thresholds of Peace*, p. 55.
39. Ibid., p. 53.
40. Kendrick to MI9 headquarters, 22 July 1941, WO 208/3455.
41. Trench Diary, 12 December 1939.
42. Ibid., 16 December 1939.
43. Trench Diary, 28 December 1939.
44. Ibid.
45. Trench visited Bletchley again on 15 August 1940. Entry in the diary for that date. There, he met with cryptographer Jos Cooper (head of Air Section), Geoffrey Tandy (marine biologist who retrieved data from waterlogged codebooks from U-boats and captured crew) and Joan Clarke (cryptanalyst).
46. The secret listeners did not know about Bletchley Park, as confirmed in interviews conducted by Helen Fry with former secret listeners Fritz Lustig and Eric Mark.
47. Trench diary, 1 January 1940.
48. SRN 1, 23 December 1939, WO 208/4141.
49. Interrogation reports dated 8 January 1940 and 19 January 1940, WO 208/5158.
50. Ibid.
51. Interrogation report, 8 January 1940, WO 208/5158.
52. Ibid.
53. Reports 9 June 1940 and 10 November 1940, WO 208/5158.
54. SRX 44, 21 February 1940, WO 208/4158.

55. Godfrey to Davidson (DMI), 7 January 1941, WO 208/5621.
56. 'W/T Procedure in German U-boat', report 11 November 1940, WO 208/5158.
57. Memo dated 31 December 1944 to Washington from director of GC&CS, HW 57/35.
58. Report contained in AIR 40/3108 and AIR 40/2394, dated 28 November 1939.
59. The hospital had 200 beds reserved for wounded axis forces awaiting process by MI9. See 'Intelligence from Prisoners of War', report by Denys Felkin, 31 December 1945, section 8, AIR 40/2636. See also pre-war preparations in a letter from MI1 via the War Office to the Admiralty, 23 March 1939, ADM 1/10579.
60. Report, 21 December 1939, AIR 40/2394.
61. Appendix to 'CSDIC Survey: 3 September 1939 to 31 December 1940', WO 208/3455. See, for example, SRA 419, 29 August 1940, AIR 40/3070.
62. 'CSDIC Survey: 3 September 1939 to 31 December 1940', pp. 2–3, WO 208/3455.
63. 'Intelligence from Prisoners of War', report by Denys Felkin, 31 December 1945, section 115, AIR 40/2636.
64. SRX 7, 23 December 1939, WO 208/4158.
65. Ibid.
66. Ibid.
67. SRA 8, 24 December 1939, WO 208/4117.
68. 'Intelligence from Prisoners of War', report by Denys Felkin, 31 December 1945, section 78–80, AIR 40/2636. See also 'SP Control and P/W Welfare Section', appendix A, WO 208/4970, and 'Section C: Stool Pigeons' in report 'P/W Interrogation 1939–1945', ADM 223/475.
69. 'Intelligence from Prisoners of War', report by Denys Felkin, 31 December 1945, section 80, AIR 40/2636.
70. SRX 9 and 10, 26 December 1939, WO 208/4158.
71. SRX 10, 26 December 1939, WO 208/4158.
72. Ibid.
73. Ibid.
74. Ibid.
75. SRA 19, 12 January 1940, WO 208/4158.
76. Ibid.
77. SRA 21, 29 January 1940, WO 208/4117.
78. Sullivan, *Thresholds of Peace*, p. 51.
79. Ibid.
80. 'Intelligence from Prisoners of War', report by Denys Felkin, 31 December 1945, section 118, AIR 40/2636.
81. Sullivan, *Thresholds of Peace*, p. 53.

3: TRENT PARK

1. 'The History of CSDIC', p. 6, WO 208/4970.
2. 'CSDIC Survey: 3 September 1939 to 31 December 1940', WO 208/3455. Copy also in WO 208/4970.
3. Ibid.
4. Appendix to 'CSDIC Survey: 3 September 1939 to 31 December 1940', p. 2, WO 208/3455. See also Minute reference number: NID 01789/39, 1 August 1940, ADM 1/23905.
5. SRN 32, 14 March 1940, WO 208/4141.
6. Ibid.
7. Ibid.
8. Interview with secret listeners, Eric Mark and Fritz Lustig.
9. Ibid.
10. 'Intelligence from Prisoners of War', report by Denys Felkin, 31 December 1945, section 116, AIR 40/2636.

11. SRA 20, 29 January 1940, WO 208/4117.
12. Ibid.
13. SR 362, 20 August 1940, AIR 40/3070.
14. SR 50, 28 March 1940, AIR 40/3070.
15. Davidson's comments in Appendix B, ref: MI9a/683, WO 208/4970.
16. 'Intelligence from Prisoners of War', report by Denys Felkin, 31 December 1945, section 117, AIR 40/2636. An early reference to X-Gerät came in January 1940 in SRA 36, 23 January 1940, AIR 40/3070. See also SRA 33, 23 February 1940, AIR 40/3070.
17. R.V. Jones, *Most Secret War*, pp. 134–50.
18. Ibid.
19. Ibid. See also WO 208/3474.
20. SRA 37, 27 February 1940, AIR 40/3070.
21. Jones, *Most Secret War*, p. 146.
22. Ibid., pp. 97–8 and 428.
23. 'Intelligence from Prisoners of War', report by Denys Felkin, 31 December 1945, section 117, AIR 40/2636.
24. Courtesy Barbara Lloyd.
25. A Minute dated 25 July 1941, WO 208/3455.
26. SR 1085, 25 April 1941, WO 208/3457.
27. The ground station's directional receiver aerial showed the plane's direction.
28. See also, for example, SRA 1612, 29 April 1941, WO 208/4123 and Felkin's summary report, 28 April 1941, WO 208/5158.
29. 'CSDIC Survey: 3 September 1939 to 31 December 1940', p. 1, WO 208/3455.
30. Ibid., p. 2.
31. See SRN 47, 17 April 1941 and SRN 297, 24 April 1941, both in WO 208/4141.
32. Trench diary, 12 March 1940. For biographical outlines of each member of NID at the bugging sites, see Derek Nudd, *Castaways of the Kriegsmarine*, pp. 61–70.
33. Interview with the author.
34. ADM 223/257 and ADM 223/472. Croghan died in an air crash on 16 December 1941 on a transport flight from Portreath to Gibraltar and is commemorated on the Chatham Naval War Memorial.
35. WO 165/39, 17 April 1940.
36. Ibid., 10 June 1940.
37. Ibid.
38. Added to the section's numbers by now were Lieutenant John Wilfred Paul de Mussenden Carey, Charles William Everett, Lieutenant R.D. Macpherson, John Stuart Marriner (formerly of Reuters), Commander Leonard Rideal (in charge of POW reports), John Mansfield Weatherby (joined April 1940) and Sub. Lt D. W. Williamson. Also information from interview with Melanie McFadyean, 2014. Ralph Izzard was the uncle of comedian Eddie Izzard.
39. Nicholas Rankin, *Ian Fleming's Commandos*.
40. After the war, Ruth Hales worked as secretary to engineer Geoffrey (Bob) Feilden who had developed the first jet engine with Frank Whittle. Esme Mackenzie married naval interrogator Brian Connell. Jean Flower married Charles Mitchel.
41. Donald Welbourn, unpublished memoirs, Imperial War Museum.
42. Interview with the author. Information confirmed in official files ADM 223/257 and ADM 223/472.
43. Nudd, *Castaways of the Kriegsmarine*, p. 70.
44. Trench diary, 12 July 1943. Wheeler was born in Bremen, Germany in 1923 where his father was employed, and lived in Hamburg until 1938.
45. ADM 223/257. McFadyean met a 19-year-old émigré (Marion Gutmann) from a prominent banking family in Berlin. A talented artist who had to flee the Nazis, she was also working for British intelligence for Sefton Delmer's propaganda unit, where she forged false ration books, SS identity cards and postcards. They later married.

46. Between 1939 and 1942, McFadyean was posted to HMS Dunnottar Castle which operated out of Freetown, then in October 1940 to HMS Seaborn, a Naval Air Service Station at Dartmouth Nova Scotia.
47. Donald Welbourn joined in March 1943.
48. Donald Welbourn, unpublished memoirs, Imperial War Museum.
49. For a detailed study of the Norwegian disaster of 1940, see John Kiszely, *Anatomy of a Campaign: The British Fiasco in Norway*.
50. Trench diary, entries for 25 May 1940 and 17 June 1940.
51. SRX 95, 25 June 1940, WO 208/4158.
52. WO 165/39, 30 April 1940.
53. Ibid., 31 May 1940.
54. Helen Fry, *The London Cage* and WO 165/39, 30 April 1940.
55. WO 165/39, 30 April 1940. Local people recall seeing Luftwaffe pilots and Italian prisoners in the grounds of Ludgrove Hall. This is now corroborated in official files by reference to POW 'Camp 1' and 'Camp 2' at Cockfosters – the two transit camps where prisoners of war were assessed for possible transfer to Kendrick's main camp. See Minutes of Meeting held at the War Office, 21 February 1940, WO 208/3458.
56. Ludgrove Hall had belonged to the Bevan family (co-founders of Barclays Bank), then became an exclusive private school which was evacuated to Sussex in 1938 and Ludgrove requisitioned for wartime use. In 1949, it was subject to a compulsory purchase order: see ED 78/418 and ED 78/419. In October 1940, Scotland transferred the cage to Kensington Palace Gardens. For a full history see Fry, *The London Cage*.
57. WO 165/39, entry for 8 May 1940.
58. Ibid., entry for 10 May 1940.
59. Ibid.
60. Ibid., entry for 18 May 1940.
61. Ibid., entry for 30 June 1940.
62. SRX 95, 25 June 1940, WO 208/4158.
63. 'CSDIC Survey: 3 September 1939 to 31 December 1940', p. 4, WO 208/3455.
64. Ibid.
65. Ibid.
66. 'CSDIC Survey: 3 September 1939 to 31 December 1940', pp. 3–4, WO 208/3455. See also Kendrick's memo of 22 January 1941, attached to this survey.
67. 'CSDIC Survey: 3 September 1939 to 31 December 1940', WO 208/3455. For examples of invasion talk: SRA 20, 29 January 1940, AIR 40/3070; SRA 918, 12 November 1940, WO 208/4121; and SRA 1323, 20 February 1941, WO 208/4123. See also decline of invasion talk in 1941: 'CSDIC Survey: 1 January 1941 to 30 June 1941', WO 208/3455.
68. 'CSDIC Survey: 3 September 1939 to 31 December 1940', p. 4, WO 208/3455.
69. Ibid. An example is SRA 1374, 2 March 1941, WO 208/4123.
70. SRA 419, 29 August 1940, AIR 40/3070.
71. 'CSDIC Survey: 3 September 1939 to 31 December 1940', WO 208/3455.
72. Ibid.
73. SRA 441, 2 September 1940, AIR 40/3070.
74. 'CSDIC Survey: 3 September 1939 to 31 December 1940', pp. 3–4, WO 208/3455.
75. 'CSDIC Survey: 3 September 1939 to 31 December 1940', p. 4, WO 208/3455.
76. Ibid.
77. 'On Talks with Prisoners of War (London Area) between 16 September and 19, 1940', Report by C.H. Brooks, FO 898/320.
78. Ibid.
79. Ibid.
80. Interview with Richard Deveson, 2013.
81. Ibid.
82. Ibid., undated notes.
83. WO 165/41, October 1942.

84. Expansion of the M Room operation had already occurred abroad with the opening of a site at Cairo. In August 1940, MI9 received a request from the commander in chief (Middle East) for a CSDIC listening station at Cairo. It was set up by Major Harrison, Captain Macmillan and Commander Rodd (RN) in readiness for successes on the battlefields of North Africa. CSDIC sites would also open in the Mediterranean (Italy) and the Far East. An assessment of their contribution is beyond the scope of this book. See history of CSDIC-Med in WO 208/3248.
85. See 'The Story of MI19', p. 4, WO 208/4970.
86. WO 165/39, 29 January 1941.
87. 'Prisoner of War Interrogation 1939–1945', p. 4, ADM 223/475.
88. Ibid. See also Richard Mayne, *In Victory, Magnanimity, in Peace, Goodwill: A History of Wilton Park*, pp. 24–8.
89. Memorandum, 7 October 1941, CAB 121/236.
90. 17 February 1941, CAB 79/9/19. See also 'Accommodation for CSDIC', p. 1, WO 208/3456. Copy also in WO 208/5621.
91. Memorandum, 7 October 1941, p. 2, CAB 121/236.
92. Ibid.
93. Letter from Archibald Boyle (Air Ministry) to Davidson (DMI), 19 December 1940, WO 208/5621.
94. Memorandum, 7 October 1941, CAB 121/236. See also 'Interference with the work of CSDIC by the Construction of the Aerodrome at Bovingdon' in WO 208/3456.
95. Memo dated 23 October 1941, WO 208/3456.
96. Kendrick to Crockatt, 26 September 1941, WO 208/3456.
97. At its meeting on 5 November 1941, CAB 121/236.
98. Ibid.
99. Minute from Crockatt to MI14, 27 July 1941, WO 208/3455.
100. MI6 to MI9, 2 March 1941, WO 208/3455.
101. Ibid.
102. Letter from Political Intelligence Department to Norman Crockatt, 24 February 1941, WO 208/3455.
103. Minute from Crockatt to MI14, 27 July 1941, WO 208/3455.
104. Letter from Room 055A [signature deleted under Section 3(4)] to Crockatt, 24 February 1941, WO 208/3455.
105. Letter 5 March 1941, Pile to Kendrick, WO 208/3460.

4: PRIZED PRISONERS, IDLE CHATTER

1. General Summary Report, September 1941, WO 208/4180.
2. SRA 1584, 27 April 1941, WO 208/4123.
3. 'CSDIC Half-Yearly Survey: 1 January 1941 to 30 June 1941', WO 208/3455.
4. Ibid.
5. Ibid., appendix B, WO 208/3455.
6. Letter 11 February 1941, John Godfrey (NID) to Francis Davidson (DMI), WO 208/4970.
7. 'CSDIC Half-Yearly Survey: 1 January 1941 to 30 June 1941', WO 208/3455.
8. MI9 frequently received 20 copies of a transcript, Admiralty 2 copies, and Air Intelligence 4 copies. Examples of this distribution can be seen in WO 208/4123 (SRA 1374, 1399 and 1617).
9. SR 1, 6 April 1941, WO 208/3455.
10. SRA 1379, 4 March 1941, WO 208/4123.
11. WO 165/39, 4 March 1941.
12. For interrogation reports of these prisoners at the London Cage, see FO 898/320.
13. WO 165/39, 31 March 1941.

14. Ibid.
15. SRA 1366, 26 February 1941, WO 208/4123.
16. WO 165/39, 30 April 1941.
17. 'CSDIC Half-Yearly Survey: 1 January 1941 to 30 June 1941', WO 208/3455.
18. SRN 224, 29 March 1941, WO 208/4141.
19. SRA 1603, 26 April 1941, WO 208/4123.
20. For interrogations of survivors of the *Bismarck*, see ADM 186/806. Bugged conversations survive in WO 208/4142 and WO 208/4143.
21. 'Summary of Reports on General Interrogation of German Naval & Air Force POWs during June 1941'. GRX 3, 9 July 1941, WO 208/4180.
22. 'CSDIC Half-Yearly Survey: 1 January 1941 to 30 June 1941', WO 208/3455.
23. Ibid.
24. Ibid., pp. 5–6, WO 208/3455.
25. NID to Davidson (DMI), 24 May 1941, WO 208/3460.
26. 'CSDIC Half-Yearly Survey: 1 January 1941 to 30 June 1941', pp. 5–6, WO 208/3455.
27. Letter dated 11 February 1941, WO 208/3460.
28. Letter 21 February 1941, Stewart Menzies (head of MI6) to Crockatt, WO 208/4970.
29. 'CSDIC Half-Yearly Survey: 1 January 1941 to 30 June 1941', WO 208/3455.
30. SR 1085, 25 April 1941, WO 208/3457; also various conversations in WO 208/4123.
31. 'CSDIC Half-Yearly Survey: 1 January 1941 to 30 June 1941', WO 208/3455.
32. SRA 1609, 28 April 1941, WO 208/4123.
33. Letter from Archibald Boyle (Air Ministry) to Francis Davidson (DMI), 19 February 1941, WO 208/3455.
34. SRA 1366, 26 February 1941, WO 208/4123.
35. 'CSDIC Half-Yearly Survey: 1 January 1941 to 30 June 1941', WO 208/3455.
36. SR 1, March 1941, WO 208/3455.
37. 'CSDIC Half-Yearly Survey: 1 January 1941 to 30 June 1941', WO 208/3455.
38. Ibid.
39. Churchill's memo of 13 May, FO 1093/1. Churchill issued instructions for Hess to be held in a house just outside London which was to be fitted with bugging appliances by 'C'.
40. FO 1093/1-16. Foley had been British passport officer in Berlin prior to 1939. See Michael Smith, *Foley: The Spy Who Saved 10,000 Jews.*
41. Ibid., pp. 188–200.
42. Felkin to F/Lt Baring, 23 May 1941, FO 1093/11.
43. Ibid.
44. Interview and correspondence with the author.
45. He is listed amongst the staff in a booklet called 'The K Album' which lists approximately 100 men and women who worked for ADI(K).
46. 'CSDIC Six-Monthly Report, 1 July 1941 to 31 December 1941', WO 208/3455.
47. 'Effect on German Troops in Occupied Countries of News about Bombings and General Conditions in Germany', p. 3, WO 208/3455.
48. 'CSDIC Six-Monthly Report, 1 July 1941 to 31 December 1941', WO 208/3455.
49. Ibid.
50. Details were picked up in the conversations of the German generals, for example SR 82, 15 April 1943, AIR 40/3106.
51. 'CSDIC Six-Monthly Report, 1 July 1941 to 31 December 1941', WO 208/3455.
52. 'Intelligence from Prisoners of War', report by Denys Felkin, 31 December 1945, section 120–125, AIR 40/2636.
53. Ibid.
54. 'Enemy Atrocities', report of 18 November 1942, WO 208/4198. For example, by November 1942, war crimes against Jews could be found in SRA 713, SRA 893, SRA 1017, SRA 1045, SRA 1142, SRA 1236, SRA 1259, SRN 750, SRN 780, SRN 794, SRN 1075, SRX 950 and SR 50. There was also an eye witness account of the Warsaw Ghetto.

55. Donald Welbourn, unpublished memoirs and SRM 1153, WO 208/4149.
56. Ibid.
57. 'CSDIC Six-Monthly Report, 1 July 1941 to 31 December 1941', WO 208/3455.
58. Jan Weber, unpublished memoirs.
59. SR 50, 13 November 1942, AIR 40/3106.
60. Catherine Jestin, *A War Bride's Story*, p. 204.
61. Ibid.
62. Copy of diary entry sent to the author by Jennifer Jestin.
63. Jestin, *A War Bride's Story*, pp. 209–10.
64. Ibid., p. 229.
65. Ibid., p. 211.
66. Ibid.
67. See WO 208/3248, Appendix C. There were CSDIC sites in Cairo, Algiers, Italy, the Middle East and the Far East: see history in WO 208/3248. On 30 September 1940, for example, 50 personnel were mobilised for CSDIC (Middle East) to be sent out the following month. For correspondence on CSDIC Algiers, see WO 208/3461. CSDIC Mediterranean was under the command of Colonel Richard Prior Edwards, a copy of whose personal army record was sent to the author.
68. WO 208/3248, Appendix C.
69. Ibid.
70. Interview with the late Elizabeth Bruegger by the author in 2011.
71. Ibid.
72. Ibid.
73. Jestin, *A War Bride's Story*, p. 210.
74. 'CSDIC Six-Monthly survey, 1 January 1942 to 30 June 1942', pp. 3 and 5, WO 208/3455.
75. Ibid., p. 2. See also 'Effect on German Troops in Occupied Countries of News about Bombings and General Conditions in Germany', p. 3, WO 208/3455.
76. 'CSDIC Six-Monthly survey, 1 January 1942 to 30 June 1942', pp. 3 and 5, WO 208/3455.
77. Bugged conversations from POWS captured in the Maaloy and Bruneval Raids are SRM 15 to SRM 63 in WO 208/4136. SRs from POWs captured in the Dieppe Raid are SRM 64–67, WO 208/4136.
78. 'CSDIC Six-Monthly survey, 1 January 1942 to 30 June 1942', p. 7, WO 208/3455.
79. Ibid., pp. 3–4.
80. Ibid., p. 3.
81. Ibid., p. 5.
82. General Summary Report, section 4, 9 July 1941, WO 208/4180.
83. 'CSDIC Six-Monthly survey, 1 January 1942 to 30 June 1942', p. 4, WO 208/3455.
84. Ibid., p. 8.
85. Lee Richards, *The Black Art: British Clandestine Psychological Warfare against the Third Reich*.
86. Ibid., pp. 179–94.
87. Kendrick's report, 24 August 1942, WO 208/4970.
88. Richards, *The Black Art*, pp. 179–94.

5: THE SPIDER

1. Letter written to Peter Quinn, copy given to the author.
2. 'The Story of MI19', pp. 8–9, WO 208/4970.
3. Fry, *The London Cage*, pp. 13–20.
4. 'The Story of MI19', WO 208/4970.
5. Report, 11 February 1945, WO 208/3451.
6. Jan Weber, extract from unpublished memoirs.
7. Sullivan, *Thresholds of Peace*, p. 53.

8. Joan Stansfield's unpublished notes, copy from his daughter, Stella MacKinnon.

9. Henry Dicks's papers survive in the Wellcome Library, London. The use of psychiatrists at CSDIC is also referenced in WO 165/41, August 1942.

10. 'The History of CSDIC', appendix J, WO 208/4970.

11. Ibid.

12. Ibid.

13. Courtesy Barbara Lloyd.

14. Letter dated April 1943, courtesy Barbara Lloyd.

15. Interview with the late Elizabeth Bruegger by the author in 2011.

16. Ibid.

17. For example: SIR 1106, 22 November 1944, WO 208/5158. CSDIC provided a summary report on codes and cyphers from a German naval deserter. See report 14 March 1943, WO 208/5158.

18. MI8 did not number their interrogation reports, only dated them. For examples of CSDIC facilitating the interrogations for MI8, see interrogation reports 23 August 1943 and 22 May 1944, both in WO 208/5158.

19. Interrogation reports 23 August 1943 and 22 May 1944, WO 208/5158.

20. Interrogation 15 January 1944, WO 208/5158.

21. Ibid.

22. Ibid.

23. Including Major Dennis Babbage (chief cryptanalyst), Nigel de Grey (cryptologist), Peter Twinn (head of Abwehr Enigma section) and William Bunty (US Army Signals Corps, later of the CIA).

24. Mayne, *In Victory, Magnanimity*, pp. 25–6.

25. Fry, *The London Cage*, p. 45.

26. Confirmed by a memo dated 1 August 1945, WO 208/5622.

27. In the inter-war period, he worked for Arnhold & Co, a major German conglomerate based in London and Shanghai.

28. Leo St Clare Grondona, 'Sidelights on Wilton Park', p. 34.

29. Ibid.

30. WO 165/41, 17 May 1943.

31. St Clare Grondona, 'Sidelights on Wilton Park', p. 35.

32. WO 165/41, June 1943.

33. Ibid.

34. Sullivan, *Thresholds of Peace*, p. 54.

35. Donald McLachlan, *Room 39: Naval Intelligence in Action 1939–45*, p. 174.

36. 'The History of CSDIC', WO 208/4970. See also WO 165/41, July 1943.

37. Jestin, *A War Bride's Story*, p. 215.

38. Ibid.

39. Ibid., p. 225.

40. A bulk of the files of Camp 020, Latchmere House, have been declassified at the National Archives in series KV. For a classic study, see John Masterman, *The Double-Cross System*.

41. Jestin, *A War Bride's Story*, pp. 230–1. See also Oliver Hoare, *Camp 020: MI5 and Nazi Spies*.

42. 'The Story of MI19', pp. 7–8, WO 208/4970.

43. Secret memo dated 28 October 1941, department not given, copy in ADM 223/475.

44. Ibid.

45. Ibid.

46. Personal citation in WO 373/148/442.

47. Ibid.

48. Jestin, *A War Bride's Story*, p. 222.

49. Letter dated September 1942 amongst Kendrick's papers.

50. WO 165/41, October 1942.

51. Visit took place at Wilton Park on 25 February 1943, see WO 165/41.

52. Visit to Latimer House and Wilton Park in March 1943, WO 165/41.
53. Visit in November 1943, WO 165/41.
54. 'Intelligence from Prisoners of War', report by Denys Felkin, 31 December 1945, section 25, AIR 40/2636.
55. Jestin, *A Memoir*, pp. 6 and 8–10.
56. Ibid., p. 12.
57. Ibid., p. 13.

6: BATTLE OF THE GENERALS

1. List of German Senior Officers at No.11 Camp, personal profiles arranged alphabetically in WO 208/3504.
2. Personal file in WO 208/3504.
3. Ibid.
4. Ibid.
5. Ibid.
6. Ibid.
7. Ibid.
8. Ibid.
9. The bugged conversations between Crüwell and von Thoma from 20 November 1942 (SRM 70) until 13 May 1943 (SRM 198) are in WO 208/4136. Their bugged conversations with a British army officer are in AIR 40/3106. Other SRs survive in WO 208/4161.
10. SRX 1504, 18 January 1943, copy in WO 208/5158.
11. SRM 160, 4 February 1943, WO 208/4136.
12. Also captured at this time were Gustav von Vaerst, Georg Neuffer, Karl Bülowius, Willibald Boroweitz, Fritz Krause and August von Quast. See WO 165/41, June 1943.
13. The transcripts from this period are contained in WO 208/4363 and WO 208/3461.
14. GRGG 1, 24 May 1943, WO 208/4363.
15. GRGG 1 and GRGG 3, 24 May 1943, WO 208/4363.
16. GRGG 2, 24 May 1943, WO 208/4363.
17. Ibid.
18. Ibid.
19. Flown to England on 16 May 1943 were Generals Hans-Jürgen von Arnim, Hans Cramer, Gustav von Vaerst, Karl Bülowius, Willibald Boroweitz, Fritz Krause, Georg Neuffer (GAF), Gerhard Bassenge (GAF) and August von Quast. See MI19 war diary, May 1943, WO 165/41.
20. Document 'Enemy Prisoners of War: Treatment on Capture', WO 32/10720. See also letter from DMI to Colonel Gatesby, 29 May 1943, WO 208/3461.
21. Generals Gotthart Frantz (GAF) and Carl Köcky, and Colonel Heinrich Hermann von Hülsen.
22. They were Schnarrenberger, Friedrich Freiherr von Broich, Kurt Freiherr von Liebenstein and Theodor Graf von Sponeck. On 2 June 1943, Generals Bülowius, Boroweitz, Köcky, von Vaerst and von Quast were taken from Trent Park, accompanied by Major D. Spencer of US intelligence (G-2 ETOUSA), to be flown to POW camps in America. War diary entry, June 1943, WO 165/41.
23. GRGG 18, 16 June 1943, WO 208/4363.
24. GRGG 54, 9 July 1943, WO 208/4363.
25. Monthly report 'German Prisoners of War in Britain,' 13 August 1943, DEFE 1/339.
26. Ibid.
27. Ibid.
28. Monthly report 'German Prisoners of War in Britain,' 17 July 1943, DEFE 1/339.
29. Ibid.

30. 'The History of CSDIC', p. 8, WO 208/4970.
31. Report on the German Senior Officer POW at No.11 Camp for the Month of June 1943, p. 1, WO 208/3433.
32. Monthly reports 'German Prisoners of War in Britain,' 13 August 1943 and 10 November 1943, DEFE 1/339.
33. Monthly report 'German Prisoners of War in Britain,' 13 August 1943, DEFE 1/339.
34. Monthly report 'German Prisoners of War in Britain,' 10 November 1943, DEFE 1/339.
35. Letter 29 May 1943, WO 208/3461.
36. Ramcke, memoirs, pp. 79–80.
37. Ibid.
38. Personal file in WO 208/3504.
39. 'The History of CSDIC', appendix M, WO 208/4970.
40. 'The History of CSDIC', p. 8, WO 208/4970. There was a similar welfare officer with the Italian senior officers at the White House, Wilton Park, although his name has not been discovered in research so far.
41. Sullivan, *Thresholds of Peace*, pp. 51–2.
42. Copy of Munro's Army Record released from Army Personnel Centre, Glasgow.
43. Ibid.
44. Sullivan, *Thresholds of Peace*, p. 52.
45. Jestin, *A War Bride's Story*, p. 232.
46. Memo to CSDIC from HQ of MI19 at Wilton Park, 30 August 1943, WO 208/5622.
47. 13 May 1965, *Radio Times*. Also, letter from Rawlinson to Kendrick amongst Kendrick's letters.
48. GRGG 57, 17 July 1943, WO 208/4363.
49. Ibid.
50. GRGG 58, 22 July 1943, WO 208/4363.
51. GRGG 57, 17 July 1943, WO 208/4363.
52. GRGG 42, 15 July 1943, WO 208/4363.
53. Ibid.
54. GRGG 52, 10 July 1943, WO 208/4363.
55. Ibid.
56. Ibid.
57. Ibid.
58. Ibid.
59. Personal file in WO 208/3504.
60. GRGG 51, 10 July 1943, WO 208/4363.
61. Letter from Norman Crockatt to DMI, 20 January 1944, WO 208/5622.
62. GRGG 49, 14 July 1943, WO 208/4363.
63. Personal file in WO 208/3504 and GRGG 46, 14 July 1943, WO 208/4363.
64. GRGG 47, 14 July 1943, WO 208/4363.
65. Ibid.
66. GRGG 55, 16 July 1943, WO 208/4363.
67. GRGG 53, 11 July 1943, WO 208/4363.
68. 'Views of German Senior Officer P/W', WO 208/5550.
69. Ibid.
70. Report on the German Senior Officer POW at No.11 Camp for the Month of June 1943, p. 2, WO 208/3433.
71. Ibid., p. 3.
72. Reference to Hamley as interpreter: CSDIC memo, ref: D11/341, 1 August 1944, WO 208/5622.
73. GRGG 57, 17 July 1943, WO 208/4363.
74. Discussions on rations, see GRGG 57, 17 July 1943 and GRGG 61, 26 July 1943, WO 208/4363.

75. Monthly report 'German Prisoners of War in Britain,' 13 August 1943, DEFE 1/339.
76. SR 4534, 8 July 1943, WO 208/5622.
77. McLachlan, *Room 39*, p. 174.
78. GRGG 72, 14–20 August 1943, WO 208/4363.
79. Ibid.
80. Eric Mark, interview with the author.
81. Interview with granddaughter, Barbara Lloyd.
82. Ibid.
83. SRGG 795, 31 January 1944, WO 208/4167. Also contained in WO 208/4363.

7: MAD HATTER'S TEA PARTY

1. GRGG 58, 22 July 1943, WO 208/4363.
2. Ibid.
3. Ibid.
4. Ibid.
5. Character study of Erich Schmidt, 1 January 1944, WO 208/3433.
6. GRGG 61, 17–23 July 1943, WO 208/4363.
7. Ibid; and a character study of General von Arnim, no date, contained in WO 208/4363.
8. Titles included: Heiden's *Europas Schicksal* (Europe's Fate), Rauschning *Vernichtung des Nihilismus* (Revolution of Destruction), Lochner *What about Germany?* and Langhoff *Moorsoldaten* (the story of a concentration camp). Crüwell borrowed Spengler's *Preussentum und Socialismus* (Prussianism and Socialism). Films were shown at Trent Park: *The Gentle Sex* and newsreel of the Free German Movement in Russia.
9. GRGG 58, 22 July 1943, WO 208/4363.
10. GRGG 61, 26 July 1943, WO 208/4363.
11. Ibid.
12. 'Views of German Senior Officer P/W', WO 208/5550.
13. GRGG 64, 23 July 1943, WO 208/4363.
14. GRGG 65, 31 July 1943, WO 208/4363.
15. GRGG 61, 26 July 1943, WO 208/4363.
16. GRGG 65, 31 July 1943, WO 208/4363.
17. GRGG 64, 30 July 1943, WO 208/4363.
18. GRGG 65, 31 July 1943, WO 208/4363.
19. GRGG 70, 14 August 1943, WO 208/4363.
20. Ibid.
21. Ibid.
22. Ibid.
23. GRGG 74, 30 August 1943, WO 208/4363.
24. GRGG 72, 21 August 1943, WO 208/4363.
25. Ibid.
26. Ibid.
27. Ibid.
28. Ibid.
29. GRGG 76, 6 September 1943, WO 208/4363.
30. GRGG 85, 26 September 1943, WO 208/4363.
31. GRGG 101, 31 October–6 November 1943, WO 208/4363.
32. GRGG 103, 7–13 November 1943, WO 208/4363.
33. GRGG 98, 2 November 1943, WO 208/4363.
34. Ibid.
35. Ibid.

36. Ibid.
37. GRGG 103, 7–13 November 1943, WO 208/4363.
38. Ibid.
39. GRGG 104, 14–27 November 1943, WO 208/4363.
40. GRGG 109, 19–25 December 1943, WO 208/4363.
41. Ibid.
42. GRGG 110, 26 December 1943–1 January 1944, WO 208/4363.
43. GRGG 111, 2–9 January 1944, WO 208/4363.

8: SECRET LISTENERS

1. Jan Weber, extract from unpublished memoirs, courtesy of Jonathan Webber. Weber was eventually posted from CSDIC (UK) to the CSDIC unit in Italy.
2. 'The History of CSDIC', appendix E, WO 208/4970.
3. Memo by Rawlinson (DDMI), 22 July 1943, WO 208/3546.
4. Jestin, *A War Bride's Story*, p. 223.
5. Ibid., p. 234.
6. Ibid., p. 223.
7. Letter, Frank Stevens to Hans Francken, 1 April 1944. Copy given to the author by Dr John Francken.
8. Jean Medawar and David Pyke, *Hitler's Gift*, p. 194.
9. Interviews with the author over a period of 15 years until his death in December 2017.
10. Fry, *Churchill's German Army*.
11. Interview with the author.
12. Information provided by Adam Ganz.
13. Copy lent to the author by John Francken.
14. Copy lent to the author by Ernest Newhouse.
15. Given to the author by Arthur Fleiss.
16. Interview with the author. Helen Fry, *Jews in North Devon During the Second World War*, pp. 125–6.
17. Interview with the author, 2013.
18. Ibid.
19. 'The History of CSDIC', The M Room: appendix E, WO 208/4970.
20. Amongst Lederer's papers is a collection of impressive medals that span his service, fighting for the Austro-Hungarian Empire in 1914–18, and the British Defence Medal for his service in the Second World War. Personal Home Guard file, County of Middlesex, served 3 years and 232 days. Copy given to the author by Helen Lederer.
21. Correspondence and interview with the author.
22. Letter dated 12 November 1944. Copy given to the author by Helen Lederer.
23. Documentary *Home Front Heroes*, BBC1 (November 2018).
24. In series WO 208 and AIR 40.
25. Correspondence with the author.
26. Interview with secret listeners Eric Mark and Paul Douglas.
27. SRM 382, 9 November 1943, WO 208/4137.
28. Peter Hart, *Journey into Freedom*, p. 100. He transferred to the Intelligence Corps in July 1944.
29. Correspondence with the author.
30. Ibid.
31. Ibid.
32. Interview with the author.
33. Ibid.
34. Ibid., and Fritz Lustig, *My Lucky Life*.

9: ROCKET SCIENCE

1. Letter dated 5 January 1943, amongst Kendrick's papers.
2. SRX 1635, 11 March 1943, WO 208/4162. Sketches of V-1 and V-2 launching equipment (ramps) contained in WO 208/4292.
3. Copies exist in RAF Medmenham archives today.
4. Chiefs of Staff memorandum, COS(43) 592 (O), entitled 'German Long Range Rockets', section 3: 'First Report of the Long range Rockets', 29 September 1943, CAB 80/75.
5. The conversation took place on 22 March 1943 and was reproduced in a memorandum to Chiefs of Staff, COS(43) 592 (O), entitled 'German Long Range Rockets', section 4: 'Von Thoma's Evidence', 29 September 1943, CAB 80/75. See also Jones, *Most Secret War*, p. 425.
6. Jones, *Most Secret War*, p. 425.
7. Ibid., p. 427.
8. Chiefs of Staff memorandum, COS(43) 592 (O), entitled 'German Long Range Rockets', section 4: 'Von Thoma's Evidence', 29 September 1943, CAB 80/75.
9. Ibid.
10. Two key reports dated 29 April 1943: 'Structures near Northern Tip of the Peninsula Peenemünde' and 'Interpretation Report of New Development at Peenemünde', AIR 40/1192.
11. Contained in AIR 40/1192 and AIR 40/2839.
12. 'Extract from an Interpretation Report of the New Development at Peenemünde', p. 1, 29 April 1943, AIR 40/1192.
13. 26 May 1943, WO 208/4165 (No SR reference on this transcript).
14. Ibid; photographs of the mission survive in this file.
15. Interview with the author.
16. Jones, *Most Secret War*, p. 438.
17. Most Secret Memo to Operations at Air Ministry from AI.3 (Air Ministry), 8 July 1943, AIR 40/1192.
18. Ibid.
19. Draft Target Information Sheet for the bombing of Peenemünde, 4 July 1943, AIR 40/1192.
20. Ibid.
21. Internal Air Ministry Memo of 8 July 1943, AIR 40/1192.
22. SRGG 319, 8 August 1943, WO 208/4166. Another conversation a few days later was recorded in GRGG 341, 11 August 1943, pp. 11–12, WO 208/4178.
23. Jones, *Most Secret War*, p. 441.
24. Ibid.
25. This was confirmed by Germany's chief project scientist there, General Walter Dornberger who was brought to Trent Park in August 1945 for interrogation and his conversations with the other generals were also bugged. See GRGG 341, 11 August 1943, pp. 11–12, WO 208/4178.
26. SRGG 980(c), 24 August 1944, WO 208/4168. See also GRGG 188, 11 September 1944, p. 9, WO 208/5017; and Felkin's series of detailed summary reports in WO 208/4292 on the locations and destruction of the launch sites of the flying bombs. All information received from the interrogation of POWs at CSDIC and the London Cage.
27. AIR 14/743, AIR 14/744 and CAB 113/41.
28. Also Jestin, *A Memoir*, p. 17.
29. 'Views of German Senior Officer P/W', section headed 'Secret Weapons – Rockets', WO 208/5550.
30. GRGG 526, 8 November 1943, WO 208/4167.
31. 'Secret Weapons – Rockets', report, pp. 8–9, in WO 208/5550.
32. Ibid.
33. SRGG 368, 23 August 1943, WO 208/4166.
34. Ibid.
35. SRGG 414, 11 September 1943, WO 208/4166.

36. 'Secret Weapons – Rockets', report, pp. 8–9, in WO 208/5550. See also SRGG 414, 11 September 1943, WO 208/4166.
37. Ibid.
38. SRGG 441, 30 September 1943, WO 208/4166. See also SRGG 414, 11 September 1943, WO 208/4166.
39. SRGG 675, 19 December 1943, WO 208/4167. See also SRM 370, 9 November 1943, WO 208/4137.
40. Ibid.
41. SRGG 494, 26 October 1943, WO 208/4166.
42. Ibid.
43. 'Secret Weapons – Rockets', report, pp. 8–9, in WO 208/5550.
44. SRGG 503, 26 October 1943, WO 208/4166.
45. GRGG 163, p. 4, 21–22 July 1944, WO 208/4363.
46. Ibid.
47. GRGG 609, 1 December 1943, WO 208/4167.
48. For example SRA 4228, 21 July 1943, WO 208/4130; SRA 4288, 30 July 1943, WO 208/4130; SRA 4291, 24 August 1943, WO 208/4130; GRGG 169, 2–4 August 1944, WO 208/4363. See also Felkin's summary report entitled 'Rocket Projectiles and Jet-Propelled Aircraft', 7 December 1943, AIR 40/2839; and 'Military Aspects of V-2', WO 208/3121.
49. Donald Welbourn, unpublished memoirs, Imperial War Museum.
50. SRA 4288, 30 July 1943, WO 208/4130.
51. Lengthy and detailed technical conversation between two POWs, SRA 4291, 24 August 1943, WO 208/4130.
52. See SRA 4287, 26 August 1943.
53. SRM 263, 27 October 1943, WO 208/4137.
54. SRA 5047, 5 March 1944 and SRA 5051, 7 March 1944 in AIR 40/3093.
55. SRX 1926, 1 February 1944, WO 208/4163.
56. SRA 5047, 5 March 1944, AIR 40/3093.
57. SRA 5051, 7 March 1944, AIR 40/3093.
58. Personal file in WO 208/3504.
59. SRGG 919, 10 June 1944, WO 208/4168.
60. SRGG 957, 10 July 1944, WO 208/4168.
61. SRGG 997(c), 25 August 1944, WO 208/4168.
62. SRGG 1001, 28 August 1944, WO 208/4168.
63. SRGG 980(c), 24 August 1944, WO 208/4168.
64. SRGG 1005, 30 August 1944, WO 208/4168.
65. GRGG 183, 29 August 1944, p. 9, WO 208/5622.
66. GRGG 188, 11 September 1944, WO 208/4363.
67. SRGG 1046(c), 17 September 1944, WO 208/4168.
68. Ibid.
69. Hart, *Journey into Freedom,* p. 103.
70. GRGG 231, 6–7 December 1944, WO 208/5018.
71. SRGG 1009, 1 September 1944, WO 208/4168.
72. SRGG 1029, 4 September 1944, WO 208/4168. See also GRGG 187(c), 10 September 1944, WO 208/5017.
73. Ibid.
74. Colin Brown, *Operation Big: The Race to Stop Hitler's A-Bomb.*
75. Damien Lewis, *Hunting Hitler's Nukes: The Secret Race to Stop the Nazi Bomb*, pp. 195–220.
76. DEFE 2/222–224, DEFE 2/1408, and AIR 20/11930.
77. Alexander Scotland, *The London Cage,* p. 167.
78. AIR 39/45, AIR 20/3648.
79. The camp operated from 1941 until 1945.
80. WO 331/16-17, WO 311/383-387.
81. Fry, *The London Cage,* pp. 176–9.

82. Discussions about the atom bomb appear in WO 208/4178.
83. GRGG 245, 5–7 January 1945, WO 208/5018.
84. Ibid.
85. GRGG 247, 10–14 January 1945, WO 208/5018.
86. Ibid. It was also published in SRGG 1118, WO 208/4169. Other references to the atom bomb appeared in SRGG 1108 and GRGG 238, WO 208/5018.
87. Ibid.
88. Dornberger's interrogation reports by British intelligence survive in WO 208/3121. See also GRGG 341, 11 August 1945, WO 208/4178 and GRGG 344, 21 August 1945, pp. 2–4, WO 208/4178.
89. GRGG 341, 11 August 1945, pp. 8–9, WO 208/4178.
90. Interrogation Report, 12 August 1945, WO 208/3121.
91. GRGG 341, 11 August 1945, pp. 8–9, WO 208/4178.
92. Brown, *Operation Big*.
93. Ibid.

10: 'OUR GUESTS'

1. GRGG 117, 30 January–5 February 1944, WO 208/4363.
2. Ibid.
3. The bugged conversations provided information on gun emplacements and their construction along the French coast. This was important intelligence to gather prior to Operation Overlord and D-Day. See SRM 382, 9 November 1943, WO 208/4137.
4. Interview with the author.
5. SRGG 755, 11 January 1944, WO 208/4167.
6. Ibid.
7. SRGG 766, 15 January 1944, WO 208/4167.
8. Ibid.
9. Summary Report dated 15 January 1944 about Dr Haccius's visit to Trent Park on 13 January 1944, WO 208/5622.
10. Ibid.
11. Ibid.
12. Another report on Haccius's visit, no date, Folio 112a, WO 208/5622.
13. GRGG 61, 17–23 July 1943, WO 208/4363.
14. Report dated 15 January 1944, WO 208/5622.
15. Ibid.
16. GRGG 113, 9–15 January 1944, WO 208/4363.
17. Ibid.
18. GRGG 114, 16–22 January 1944, WO 208/5016.
19. Ibid.
20. Ibid.
21. Ibid., copy also in AIR 40/3104.
22. GRGG 115, 23–29 January 1944, WO 208/5016.
23. GRGG 117, 30 January–5 February 1944, WO 208/5016.
24. GRGG 121, 6–12 February 1944, WO 208/4363.
25. SR 82, 15 April 1943, AIR 40/3106.
26. Ibid.
27. SRN 1729, 3 May 1943, WO 208/4145.
28. Ibid.
29. Ibid. Information about U-boat shelters was picked up in SRM 444, 31 December 1943, WO 208/4137.
30. GRGG 113, 9–15 January 1944, WO 208/4363.

31. WO 165/41, January 1944. See also Nudd, *Castaways of the Kriegsmarine*, pp. 107–13.
32. A full account can be read in Kendrick's biography, *Spymaster*, pp. 155–6.
33. Letter dated 17 January 1944, copy sent to the author by Derek Nudd.
34. SR 231, 19 January 1944, AIR 40/3104. Another example of a conversation about the *Tirpitz* is in SRN 224, 29 March 1941, WO 208/4141.
35. SR 683, 30 March 1945, AIR 40/3104.
36. Sketch contained in AIR 40/3104.
37. SR 2065, 2 March 1944, AIR 40/3105.
38. 'Intelligence from Prisoners of War', report by Denys Felkin, 31 December 1945, section 152, AIR 40/2636.
39. Ibid., section 152–154. See also GRGG 344, 21 August 1945, pp. 14–15, WO 208/4178.
40. 'Intelligence from Prisoners of War', report by Denys Felkin, 31 December 1945, section 154, AIR 40/2636.
41. GRGG 123, 20–26 February 1944, WO 208/4363.
42. Ibid.
43. Ibid.
44. Ibid.
45. Ibid.
46. Ibid., p. 2.
47. Ibid., p. 2.
48. Personal file in WO 208/3504.
49. GRGG 123, 20–26 February 1944, p. 2, WO 208/4363.
50. Ibid., pp. 2–3.
51. Ibid., p. 3.
52. GRGG 125, 12–18 March 1944, WO 208/4363.
53. GRGG 124, 27 February 1944, WO 208/4363.
54. GRGG 129, 10–16 April 1944, WO 208/5016.
55. GRGG 130, 17–23 April 1944, WO 208/5016.
56. GRGG 175, 17–18 August 1944, WO 208/4363.
57. Ibid.
58. Jestin, *A Memoir*, p. 18.
59. Patrick Leigh Fermor, *Abducting a General: The Kreipe Operation and SOE in Crete*; W. Stanley Moss, *Ill Met by Moonlight*.
60. Personal file in WO 208/3504. See also GRGG 135, 25 May 1944, WO 208/4363.
61. Personal file in WO 208/3504.
62. Ibid.
63. GRGG 135, 24 May 1944, GRGG 136, 26 May 1944, GRGG 137, 29 May 1944 WO 208/5017.
64. Copy of the questionnaire in WO 208/4208.
65. His account is preserved in SRGG 910 and also summarised in WO 208/5017.
66. GRGG 138, p. 4, 1 June 1944, WO 208/5017.
67. GRGG 135, 24 May 1944, p. 5, WO 208/5017 and GRGG 138, p. 5, 1 June 1944, WO 208/5017.
68. Correspondence from Ken Walsh with the author from South Africa prior to his death in 2017.
69. Ibid.
70. SRGG 135, 25 May 1945, p. 4, WO 208/5017.
71. Ibid.
72. SRA 5020, 24 February 1944, AIR 40/3093.

11: SAGA OF THE GENERALS

1. Article entitled 'D-Day: 150,000 Men and One Woman' in the *Huffington Post*, 5 May 2014.

2. WO 165/39, June 1944.
3. His original name was Hans Joachim Colman, later anglicised to Hugh John Colman.
4. Copy of personal army record from daughter Andrea Evers. After joining the Intelligence Corps, Colman received training in interrogation and initially served with the interrogation team of the 62nd Army.
5. Entries for October and November 1944, WO 165/39.
6. Letter from DNI to Lieutenant Commander Cope, 28 October 1944, ADM 223/475.
7. Entries for June, July and August 1944, WO 165/41.
8. Personal files in WO 208/3504.
9. Diary entries for June, August and September 1944, WO 165/41. Others senior German officers captured after D-Day included, with place of capture in brackets: General Hermann Ramcke (Brest), General Erwin Vierow (Arras), General Heinrich Eberbach (commander of a Panzer division, captured at Amiens); General Lieutenants Kurt Badinsky (Bailleul), Wilhelm Daser (Middelburg), Otto Elfeldt (Trun), Rüdiger Heyking (Mons), Erwin Menny (Maguy), Erwin Rauch (Brest), Paul Seyffardt (Marbaix), Karl Spang (Brest); Major Generals Bock von Wülfingen (Liège), Kurt Eberding (Knocke), Alfred Gutknecht (Soissons-Rheims), Hans von der Mosel (Brest), Robert Sattler (Cherbourg), Hans Schramm (Creney-Troyes), Stolberg (Antwerp), Carl Wahle (Mons), SS Oberführer Kurt Meyer (Liège); Colonels Ludwig Krug (Normandy), Rolf Müller-Römer (Paris), Hans Jay (Paris), Helmuth Rohrbach (St Gabriel), Karl von Unger (Paris), Ernst Herrmann (Cherbourg), Gerhard Wilck (Aachen), Eberhard Wildermuth (Le Havre), Vice Admirals Schirmer (Brest), Otto Kähler (Brest), Hans von Tresckow (Le Havre) and Carl Weber (Loire).
10. Report by Rushbrooke, 23 July 1944, ADM 223/475.
11. Ibid.
12. GRGG 159, 15–16 July 1944, WO 208/4363.
13. Ibid.
14. Ibid.
15. GRGG 146, 11–16 June 1944, WO 208/5017.
16. Ibid.
17. Ibid.
18. Ibid.
19. Ibid.
20. Ibid.
21. Memo dated 2 December 1944, WO 208/5622. It was originally the idea of SHAEF with the support of MI19.
22. *Lord Glenaldy*, copy in BBC Archives, originally transmitted May 1965.
23. The author has successfully found all the scenes that are written in it, in declassified files at the National Archives. As such, it is possible to say that this play is remarkably close to the facts.
24. *Lord Glenaldy*, Part III, pp. 22–6.
25. Ibid., pp. 23–4.
26. *Radio Times*, 13 May 1965.
27. 'Summary of SR Information concerning the departure of Generals Arnim and Crüwell', 17 June 1944, WO 208/5622.
28. Ibid.
29. Ibid.
30. GRGG 44, 15 July 1943, WO 208/4363.
31. 'Summary of SR Information concerning the departure of Generals Arnim and Crüwell', 17 June 1944, WO 208/5622.
32. Ibid.
33. GRGG 160, 25 July 1944, WO 208/4363.
34. Inserted as 'News Press' at end of GRGG 160, 25 July 1944, WO 208/4363.
35. 'Attempted Assassination of Hitler and Subsequent Events', GRGG 161, no date, WO 208/4363.

36. The failed assassination was still being talked about in some detail that autumn. See GRGG 186, 4–5 September 1944, WO 208/4363.
37. Jestin, *A War Bride's Story*, p. 250.
38. Ibid.
39. SRGG 962, 21 July 1944, WO 208/4168.
40. GRGG 180, 25–26 August 1944, WO 208/5017.
41. GRGG 160, 25 July 1944, p. 6, WO 208/4363.
42. Ibid., p. 11.
43. GRGG 161, no date, p. 6, WO 208/4363.
44. GRGG 183, 29 August 1944, p. 13, WO 208/5622.
45. Ibid., p. 9.
46. SRGG 962, 21 July 1944, WO 208/4168.
47. GRGG 167, 28–30 June 1944, WO 208/4363.
48. SRGG 167 and SRGG 171, 28–30 July 1944, WO 208/4363.
49. GRGG 197, 20–21 September 1944, WO 208/5018.
50. Appendix B to SRGG 171, 28–30 July 1944, WO 208/4363.
51. Interview with the author.
52. Memo from DMI, 7 September 1944, Folio 122B, WO 208/5622.
53. Personal file in WO 208/3504.
54. Ibid.
55. Ibid.
56. Report, 30 September 1944, WO 208/5622.
57. GRGG 188, 5–7 September 1944, WO 208/5017.
58. Ibid.
59. Personal file in WO 208/3504.
60. Ibid.
61. Ibid.
62. Ibid.
63. Ibid.
64. Ibid.
65. GRGG 184, 30 August 1944, pp. 3–4, WO 208/4363.
66. Ibid.
67. Personal file in WO 208/3504.
68. Ibid.
69. Ramcke, memoirs, p. 77.
70. Memo from CSDIC, 5 December 1944, WO 208/5622.
71. Ramcke, memoirs, p. 77. Kindly translated from the original German by Fred Judge.
72. Personal file in WO 208/3504.
73. Ibid.
74. Ibid.
75. Memo from Lieut. Colonel Corner to MI19, 12 October 1944, WO 208/5622.
76. GRGG 209, 12 October 1944, WO 208/5622.
77. Personal file in WO 208/3504.
78. Ramcke, memoirs, p. 77.
79. Ibid., p. 78.
80. GRGG 198, 24 September 1944, WO 208/5018.
81. Jestin, *A Memoir*, pp. 19–20.
82. Jestin's account of Ramcke's award is borne out in official files, see GRGG 198, 24 September 1944, WO 208/5018.
83. Jestin, *A Memoir*, p. 20.
84. Ibid.
85. Ramcke, memoirs, pp. 77–82.
86. Personal file in WO 208/3504.
87. GRGG 178, 23 August 1944, WO 208/5017.

88. Personal file in WO 208/3504.
89. Ibid.
90. Ibid.
91. Ibid.
92. Ibid.
93. Jestin, *A Memoir*, p. 24.
94. Jestin, *A War Bride's Story*, p. 254.
95. Jestin, *A Memoir*, p. 24.
96. Ibid., p. 18.
97. Personal file in WO 208/3504.
98. Ibid.
99. GRGG 278, 1 April 1945, pp. 4–5, WO 208/4177.
100. Personal file in WO 208/3504.
101. GRGG 330(c), 1 August 1945, WO 208/4178.
102. Ibid.

12: WAR CRIMES AND THE HOLOCAUST

1. Report dated 18 November 1942 entitled 'Enemy Atrocities', WO 208/4198. See also report dated 7 December 1942, WO 208/4202 and, for example, GRGG 245, 5–7 January 1945, WO 208/5018.
2. 'CSDIC Six-Monthly survey, 1 January 1942 to 30 June 1942', p. 8, WO 208/3455. See also reports on the German generals and their reaction, report, 7 December 1942, WO 208/4202.
3. Report dated 7 December 1942, WO 208/4202.
4. Ibid.
5. Martin Gilbert, *Auschwitz and the Allies*.
6. SRN 2528, 19 December 1943, WO 208/4148. See also SRA 4604, 27 October 1943, WO 208/4131.
7. 'CSDIC Six-Monthly survey, 1 January 1942 to 30 June 1942', p. 8, WO 208/3455.
8. Ibid.
9. Ibid.
10. SRX 1876, 10 October 1943, WO 208/4137. For massacres in Lublin, see also SRA 4820, 13 January 1944, WO 208/4132.
11. SRX 1914, 22 January 1944, WO 208/4163.
12. SR 120, 20 November 1943, AIR 40/3106.
13. SR 121, 22 November 1943, AIR 40/3106.
14. SR 123, 22 November 1943, AIR 40/3106.
15. Ibid.
16. SRM 426, 28 December 1943, WO 208/4137.
17. SR 128, 5 January 1944, AIR 40/3106.
18. Ibid.
19. SRGG 670, 17 December 1943, WO 208/4167.
20. SRA 3468, 30 December 1942, WO 208/4128.
21. SRX 1880, 12 October 1943, WO 208/4163.
22. SR 132, 5 March 1944, AIR 40/3106.
23. SR 128, 5 January 1944, AIR 40/3106.
24. SR 131, 23 February 1944, AIR 40/3106.
25. SRGG 756, 12 January 1944, WO 208/4167.
26. GRGG 272, 13–16 March 1945, WO 208/4177.
27. Ibid.
28. Ibid.

29. SR 111, 5 July 1943, AIR 40/3106.

30. Ibid.

31. Ibid.

32. SIR 557, 12 July 1944, WO 208/4295.

33. SIR 931, 9 September 1944, WO 208/4296. His testimony was noted to corroborate information received in SIR 447, 692 and 696, WO 208/4295. Another prisoner provided details of Auschwitz: SIR 938, 14 September 1944, WO 208/4296.

34. WO 311/54.

35. SIR 931, 9 September 1944 and SIR 938, 14 September 1944, WO 208/4796.

36. Sönke Neitzel, *Tapping Hitler's Generals : Transcripts of Secret Conversations, 1942–45*, pp. 50–2.

37. GRGG 195, 16–17 September 1944, WO 208/5018.

38. SRX 1739, 17 April 1943, WO 208/4163.

39. SRGG 209, 10 July 1943, WO 208/4165.

40. SRGG 676, 19 December 1943, WO 208/4167. Similar conversations about killings in Russia had taken place between von Thoma and Hubbuch, see SRGG 647, 10 December 1943, WO 208/4167.

41. Letter dated 11 February 1944, WO 208/5622. Also of relevance is SRGG 815, 2 February 1944 and MI9 memo of 13 February 1944, both in WO 208/5622. See also GRGG 230, 2–4 December 1944. The Katyn Massacre is discussed by the generals in GRGG 288, 24–26 April 1945, WO 208/4177.

42. SRGG 1086(c), 28 December 1944, WO 208/4169.

43. Ibid.

44. Ibid.

45. GRGG 271, 15 March 1945, WO 208/4177.

46. Ibid.

47. Ibid.

48. SRM 175, 14 February 1943, WO 208/4136.

49. GRGG 169, 2–4 August 1944, WO 208/4363.

50. GRGG 230, 2–4 December 1944, WO 208/5018.

51. GRGG 189, 8–9 September 1944, WO 208/4363.

52. GRGG 211, 14–17 October 1944, p. 5, WO 208/4364.

53. SRGG 796, 25 January 1944, WO 208/4167.

54. Ibid.

55. Conversation in January 1944.

56. GRGG 197, 20–21 September 1944, WO 208/5018.

57. GRGG 199, 17–21 September 1944, WO 208/5018. For another bugged conversation about the Warsaw Ghetto, see SRGG 1089(c), 27 December 1944, WO 208/4169.

58. GRGG 301, 18–19 May 1945, WO 208/4178.

59. Ibid.

60. GRGG 306, 28–31 May 1945, WO 208/4178.

61. Ibid.

62. GRGG 274, 24 March 1945, p. 4, WO 208/4177.

63. GRGG 286, 23 April 1945, WO 208/4177.

64. GRGG 197, 20–21 September 1944, WO 208/5018.

65. SRGG 194(c), 20 September 1944, WO 208/4363.

66. This harks back to Kendrick's first intelligence report of the war in WO 208/4970.

13: BREAKING THE GERMAN WILL TO RESIST

1. Sullivan, *Thresholds of Peace*, pp. 56–8.

2. Ibid.

3. Ibid.

4. Ibid.
5. Ibid.
6. 'Report on Visit to No.11 Camp of Representatives of the Swiss Red Cross, Folio 136A', WO 208/5622.
7. Ibid.
8. His full lecture survives in CSDIC files, WO 208/5622.
9. Letter from Lord Aberfeldy to Captain Evans, 2 March 1945, WO 208/5627.
10. Ibid.
11. 'The Utilization of Captured German Generals as Envisaged in the Bruce-Lockhart Committee Plan', WO 208/5627.
12. They were Broich, Neuffer, Bassenge, Reimann, Schlieben, Elfeldt, Eberbach, Wahle, Heim, Wilck, Wildermuth, Daser, Felbert, Bruhn, Vaterrodt, Schaeffer, von der Heydte and Rothkirch.
13. Report ref: D11a/11/2, 5 April 1945, WO 208/5627.
14. 'Report by General Sir A. Thorne on his Visit to German Senior Officer Prisoners of War at No.11 Camp on 3 April 1945', WO 208/5627.
15. Report D11a/11/3, pp. 9–10, 6 April 1945, WO 208/5627.
16. 'Report by General Sir A. Thorne on his Visit to German Senior Officer Prisoners of War at No.11 Camp on 3 April 1945', WO 208/5627.
17. WO 165/41, April 1945. They were Generals Walter Somme and Johannes Fink of the German air force; General O. Hitzfeld, Major Generals: Alexander von Pfuhlstein, Ludwig Hellmann, Gerhard Fischer, Wilhelm Kohlbach, Walter Lindner; Erich Büscher, Wilhelm Viebig, Paul Goerbig, Maximilian Jais, Paul Steinbach, Heinrich Hoffmann, Otto Schneider, Heinrich Bruns, Richard Habermehl, Hubert Lütkenhaus, Hans Erxleben, Gerhard Franz, H. Kokott, E. König, A. Kuen, E. Stahl and Rudolf Petrauschke. Captured Lieutenant Generals were: Kurt Gerlach, Karl Veith, Erwin Leister, Walter Friedensburg, Fritz Pauer, Wolgang Lange, Fritz Neidholdt, Ralph von Oriola, Richard Schimpf, Alfred Sturm, Franz Sensfuss, Hans von Boineburg, Hans von Sommerfeld, Horst von Uckermann, Karl Burdach, Max Siry, Karl Reiter, von Hernekamp (in hospital), von Kirchheim; also Colonels J. Harpe and K. Hollidt; and Vice Admirals Wilhelm Tackenberg, Kurt Utke and Siegfried Engel.
18. Personal file in WO 208/3504.
19. GRGG 301, 23 May 1945, pp. 8–9, WO 208/4178.
20. Ibid.
21. GRGG 306, 2 June 1945, pp. 2–3, WO 208/4178.
22. Ibid.
23. Ibid.
24. Personal file in WO 208/3504.
25. Ibid.
26. Ibid.
27. Ibid.
28. GRGG 281, 11 April 1945, WO 208/4177.
29. Personal file in WO 208/3504.
30. Hugh Trevor Roper, The Last Days of Hitler, p. 101.
31. GRGG 286, 23 April 1945, p. 5, WO 208/4177.
32. Roper, The Last Days of Hitler, p. 107.
33. GRGG 292, 4 May 1945, pp. 3–9, WO 208/4177.
34. Ibid., p. 3.
35. Interview with the author.
36. Reported in GRGG 323, 30 June–5 July 1945, WO 208/4178.
37. GRGG 329, 6–20 July 1945, WO 208/4178.
38. Personal file in WO 208/3504.
39. Ibid.
40. Ibid.
41. SRGG 1209(c), 13 May 1945, WO 208/5622.
42. Personal file in WO 208/3504.

43. Ibid.
44. St Clare Grondona, 'Sidelights on Wilton Park', p. 35.
45. Ibid.
46. Ibid., pp. 36–7.
47. Ibid. Kurt Dittmar overlapped at Wilton Park with von Rundstedt in May 1945. Dittmar was transferred to Trent Park at least two months before the field marshal.
48. Ibid.
49. Copy sent to the author.
50. St Clare Grondona, 'Sidelights on Wilton Park', p. 37.
51. Ibid., p. 36.
52. Ibid.
53. Ibid.

14: BRITISH INTELLIGENCE, POWS AND WAR CRIMES TRIALS

1. Interview with the author.
2. Hart, *Journey into Freedom*, p. 102.
3. Interview with the author.
4. GRGG 314, 15 June 1945, p. 4, WO 208/4178.
5. GRGG 311, 7 June 1945, WO 208/4178.
6. The belief that the photographs were faked was still circulating that summer. See GRGG 344, 21 August 1945, p. 14, WO 208/4178.
7. GRGG 311, 7 June 1945, WO 208/4178. Felbert had previously denied any knowledge of the killings: see GRGG 253, 26–27 January 1945, WO 208/5018.
8. GRGG 311, 7 June 1945, WO 208/4178.
9. Terence Prittie, *Germany Divided*, p. 53.
10. GRGG 297, 10 May 1945 and GRGG 300, 20 May 1945, both in WO 208/4177.
11. GRGG 281, 8–9 April 1945, pp. 5–6, WO 208/4177.
12. Ibid.
13. GRGG 302, 25 May 1945, WO 208/4178.
14. Memo entitled 'German Atrocities' from MI14, dated 14 May 1945, which comments on the subject to be discussed at the forthcoming Joint Intelligence Committee, on 15 May 1945, copy in WO 208/3466.
15. Ibid.
16. GRGG 314, 7–30 June 1945, WO 208/4178.
17. Interview with Eric Mark.
18. GRGG 314, 7–13 June 1945, WO 208/4178.
19. GRGG 265, 7 Feb–1 March 1945, WO 208/4178.
20. GRGG 292, 4 May 1945, WO 208/4177.
21. GRGG 363, 9 October 1945, WO 208/4178.
22. Ibid.
23. Ibid.
24. Ibid.
25. Ibid.
26. Ibid.
27. GRGG 264, 24–26 February 1945, WO 208/4177.
28. Ibid. For mass killings at Rostov, see also SRGG 1089(c), 27 December 1944, WO 208/4169.
29. SRGG 275, 26 March 1945, pp. 3–6, WO 208/4177.
30. Ibid.
31. GRGG 277, 1 April 1945, pp. 2–3, WO 208/4177.

32. GRGG 271, 10–12 March 1945, WO 208/4177.
33. Interview with Fritz Lustig and Eric Mark.
34. Minutes of both meetings in WO 208/3466.
35. Memo entitled 'German Atrocities' from MI14, dated 14 May 1945, which comments on the subject to be discussed at the forthcoming Joint Intelligence Committee, on 15 May 1945.
36. Note JIC/731/45, 4 June 1945, WO 208/3466.
37. Ibid.
38. Ibid.
39. During the war, Derry had escaped twice as a prisoner of the Germans, having jumped once from a moving train on its way to Auschwitz, and the second time tunnelling out of Camp 21 in Italy. He became head of the Rome Organization and coordinated the escape and evasion of over 3,000 Allied airmen and soldiers. He was awarded the DSO and MC.
40. Directive from Derry, 16 November 1945, WO 311/632.
41. Ibid.
42. Ibid.
43. Ibid.
44. Minute dated 28 November 1945 issued by Judge Advocate General, WO 311/632.
45. Personal file in WO 208/3504.
46. WO 208/3466.
47. Personal Minute, Winston Churchill to General Ismay (for Chiefs of Staff), 16 February 1944, CAB 121/236.
48. WO 165/41, March 1944.

15: ALWAYS LISTENING

1. Helen Fry, *Denazification*.
2. Fry, *The London Cage*, pp. 126–92.
3. Jeremy Bernstein, *Hitler's Uranium Club: The Secret Recordings at Farm Hall* and Brown, *Operation Big*. See also Jim Baggott, *Atomic: The First War of Physics and the Secret History of the Atom Bomb, 1939–1945*, pp. 339–56.
4. The other scientists held at Farm Hall were Werner Heisenberg, Paul Harteck, Erich Bagge, Kurt Diebner, Walther Gerlach, Horst Korsching, Carl Friedrich von Weizsäcker and Karl Wirtz.
5. File containing solely material on Operation Epsilon, WO 208/5019.
6. Bernstein, *Hitler's Uranium Club*, p. 73. Lieutenant Commander Eric Welsh was based with Naval Intelligence Division at the Admiralty.
7. WO 165/41, July 1944.
8. Hoare, *Camp 020*.
9. FO 1060/11.
10. See Ian Cobain, *Cruel Britannia: A Secret History of Torture*, and Dominic Streatfeild, *Brainwash: The Secret History of Mind Control*.
11. They were Fritz Lustig, Eric Mark, Peter Baines, Peter Bendix, Oscar Hamm, Walter Beevers, Richard Stern, Franz Huelsen, Peter Türkheim, Walter Hellier, Rees Nichols, Wolfgang Meyer and Freddie Katz.
12. Independent interviews with Fritz Lustig and Eric Mark.
13. Information provided by the family.
14. Ibid.
15. Their bugged conversations survive in WO 208/4178.
16. Personal file in WO 208/3504.
17. GRGG 341, 28 July–7 August 1945, WO 208/4178.
18. Dornberger's interrogation reports survive in WO 208/3121.
19. GRGG 341, 11 August 1945, pp. 10–11, WO 208/4178.

20. Ibid.
21. Personal file in WO 208/3504.
22. WO 208/4178.
23. Personal file in WO 208/3504.
24. Ibid.
25. Ibid.
26. Personal file in WO 208/3504.
27. Personal file in WO 208/3504.
28. Ibid.
29. Ibid.
30. Letter dated 29 September 1945, in papers of Captain Hamley, National Army Museum, ref: 1993-10-162.
31. Sullivan, *Thresholds of Peace*, pp. 356–8; and Mayne, *In Victory, Magnanimity*, p. 28.
32. Derek R. Mallett, *Hitler's Generals in America: Nazi POWs and Allied Military Intelligence*, pp. 107–32.
33. Overseen by the Trent Park Museum Trust; www.trentparkmuseum.org.uk
34. 'Report and Proceedings', 21 May 1945, ADM 1/18422.
35. The White House has had various name changes. It was previously called West Farm Place and Norrysbury; and once belonged to the Bevan family who had owned Trent Park and Ludgrove Hall.
36. Nancy Clark, *Hadley Wood: Its Background and Development*, pp. 88–9.
37. 'Report and Proceedings', 21 May 1945 and 23 June 1945, ADM 1/18422.
38. Interview with Melanie McFadyean, 2013.
39. Other members of FIU were Julius Lunzer, Brian Connell, Charles Mitchell, Patrick Dalzel-Job, Lt T.W. Broecker (USNR) and Lt Kaminada (RNVR). Charles Everett became Staff Officer (Security) at Emden, and Donald Welbourn interviewed scientific and technical sources in Germany. Information kindly provided by Derek Nudd.
40. 'Report and Proceedings', 21 May 1945 and 23 June 1945, ADM 1/18422.
41. Roger Hermiston, *The Greatest Traitor: The Secret Lives of Agent George Blake*, pp. 170–1.
42. Ibid.
43. Richard Davenport-Hines, *Enemies Within: Communists, the Cambridge Spies and the Making of Modern Britain*; and Andrew Lownie, *Stalin's Englishman: The Lives of Guy Burgess*.
44. Summary report of the Joint Intelligence Sub Committee meeting, 1 May 1945 to form CSDIC (WEA) and wind down CSDIC (UK), WO 208/3451.
45. 'Intelligence from Prisoners of War', report by Denys Felkin, 31 December 1945 section 288, AIR 40/2636.
46. Ibid., section 289, AIR 40/2636.
47. Ibid., section 297, AIR 40/2636.
48. Ibid.
49. Ibid.
50. Adolf Galland, *The First and the Last: The German Fighter Force in World War II*, p. 125. Galland's interrogation reports survive in WO 208/4292: in particular ADI(K) report No.311, 1945.
51. 'Intelligence from Prisoners of War', report by Denys Felkin, 31 December 1945, section 253 and 254, AIR 40/2636.
52. AIR 29/1104.
53. Ibid.
54. Ibid.
55. For official file on Inkpot, see AIR 40/1178.
56. Crockatt to C, 1 September 1945, WO 208/5622.
57. This included appointments as lecturer at Royal Holloway College, London; lecturer in German Philology and Medieval Literature at Westfield College (London); Reader in German at Oxford University, then Emeritus Professor of German; Fellow of Hertford College, Oxford; and Resident Fellow at Herzog August Bibliothek (Wolfenbüttel). During

his time at Oxford, Ganz acted as facilitator in establishing contacts between German studies in England and Germany. In recognition of this, in 1973 he received the Grosses Bundesverdienstkreuz by the Federal Republic. He died on 17 August 2006.

58. Hart, *Journey into Freedom*, p. 112.
59. Interview with the author.

EPILOGUE: SECRETS TO THE GRAVE

1. Fritz Lustig, interviews with the author; and his interview with Sir David Jason for the documentary series *David Jason's Secret Service*, Channel 4, 2017.
2. Official report of 14 February 2017 by Historic England to Enfield Council's Planning Department in relation to the housing development at Trent Park in North London (MI9's former site).
3. 'Intelligence from Prisoners of War', report by Denys Felkin, 31 December 1945, section 112–125, AIR 40/2636.
4. Extract of Report by the Joint Intelligence Sub Committee, 15 February 1945, copy amongst Kendrick's personal papers.
5. 'Intelligence from Prisoners of War', report by Denys Felkin, 31 December 1945, section 122, AIR 40/2636.
6. Ibid.
7. 'Prisoner of War Interrogation 1939–1945', p. 11, ADM 223/475.
8. Interview with Tom Deveson, 2013.
9. Letter amongst Kendrick's personal papers.
10. Official report of 14 February 2017 by Historic England to Enfield Council's Planning Department in relation to the housing development at Trent Park.
11. St Clare Grondona, 'Sidelights on Wilton Park', p. 35.

Bibliography

PAPERS AND ARCHIVES

Archives at the Military Intelligence Museum and Archives, Chicksands; RAF Medmenham Archives; the papers of Lieutenant Colonel Henry Dicks (ref: PP/HVD) at the Wellcome Library (London); private papers and photographs from the family of the late Colonel Kendrick; unpublished memoirs of Lieutenant Commander Donald Burkewood Welbourn, RNVR (ref: 99/6/1) at the Imperial War Museum; and uncatalogued war diaries of Bernard Trench, at the National Museum of the Royal Navy, Portsmouth. Papers of Captain E.A. Hamley at the National Army Museum (refs: 1993-10-162 and 1993-10-163).

INTERVIEWS

This book draws on interviews with: Thomas Joseph Kendrick's grandchildren, Barbara Lloyd and Ken Walsh; secret listeners, Paul Douglas, Fritz Lustig and Eric Mark; surviving relatives of secret listeners and intelligence staff, Dudley Bennett, Otto Bennett, Richard Benson, Richard Deveson, Liz Driscoll, Adam Ganz, Roger Lloyd-Pack, Derek Nudd, Jessica Pulay and Anne Walton; former female intelligence staff, Evelyn Barron, Elizabeth Bruegger (née Rees-Mogg), Susan Lustig (née Cohn) and Cynthia Turner (née Crew).

THE NATIONAL ARCHIVES

ADM 1/10579, ADM 1/18422, ADM 1/23905, ADM 116/4572, ADM 186/805, ADM 186/809, ADM 223/257, ADM 223/472, AIR 14/743, AIR 14/744, AIR 29/1104, AIR 40/2394, AIR 40/2572, AIR 40/2636, AIR 40/2839, AIR 40/3070, AIR 40/3093, AIR 40/3102, AIR 40/3106, AIR 40/3108, CAB 113/41, CAB 121/236, DEFE 1/339, ED 78/418, ED 78/419, FO 371/21691, FO 371/22321, FO 898/320, HW 57/35, KV 2/3766, KV 2/3767, KV 4/302, PREM 3/219/5, WO 32/10720, WO 94/105, WO 165/39, WO 165/41, WO 208/3433, WO 208/3451, WO 208/3455, WO 208/3456, WO 208/3457, WO 208/3466, WO 208/3474, WO 208/3504, WO 208/3582, WO 208/4202, WO 208/4117, WO 208/4121, WO 208/4123, WO 208/4128, WO 208/4131, WO 208/4136, WO 208/4137, WO 208/4141, WO 208/4148, WO 208/4158, WO 208/4165, WO 208/4166, WO 208/4167, WO 208/4168, WO 208/4169, WO 208/4177, WO 208/4178, WO 208/4196, WO 208/4292, WO 208/4363, WO 208/4364, WO 208/4471,

BIBLIOGRAPHY

WO 208/4796, WO 208/4970, WO 208/5016, WO 208/5017, WO 208/5018, WO 208/5019, WO 208/5158, WO 208/5550, WO 208/5621, WO 208/5622, WO 208/5623, WO 311/54, WO 311/632.

PUBLISHED WORKS

Andrew, Christopher. *Secret Service*, Book Club Associates: 1985.

Baggott, Jim. *Atomic: The First War of Physics and the Secret History of the Atom Bomb, 1939–1945*, Icon: 2015.

Bernstein, Jeremy. *Hitler's Uranium Club: The Secret Recordings at Farm Hall*, Copernicus Books: 2001.

Brown, Colin. *Operation Big: The Race to Stop Hitler's A-Bomb*, Amberley Publishing: 2016.

de Burgh, Lucy. *My Italian Adventures: An English Girl at War 1943–47*, The History Press: 2013.

Clark, Nancy. *Hadley Wood: Its Background and Development*, Ward Lock: 1968.

Cobain, Ian. *Cruel Britannia: A Secret History of Torture*, Portobello Books: 2013.

Collins, Damian. *Charmed Life: The Phenomenal World of Philip Sassoon*, William Collins: 2016.

Davenport-Hines, Richard. *Enemies Within: Communists, the Cambridge Spies and the Making of Modern Britain*, William Collins: 2018.

Fermor, Patrick Leigh. *Abducting a General: The Kreipe Operation and SOE in Crete*, John Murray: 2015.

Fraser-Smith, Charles. *The Secret War of Charles Fraser-Smith*, Michael Joseph: 1981.

Fry, Helen. *Churchill's German Army*, second edition: Thistle Publishing: 2015.

——. *Denazification*, The History Press: 2010.

——. *Jews in North Devon During the Second World War*, Halsgrove: 2005.

——. *The London Cage: The Secret History of Britain's World War II Interrogation Centre*, Yale University Press: 2017.

——. *Spymaster: The Secret Life of Kendrick*, Thistle Publishing: 2015.

Galland, Adolf. *The First and the Last: The German Fighter Force in World War II*, Methuen: 1955.

Gilbert, Martin. *Auschwitz and the Allies*, Michael Joseph: 1981.

——. *Beyond the Call of Duty: British Diplomats and Other Britons Who Helped Jews Escape from Nazi Tyranny*, Foreign and Commonwealth Office: 2008.

Hart, Peter. *Journey into Freedom*, Authors OnLine: 2003.

Hermiston, Roger. *The Greatest Traitor: The Secret Lives of Agent George Blake*, Aurum Press: 2014.

Hoare, Oliver. *Camp 020: MI5 and Nazi Spies – The Official History of MI5's Wartime Interrogation Centre*, Public Record Office: 2000.

Jackson, Sophie. *Churchill's Unexpected Guests: Prisoners of War in Britain in World War II*, The History Press: 2010.

Jeffery, Keith. *MI6: The History of the Secret Intelligence Service, 1909–1949*, Bloomsbury: 2010.

Jestin, Catherine. *A War Bride's Story*, privately published.

Jones, R.V. *Most Secret War*, Coronet: 1978.

Kenyon, David. *Bletchley Park and D-Day*, Yale: 2019.

Kiszely, John. *Anatomy of a Campaign: The British Fiasco in Norway, 1940*, Cambridge University Press: 2017.

Leighton-Langer, Peter. *The King's Own Loyal Enemy Aliens*, Vallentine Mitchell: 2006.

Lewis, Damien. *Hunting Hitler's Nukes: The Secret Race to Stop the Nazi Bomb*, Quercus: 2016.

Lownie, Andrew. *Stalin's Englishman: The Lives of Guy Burgess*, Hodder: 2016.

Lustig, Fritz. *My Lucky Life*, privately published: 2017.

McLachlan, Donald. *Room 39: Naval Intelligence in Action 1939–45*, Weidenfeld & Nicolson: 1968.

BIBLIOGRAPHY

Mallett, Derek R. *Hitler's Generals in America: Nazi POWs and Allied Military Intelligence*, University Press of Kentucky: 2013.

Masterman, John. *The Double-Cross System*, Vintage: 2013.

Mayne, Richard. *In Victory, Magnanimity, in Peace, Goodwill: A History of Wilton Park*, Whitehall History Publishing: 2003.

Medawar, Jean and David Pyke. *Hitler's Gift*, Richard Cohen Books: 2000.

Moss, W. Stanley. *Ill Met by Moonlight*, Weidenfeld & Nicolson: 2014.

Neitzel, Sönke (ed.). *Tapping Hitler's Generals: Transcripts of Secret Conversations, 1942–45*, Frontline: 2007.

Nudd, Derek. *Castaways of the Kriegsmarine: How Shipwrecked German Seamen helped the Allies Win the Second World War*, CreateSpace: 2017.

Prittie, Terence. *Germany Divided*, Hutchinson: 1961.

Rankin, Nicholas. *Ian Fleming's Commandos: The Story of the Legendary 30 Assault Unit*, Faber: 2011.

Richards, Lee. *The Black Art: British Clandestine Psychological Warfare against the Third Reich*, 2010: available at www.psywar.org

Sanders, Eric. *From Music to Morse*, privately published autobiography.

Scotland, Alexander P. *The London Cage*, Evans Brothers Ltd: 1957.

Smith, Michael. *Foley: The Spy Who Saved 10,000 Jews*, Politico's Publishing: revised edition, 2004.

———. *The Secrets of Station X: How the Bletchley Park Codebreakers Helped Win the War*, Biteback Publishing: 2011.

Streatfeild, Dominic. *Brainwash: The Secret History of Mind Control*, Hodder & Stoughton: 2007.

Sullivan, Matthew Barry. *Thresholds of Peace: German Prisoners and the People of Britain*, Hamish Hamilton: 1979.

Trevor Roper, Hugh. *The Last Days of Hitler*, Pan Books: 2002 edition.

Weidenfeld, George. *Remembering My Good Friends: An Autobiography*, HarperCollins: 1994.

West, Nigel (ed.). *The Guy Liddell Diaries, Vol. 1, 1939–1942*, Routledge: 2009.

———. *The Guy Liddell Diaries, Vol. 2, 1942–1945*, Routledge: 2009.

———. *Historical Dictionary of International Intelligence*, Scarecrow Press: 2006.

ARTICLES AND UNPUBLISHED WORKS

Hayward, Gil. 'Dollis Hill in the Desert, 1940–44' (CSDIC Cairo), copy in the Intelligence Corps Archives, Chicksands.

Jestin, Heimwarth. *A Memoir, 1918–1946*, unpublished memoirs, copy provided to the author by the family.

McFadyean, Melanie. 'A Private War', *Guardian*, 6 July 2002.

St Clare Grondona, Leo. 'Sidelights on Wilton Park', *RUSI Journal*, December 1970, pp. 34–7.

Vincent, Jeff. 'The Combined Services Interrogation Centre', in *After the Battle*, no. 70, 1990.

Weber, Jan August. Unpublished memoirs.

IN THE MEDIA

Home Front Heroes, episode 5, BBC1, 2018 with Helen Lederer.

David Jason's Secret Service, episode 3, Channel 4, 2017.

Spying on Hitler's Army, documentary for Channel 4 and PBS, 2013.

Britain's Secret Homes, ITV, 2013 with Sir David Jason, filmed at Latimer House.

Lord Glenaldy, a play in three parts, BBC Radio 4, transmitted May 1965.

Index

INDEX

INDEX